*Vietnam's Children in a Changing World*

The Rutgers Series in Childhood Studies

Edited by Myra Bluebond-Langner

Advisory Board

Joan Jacobs Brumberg

Perri Klass

Jill Korbin

Bambi Schiefflin

Enid Schildkraut

# Vietnam's Children in a Changing World

*Rachel Burr*

*Rutgers University Press*

New Brunswick, New Jersey, and London

**Library of Congress Cataloging-in-Publication Data**

Burr, Rachel.
    Vietnam's children in a changing world / by Rachel Burr.
        p. cm. — (The Rutgers series in childhood studies)
    Includes bibliographical references and index.
    ISBN-13: 978-0-8135-3795-5 (hardcover : alk. paper)
    ISBN-13: 978-0-8135-3796-2 (pbk. : alk. paper)
    1. Children—Vietnam—Social conditions.  2. Street children—Vietnam.
3. Children's rights—Vietnam.  4. Child labor—Vietnam.  5. Child welfare—
Vietnam.  6. Humanitarian assistance—Vietnam. 7. North and south.
I. Title. II. Series.
    HQ792.V5B87 2006
    362.7'09597—dc22

                                                                    2005023052

A British Cataloging-in-Publication record for this book is available from the
British Library.

Manufactured in the United States of America

*To Mum and Dad,*
*with much gratitude and love*

*And in memory of Father Charlie Robak,*
*who was a great friend and inspiration*

# Contents

# Acknowledgments

My grateful thanks go to all the children who informed my research, especially the boys with tattoos and those who were making their living on the streets of Hanoi.

Most importantly I must thank my doctorate supervisors, Ronnie Frankenberg, Ian Robinson and Alison Shaw, without whose insightful encouragement I could not have embarked on this project. At the outset of my work Erica Burman and Jo Boyden were very encouraging. Special thanks also go to Barrie Thorne, who encouraged me to send a book proposal to Rutgers University Press. Thanks to Judith Justice, who also supported my proposal. The writing of this book would have been impossible without the ongoing support of Kristi Long, who gave me many insightful comments during the editing process and encouraged me to remain true to my original work.

I would very much like to thank Dr. Gill Tipping of the Institute of Development Studies at Sussex University, who became my Hanoi-based mentor and copious tea drinking companion and friend.

There is insufficient room to thank all the NGO workers and Hanoi-based friends who informed my study. However, I must single out "Jack," whose strength of character and compassion was truly inspiring. I also wish to thank Alison Purvis, who taught me much about Vietnam, and Tim Bond for his encouragement. Jane McClennan at The School of Oriental and African Studies, London University, must also be thanked for her interest in my work.

Nguyen Thuy Hien, Vu Thu Hong, Nguyen Hong Ngoc, and my professor at Hanoi National University, were more than generous with their friendship and time.

I would like to thank my good friend Emma Williams and also Vu Kanh Thanh at the An Viet Foundation, London, who gave me the opportunity to get involved in the Viet Kieu community.

My colleagues at the Open University provided a rich and stimulating environment in which to develop my ideas. I am particularly grateful to Heather Montgomery, Martin Woodhead, Peter Barnes, Mary Jane Kehily, Wendy Stainton-Rogers, Janet Maybin, Donald Mackinnon, and Jeremy Roche. Thanks too to Virginia Morrow, who edited my first publication. Between 2003 and 2005 the anthropology department at the University of Wisconsin generously provided me with a visiting fellowship specifically so that I could work on this book.

Writing a book of this length inevitably takes time, and over the years particular friends and family members have provided me with support. Kristin Liabo has shared her insights into the study of childhood, while Jon Braman encouraged me from the very beginning of this project right to the end. Victoria Cardin's support has been unwavering during the writing of this book. Eliot Freidson and Helen Giambruni offered comments on early manuscripts. Judith Lorber gave me much encouragement in seeing this project through to completion. Simon Burr has offered empathetic words of encouragement. Both my parents, Mike and Pamela Burr, have offered immeasurable support and interest in my work, even going as far as to visit me while I was living in Hanoi and going on to read countless drafts of this book.

Gratitude also to my mother, Vicki Dobski, and Megan Chaloupka for caring for my children while I was writing.

Finally, my thanks go to my partner, Matt Freidson, whom I met when we were both living in Hanoi. Our shared passion for Vietnam has inspired me during the writing of this book.

*Vietnam's Children in a Changing World*

*One*

*"Neither the life of an individual nor the history of a
society can be understood without understanding both."*
—(Muncie 1999, 205)

# What Is Childhood?

For two years, between 1996 and 1998, I lived in Hanoi, Vietnam,
where I did anthropological fieldwork with a focus on childhood. I had originally intended to concentrate my research on the everyday experiences of
working children. But on arriving in Hanoi it soon became clear to me that
local children's experiences could not be adequately represented or explained if I only looked at their immediate environment at the local level.
Instead, if I were to represent their experiences properly I would also need
to take into account global influences at work at the local level, and particularly the impact of the internationally led child-focused aid programs now
being mounted in Vietnam. The end result is a broadly based analysis
founded on anthropologically based fieldwork but informed by an examination of international development, human rights, and, because my interest is in childhood, the United Nations Convention on the Rights of the Child
(UNCRC). Nonetheless, at the core of this book are the voices and experiences of the Vietnamese children I met. Their experiences inspired the direction in which this body of work has gone, and it is because of them, and
my desire that they be heard, that I have felt so determined to make my
findings public.

On the face of it, a revolution in attitudes toward children has taken place
across the globe, stimulated particularly by the UNCRC. During the first

1

four years after the convention's publication in 1989, 128 countries became signatories, making it the most swiftly signed human rights convention to date. In 1990, only three years after it had loosened its ties with the Soviet Union, Vietnam became the first country in Asia to ratify the UNCRC, embracing a child-focused human rights agenda that under the charter places emphasis on the rights of each child. As a result, Vietnam's social policy toward its children is currently dominated by the UNCRC and is applied both by the government and by the most dominant aid agencies presently working in Hanoi.

The key question that this book examines at the macro-sociological level is whether the UNCRC offers Vietnam a relevant set of guidelines for the raising of its children. As I show in chapter 3, the UNCRC embraces a model of a particular kind of Western childhood that is erroneously assumed to be universally and globally applicable, thus making no concessions to cultural or economic differences between states. For example, the UNCRC requires signatory countries to have adequate funding available to provide all of their people with a good standard of health care and universally accessible free primary education, but most countries in the Southern Hemisphere are economically incapable of offering this or can only do so during temporary periods when they are recipients of international funding.

To gain an insight into this question, I compared the work of a cross-section of child-focused organizations based in Hanoi: the aid agencies and non-government organizations (NGOs) whose work is informed by the UNCRC, alongside those NGOs that were not working to the UNCRC remit but were nevertheless setting up projects that seemed to be helpful and relevant to the same children. As I now briefly show and demonstrate in detail in chapter 3, the UNCRC's objectives are being implemented with difficulty at the local level.

One problem with implementing the UNCRC is that it is a legal document that is meant to be applicable to all children in the world. In reality children's lives do not neatly map onto the theories that are shaped around them or created about them. Because of my experiences working as both a practitioner and an academic in the field of childhood I am sympathetic both in practice and in theory to the treatment of childhood and children's experiences. But I have also become increasingly frustrated by the manner in which theoretical ideas about the child, children, and childhood often unsatisfactorily shape the social policies that affect the work of practitioners, and vice versa. My academic training is in anthropology, but I am at once an anthropologist, a social economist, and a trained and practicing social worker. This means that I have both an academic's interest in childhood studies and a practitioner's experience of working directly with children. Until my children were born I was a lecturer in childhood studies at the Open University in Britain, where I sometimes attended the meetings of academics in the social work school. At these meetings I listened with interest to the ideas generated around the table but usually withdrew in frustrated silence after hearing academics complain that practicing social workers did not keep up to date with their research findings in the field and therefore did not apply them. Meanwhile, in my previous social work job, my manager always put academic papers on the agenda for us to discuss at the end of our case study meetings. On one occasion the social work team discussed the findings of an academic who had suggested that community centers be set up in areas where more vulnerable and poverty-affected families were living, because such a resource could improve early intervention in instances where a child might be at risk. While this was a sensible and well-researched proposal backed up by thorough fieldwork, everyone present at the team meeting was already aware that in our daily work we were struggling to find the money to adequately fund good-quality foster care support provided by families in the community. It was hard enough to get the basic cover to protect the children who were already on our child protection case list without finding the funds to set up an entirely new set of resources. Time and again it seemed that when academic and practitioner worlds collided they created frustration and disillusionment on both sides. Here and in the chapters that follow I show why, in the Vietnamese context, this gap between theoretically informed treatment of the child, practitioner-based policies, and the experiences of children has added to the failure of child rights aid programs to achieve their goals.

## *The Anthropological Approach*

As an anthropologist I felt well equipped to discover some of the problems that occur when globally led agendas take effect at the local level. This is because anthropology developed as a discipline out of a desire to understand other people's social processes and to discover the cultural practices and expectations that give meaning to people's lives. Good anthropologists expect to discover the unexpected and thus will observe and allow issues that might entirely change the direction of their work to emerge during the fieldwork process without intervention. The central research tool of the anthropologist is the technique of participant observation, in which the emphasis is on allowing critical categories and meanings to emerge from the ethnographic encounter. To develop an understanding of what it is like to live in a particular setting, the researcher must become a participant in the life of people in that setting while maintaining the stance of an observer, someone who can describe the experience objectively. This process usually requires anthropologists to become such a familiar presence in people's daily lives that life goes on around them virtually as it would if they were not there. Some anthropologists also interview a selection of the people they meet during fieldwork, but even then interviews lean toward being semistructured and open ended rather than formal and questionnaire based. Allowing for some flexibility during the interview process provides the opportunity for unexpected information—information that as an outsider one might never have known existed—to come to light. Thus, my fieldwork among children shifted direction once I had completed some open-ended interviews among a group who worked on the streets; from this process I learned that out of the seven children present, four had been arrested and put in a children's detention center during the past six months. Until that point I had not known that being arrested by the police was such a regular occurrence in these children's lives. Armed with this knowledge I then broadened my fieldwork settings to include experiences among children living in a reform school. Most of these children had previously worked or stolen to earn a living and told me that because of the poverty their families were in most of them could see no end to that way of life after leaving the reform school. Understanding this gave me insight into the argument for children's viewpoints on the subject of work to be properly acknowledged by policy makers (no matter what the policy makers' own stand on the subject might be). This argument is set out in detail in chapter 3.

Across the Northern Hemisphere childhood is generally regarded as the one period in life when people are not expected to work to support themselves. Within the international aid community and governments of the developed nations, child work has become synonymous with deprivation. This received wisdom makes writing about the positive experiences reported by working children, some of which I observed during my time in Vietnam, quite difficult. Because of my own street-level observations, I have come to challenge this received wisdom, and as a consequence my critics ask me if I am advocating for children to continue to work, or live on the streets, or leave their family home to find work in the city. I reply that of course I am not an advocate of child work, but there is a need for pragmatism if any improvements are to be made: the low family incomes of most countries of the South place demands upon children to work, and this cannot be changed overnight by attempting to apply unworkable reform programs conceived by the West. To support my argument, I draw upon children's own experiences at the local level to explain why they need to continue working. But I also argue that international aid and international human rights conventions will continue to have little impact on such children's lives unless something is also done to change the bias of the global market, which is grossly distorted in favor of Western economies. It is this economic bias in favor of the West that allows for the disparities of wealth to continue and for the stopping of work to be an impossibility for many children living in the South. The part that the Western world plays in this is all the more unsettling because antichild work policies also find their roots in the West.

To understand some of these contradictions, let us examine how particular social developments have contributed to theoretical treatments of childhood. Many others have written on this subject, and whole books and university courses have been developed that address the theory of childhood, so for the purpose of this book I will provide only a brief introduction to the subject to provide a clearer idea of why the UNCRC now dominates the global arena. In the next section I examine how early theories about the state of childhood evolved into the protectionist approach to child welfare stimulated by the nineteenth-century Western Industrial Revolution, as a precursor to the evolution of the present child rights approach on the contemporary treatment of childhood as expressed by the UNCRC.

### Defining the Child

A wealth of academic material provides us with particular ways of looking at the individual child. In brief we may think of a child in purely biological terms as physically developing (therefore physically vulnerable because of size and strength) and thus always in a state of change and growth. In developmental psychology, children are also referred to as being incomplete from a cognitive and emotional perspective, because they are still undergoing the emotional and intellectual development that marks them as separate from adults. Erica Burman explains:

> Childhood is celebrated as a universal stage or period of life which is characterized by protection and freedom of responsibilities. But although it purports to be universal, this representation of childhood turns out to be specific and geographically distributed. In this view, childhood becomes an entity the deprivation of which constitutes a violation of human rights. The polarities set up between this supposedly universal stage and those deemed to lack it map, of course, onto the North-South divide: in the North children develop, and in the South they merely survive if they are lucky . . . this life stage that we all have a right to enjoy is in fact an idealized representation of Northern models of childhood. It achieves a globalized status through its inscription within international aid and development policies and legislation. (Burman 1994b, 32)

To find out why this particular treatment of childhood has taken hold at a global level it is necessary to examine historical influences more closely. One of the most surprising aspects of all of this is that what we consider a normal childhood—filled with school and play—is actually a relatively new phenomenon in the Northern Hemisphere or the West as well as in the rest of the world. If any of us had been born just a hundred years ago our experiences of being children would in all likelihood have had many more parallels with those of the children you will meet in later chapters of this book. The sociologists James and Prout (1990) make the point that the immaturity of children is a biological fact of life but the way in which this immaturity is understood and made meaningful is a fact of culture. In other words their worlds are defined by the society in which they live. Within the theory of childhood this is referred to as the *social construction of childhood*. There is now a large body of work written about childhood, and the argument that it is socially constructed and that the treatment of the subject is dominated by relatively recent Western influences is widely accepted.

It was Philippe Ariés (1973) who set in motion the present debate about whether childhood as a distinctive life phase is a recent invention. Ariés claimed that people of the Middle Ages had no understanding of the child as anything other than an "adult in waiting." He based his theory on historical iconographic evidence that depicted children as miniature adults. Other historians have challenged this view, and there is now more of a consensus among them that the origins of a recognized "theoretical" conceptualization of childhood are generally attributed to the early seventeenth century (Hendrick 1997). This more theoretically oriented discourse on childhood originated in religious thinking of the period, when images of childhood came to be dominated by Puritan dogma. This was based on the belief that children were innately evil, born with "original sin" that must be purged from them. By the end of the seventeenth century, secular discourse had replaced religious dogma and a new notion of childhood innocence had replaced the concept of "evil" children who had to be saved from corruption and molded into responsible adults. One of the principal proponents of this secular discourse was John Locke, who in 1690 wrote an essay challenging the idea that children were innately evil, or innately anything for that matter, arguing instead that they were merely products of their environment. He posited the image of children as "blank slates" ("tabula rasa") capable of being shaped by their environment and experiences. The development of logic and reasoning was a key element of this process. Childhood was still considered a preparatory stage in a person's life cycle. Later, in 1762, Emile Rousseau proposed a construction of childhood that presented an idyllic image of childhood as a time of innocence and posited that the progression through to adulthood represented a process of steady decline from innocence to corruption.

Despite these philosophical insights, such ideas about childhood were clearly only taking effect among the minority of children who came from the upper classes. Throughout this period in Europe societies were still based upon rigidly hierarchical class structures; the majority of children still received little or no education, and they had to work. During the Industrial Revolution, which began in Europe and North America during the late eighteenth century, harsh economic reality put paid to any notions of childhood innocence or the preservation of a special child identity. With industrialization, women and children could now undertake work that had previously required the strength of an adult male. Indeed, some of the early spinning machines in cotton mills were designed to suit the smaller fingers of children, thus also benefiting the mill owners who paid children much less than adults although effectively they were often doing the same jobs. Thus, children were recognized as an important economic commodity, and because of the subsistence wages generally paid to adults, the survival of many families depended on their children's incomes, however small. These conditions were not conducive to the spread of idealized images of childhood, and "childhood" as we understand it in the West was delayed for the poorer classes until social and work-related reforms in the middle of the nineteenth century began to have a real impact on the lives of children generally, promoted not only by intellectual thinkers such as John Ruskin (1819–1900) but also by enlightened industrialists such as Robert Booth (1771–1858).

## Work-Related Reform

In Britain, the Factory Act of 1819 laid down work restrictions for the first time so that no children under the age of nine could work in factories, and children aged from nine to sixteen were "only" allowed to work a maximum of seventy hours per week with one and a half hours a day for meals. Other acts followed: for example, the 1842 Mines and Collieries Act banned employment of those under the age of ten, significantly reducing the number of young children working in coal and lead mines. The introduction of half-time working for school-age children in Britain's Factory Act of 1844 caused numbers to dwindle further and to all but disappear when compulsory schooling was introduced in Britain in1880. Indeed, by this time most industrializing countries had some sort of child labor laws in operation at national level, with the notable exception of the United States.

The historian David Cunningham points out, however, that there have also always been supporters of child work (1995). Opposition to child labor was always contested by those who felt that children could or should work; the existence of a labor market for children living in Britain today serves as a useful reminder that those who campaigned against child work did not win all the arguments (see chapter 4). So what was the impetus for pioneering child labor legislation in Europe rather than anywhere else in the world? There are no absolute explanations, and the decline in child labor was far from straightforward, unanimously supported, or absolute. Some point to the rise in adult wages as a precursor to the decline in child labor because the family no longer had to rely on the children's contribution to family income to survive (Nardinelli 1990). Others point to the increasing emphasis placed on education as a means of pulling children out of work, while yet others point to cultural differences. Cunningham argues that countries that have passed through similar stages of economic development have made use of different levels of child labor.

## The Protectionist Approach

The aftermath of World War I and anti-work legislation led to a reappraisal of childhood and its importance. Children were now viewed as the future of the nation, valuable commodities to be emotionally prized and preserved at all costs, and were seen to have a singular identity with particular physical, mental, and emotional needs that had to be satisfied. This era of preserving and protecting children generated research in aspects of nutrition, health, and preventive medicine such as childhood vaccinations. Comparative studies of children's physical well-being and mortality rates also exposed inequalities among the different social class structures and heralded a new wave of research spearheaded by politicians and welfare reformers. Previously, children had been educated through apprenticeships and charity schools and parents had managed to retain a modicum of control and influence. Now a high level of control passed into the hands of the state, and a protectionist approach dominated in the treatment of childhood.

Thus, childhood was now viewed as a time of innocence and of vulnerability, which in some ways it self-evidently is. That being said, there are very particular periods in a child's life when he or she is more vulnerable than at other times and in need of particularly protective care. This protectionist model of childhood dictated that adults were the experts and the great protectors of children's needs, and this resulted in children having little opportunity under law and in wider society to express their views concerning their welfare or that of others. Within this treatment of childhood children were considered immature and lacking the competence of adults, which meant that decisions were often made on their behalf without their opinions being taken into account. Once children were removed from the workplace and given an education, childhood became a time of preparation for entering adulthood. The distinctions between children and adults became formalized. Today one of the central components of Western thinking about childhood is the idea that childhood should be seen as a period of "becoming": as a period that shapes each person's opportunities later in life. During a conversation I once had with the anthropologist Ronnie Frankenberg, he argued that it is too restrictive to assume that the period of "becoming" will end once childhood is over. As he put it, "Are we not all always in a process of flux and change?" No one can ever consider him- or herself complete in the way that is implied by the notion that a child is preparing to become an adult. All the same, during childhood there are clearly significant and lasting influences at work that contribute to the shaping of later experiences. If, as we believe in the West, the psyche of a person is laid down in childhood, then it is easy to see why we are generally so protective of children's lives. It also makes sense that we should have put legal apparatus in place to protect children and to ensure that they do not have to take on responsibilities now associated with adulthood. But this understanding of childhood as a time of immaturity and preparation for adulthood has developed out of a very particular set of historical, political, economic, and social developments that are peculiar to Western Europe and North America and that have led directly to the philosophy that underpins the development of child rights and the UNCRC.

## The Origins of Child Rights and the UNCRC

The UNCRC, with its emphasis on child rights and the child as an autonomous individual, only came into existence in 1989, but questions began to be raised in the first half of the twentieth century (even as the protectionist model of childhood dominated general attitudes toward children) by a small minority in Western Europe about the right of children not only to protection but also to self-expression and their own set of basic human rights. As early as 1909, the Swedish reformer Ellen Key claimed that the twentieth century would be the century of the child. She envisioned a world where children would take their place alongside adults as full and equal participants in society. This was very much a minority view of childhood at the time, however, and had no social or political sway. The twentieth century did see the recognition of the idea that children have rights, beginning with the Geneva Declaration of the Rights of the Child in 1924, but it was not until 1948, in the aftermath of World War II, that international human rights were first codified. Even then the powerlessness of children was largely absent from the declaration. It is the absence of any focus on children's rights from the 1948 Universal Declaration of Human Rights that the UNCRC addresses.

In 1989 the United Nations formally adopted the fifty-four principles that make up the UNCRC, from the right of a child to a nationality and name to the right to education and play and special protection for children removed from their family of origin and in some cases being put up for adoption.

On the face of it this child-focused convention has achieved unprecedented international recognition. Today 191 of the world's 193 countries have ratified the UNCRC, making themselves legally bound to comply with its obligations; the only exceptions are the United States and Somalia. While the United States has not signed the UNCRC it has agreed to uphold a number of its articles, notably those relating to child labor. Although the UNCRC is still not considered important on the American domestic front it does inform the international work of U.S. nonprofit aid and welfare groups, including some of the NGOs I encountered in Vietnam, which are often active in areas of the world where the UNCRC has a high profile. Its supporters consider it to be universally applicable. The developmental psychologist Mary John explains that the UNCRC represents decades of careful thought and drafting by the working group of the Human Rights Commission in establishing a common basis for agreement of what these rights should be. It establishes a vision of the kind of life every child should be entitled to (2003).

### Principles of the Charter

The intentions set down in the UNCRC indicate a genuine desire to avoid situations in which children become victims of both manufactured and natural difficulties. Archbishop Desmond Tutu makes this clear in his introduction to a children's book about the UNCRC published by the United Nations International Children Education Fund (for more about UNICEF, see chapter 3), which oversees it:

> In this book you will see many pictures of children as they should be—happy, healthy, laughing, learning, holding securely to adults they could trust, who would protect and uphold their inalienable rights—the rights formally laid out in the UNCRC.... There have been pictures to appall us, showing children as they should not be, hollow eyed and pot bellied, as victims of malnutrition, famine and disease.... We have seen children

benumbed after witnessing the mass killings of relatives. . . . children abused and raped. . . . Let us commit ourselves to outlaw the conditions that have made the second kind of pictures possible. (UNICEF 2002, iv)

But the UNCRC is not only designed to deal with such extreme childhood experiences. Its advocates intend that it should also be used to give children rights that impact upon everyday life experiences. In doing so they embrace a particular view of what childhood should be like: for example under the UNCRC all children are expected to receive a formal education at primary level, and they should as much as possible reside in a family home with adults to support them.

The procedure of national ratification requires state representatives from each ratified country to examine their laws and bring them in line with the UNCRC. Article 3 of the UNCRC requires governments to fulfill their commitment that judicial and administrative agencies will make the best interests of children a primary concern. The United Nations established a monitoring committee to follow the performance of each of these signatory states. The committee is empowered to obtain periodic reports from these states, initially after two years and then at five-year intervals, on the steps they have taken to realize their commitments under the UNCRC. Notwithstanding this, countries are also given the option of opting out of certain articles that they feel they are not yet able to comply with.

### Child Rights under the UNCRC

The UNCRC treats children as autonomous individual rights-bearing citizens by defining four different types of rights for them. *Provision rights* allow for growth and development: they include the rights to food, housing, and education. *Prevention rights* are concerned with putting systems in place that prevent abuse of children or infringements of their rights, for example, legal representation or the right to privacy. *Protection rights* are concerned with protecting children against exploitation and abuse and intervening once their rights have been infringed (for example, children who have suffered abuse in the home can be given state protection). The fourth and final category is probably the most contentious: *Participation rights* enable children to take part in decisions being made on their behalf and include freedom of conscience and the right to hold an opinion. The rights laid down in the UNCRC obviously overlap and are not meant to be mutually exclusive, but by ratifying the UNCRC, governments have agreed to incorporate its provisions into their national laws and to place children's interests at the center of policymaking.

The UNCRC asks that children's best interests be set above those of adults to a greater or lesser degree depending on each child's level of competence, and it is this aspect of the UNCRC that is proving to be problematic in all parts of the world. In practice there may be clashes between adults and children about children's rights to participate in decisions made about them. Even the most ardent supporters of child rights acknowledge how difficult it has been to properly support such rights, not least because such debates are usually held within the family circle and away from the public gaze.

While working for the Open University in England, I interviewed Gerison Lansdown, an academic who keenly promotes the UNCRC with specific reference to its influence in Great Britain. She noted that the "UNCRC supports the rights of children to be heard, to express their views and freedom of religion and so on. And in that respect there is a challenge to every society in the world in relation to children because children have traditionally not had rights to articulate their views, to be heard properly in political decisions, in social decisions, in family decisions, in education and so on" (January 2002). While Lansdown makes a valid point, the same arguments could be applied to the experiences of most adults, to the elderly, or to people from ethnic minorities, many of whom would find it difficult to articulate their rights. If many adults find it hard to articulate their own rights, is it not wishful thinking to expect children to be able to do so, particularly because children's positions in society remain so contradictory? Children are at once considered in need of protection and adult-led nurturing while at the same time it is possible, under the UNCRC, for them to stand up and have their viewpoints properly heard, sometimes by the very people who might be protecting them.

As I found out, many children I worked with had experienced difficulties in their lives and lacked the confidence to verbalize their wants in formal settings. Moreover, they would have been scared to do so because of their vulnerability: fear of arrest, fear that formal services aimed at them would change the face of their lives, remove them from the street, or put them in reform settings. In fact the very convention that is credited with introducing child participatory rights on a global scale is itself deeply flawed on this issue. As John asserts, "it is interesting that those responsible for drafting the UNCRC, while emphasizing in Article 12 the importance of involving children in all matters that concern them, failed to practice what they preached. Children did not participate in the deliberations or the drafting of the UNCRC. This alone indicates how the international community still implicitly regards children" (2003, 104). The fact that children did not contribute to the drafting of the one internationally recognized human rights bill that purports to support their interests indicates a disturbing level of hypocrisy.

Such experiences of disempowerment at the local level are not only felt by the individual. One of the problems with living in a globalized world is that, on the surface, the same level of opportunities seems to exist across the world and the differences of opportunity between states becomes less obvious. Gilbert and Gugler have stated, "The process of incorporation into the world system has spread across the entire globe. The self-centered society that had only limited contact from the outside world has virtually disappeared" (1992, 63). This does not mean, however, that everyone has achieved the same level of access to the world system and global economic development, or that greater knowledge about what is taking place throughout the world has led to a growing consensus among countries desiring to change. As Anthony Giddens argues, "In circumstances of accelerating globalization the nation-state has become too small for the big problems of life, and too big for the small problems of life" (1990, 65). The argument that nation-states are being simultaneously weakened and strengthened by globalization depending on their political allegiances and the stance that they take on individual issues might prompt greater faith in the international bodies such as the United Nations. But Giddens goes on to argue, "The global influence of the United Nations is not purchased solely by means of diminution of the sovereignty of nation-states" (73). It should be noted as well that programs often have to be deliberated over long periods because of the time it takes for member states to reach a consensus, and the resulting declaration can be so compromised that the clarity of the original intention is significantly reduced.

The drafting of the UNCRC is a case in point: those who drafted the

UNCRC wrote in very broad terms under each article, and because of this the entire convention is open to interpretation. As Murray Last explains, UNCRC articles offer party states agreement flexibility in accordance with their national laws. Britain, for example, has not agreed to uphold articles that refer to child labor. Last writes, "On the sensitive issue of how far a child had a right to express his views and a right to freedom of thought, conscience and religion, the degree of maturity was left as the crucial variable" (1994, 196). The UNCRC also leaves it to national governments to sort out the sticky problem of how to find the necessary resources to implement the stated goals. All that the UNCRC says is "The State must do all it can to implement the rights recognized by the convention and contained in it" (UNCRC 1989).

This also begs the question of whether the level of resources needed to effect real improvement would ever become available. National governments may attract international funding and charity assistance, but such money is too limited to alter people's lifestyles significantly. For example, people who live in poverty are unlikely to ever achieve the objectives of Article 24 of the UNCRC, which states that children should have adequate nutrition and education. Articles are also often unsystematically applied, and piecemeal solutions are offered where a comprehensive program of development and investment would be more appropriate. Of course, with the declaration in February 2005 by the G7 nations of their intention to write off third world debt there may be some hope for the future, but even here the United States has declined to join with the other countries, and some commentators do not believe that anything collective will actually happen (BBC News Ten O'Clock Report, February 5, 2005). So we can talk about child rights and show concern about conditions under which children in the so-called third and second worlds sometimes operate, but the laudable notion that all children should have primary education or adequate health care does not stand a chance of being achieved until adequate resources are put in place to make that happen. The UNCRC makes no attempt to acknowledge or address the current distorted global distribution of wealth in its list of factors that need to change if improvements are going to be made in children's lives.

For the philosophy of the UNCRC to take effect it must have popular local support and influence-changing values from within a society rather than being externally imposed. But when, for example, the UNCRC was ratified in Vietnam it was done in such a way that it immediately took precedence over existing policies on childhood without any attempt being made by the Vietnamese government or UNICEF to address or reconcile the differences that existed. Officially the UNCRC carries weight, but it is difficult to measure whether it has had real impact at the local level. Local officials and charity workers may have mouthed the rhetoric, but as I discovered and discuss in chapter 3, it did not follow that they fully supported or understood that children had particular rights. And my findings show that work with children has become confused by the existence of a disparate range of organizations that often hold conflicting ideas about their circumstances and needs.

One of the biggest sticking points for supporters of child rights is that, wherever they are based, society at large does not show consistent commitment to their cause, because so many contradictory ideas about children jostle inconsistently alongside each other. But child rights workers are also inconsistent in their support of particular aspects of the UNCRC.

I raise these issues because the enunciation of the laudable principles contained within the UNCRC carries with it high expectations. While it may provide signatory states with a set of universal objectives, its real impact will depend on the validity of its application and on the level of local support that it receives. Like other critics (for example, Alston 1994), I argue that the UNCRC presents a particular view of childhood that is not universally applicable, and so it is ineffective at the local level. I therefore question whether the UNCRC can ever live up to its supporters' expectations. With that in mind, let us now look at some of the key societal differences that exist between the West and other parts of the world, differences that challenge the UNCRC's claim to universality.

### Collectivist and Individualistic Societies

The UNCRC is a human rights convention of international standing. The anthropologist Richard Wilson points out that "the past few decades have witnessed the inexorable rise of the application of international human rights law as well as the extension of a wider public discourse on human rights, to the point where human rights could be seen as one of the most globalized political values of our time." (1997, 1) The universalists who uphold the UNCRC perceive human rights as self-evident universal norms.

Sitharamam Kakarala (1989) points out that human rights laws are founded on the Western philosophy that each person is an autonomous individual, while relativists point out that the human rights agenda was developed in Western Europe largely in response to the human abuses that occurred during World War II. Thus the concept of what it is to be a human and to have rights is bound to a particular point in history and to the principle that individuals bear rights.

Influenced as it is by "Western" notions of individuality, the United Nations' thinking deals less well with societies whose social rules are grounded in the concepts of collective responsibility, such as those that espouse Confucianism. This has led to an overemphasis on the individualistic conceptions of rights in its development of human rights procedures. The anthropologist Roger Goodman notes that when the concept of "rights" was introduced to Japan, "a whole new vocabulary had to be developed to explain it, as did the idea of the individual who could be endowed with such rights. Even today, individualism has strongly negative connections in Japan and is frequently associated with Western selfishness" (Goodman and Neary 1996, 131). Most Southeast Asian countries have a collective sense of self (albeit one that is not static) that comes from a fundamentally different understanding of family and society. So in places like China and Vietnam, where individual human rights are still largely subordinate to those of the needs of the family (and sometimes the state), the idea of the individual autonomous self is not nearly so well understood as in the West. But to locate individualistic and collectivist societies in rigidly opposed camps would be an overreaction: as Richard Wilson states, "the universalist/relativist polarity is too totalizing . . . what is needed are more detailed studies of human rights according to the actions and intentions of the social actors within wider historical constraints of institutionalized power" (1997, 3).

It is too simplistic to conclude merely that cultural misunderstandings are central to the failure of the UNCRC to take effect. In chapter 3 I show that it was the practitioners in charge of applying the UNCRC to the Vietnamese setting who had a tendency to introduce the concept of rights without simultaneously familiarizing themselves with Vietnamese ideas of rights and selfhood, a failing that was not so much about cultural misunderstanding as about operating with imperialistic notions of power. This situation is further complicated by the fact that in countries that were once colonized

much of what still stands for national law was introduced by the former colonial powers and reflects Western notions of individual rights; with growing globalization, internationally led influences are inevitably set to continue
and grow. This does not mean that these same laws will be understood or
applied in the same way in different countries, particularly those of the
South, but there are particular influences of agency and power at work in
the development of globally developed human rights that under certain conditions make compromise on their principles nonnegotiable, by the insistence of linking of aid to government reform. Of late, as with the putative
cancellation of third world debt, there have been some encouraging signs
that donor countries are starting to relax their insistence on such links
(Morrissey, 2004).

Similarly, I observed while in Vietnam that such linking can make it difficult for individuals operating under such circumstances to retain a level
of objectivity about their work. Some child rights–focused expatriate NGO
workers I interviewed gave the impression that they held the moral high
ground in all that they did simply because they were trying to enforce a
new set of standards for Vietnam's children. Their approach was to attempt
to introduce the UNCRC rapidly, and in opposition to local cultural mores
and values, rather than introduce its principles gradually in sympathy with
local value systems.

### Ripostes from the South

These attempts by the UN to apply universal edicts have provoked
the elites of the South to create alternative forms of human rights, which
creates further ambiguity in the application of human rights (Kakarala 1996).
One of the most prominent of these is the African Charter on the Rights
and Welfare of the Child, which came into force in 1990. It was developed
and promoted by the Organization of African Unity, a group made up of African governments that provides a regional forum for African needs. The
various member states in this organization felt that the UNCRC needed to
be made more relevant to the concerns of the region (confirming my as-
sertion that not everyone agrees that the UNCRC is universally applicable).
The charter recognizes the particular quality of an African childhood. It
stresses both the rights and the *responsibilities* of the child and also gives
equal weight to the concurrent responsibilities of the community toward

the child. In contrast, in the UNCRC, the words "responsibilities" and "duties" never feature in relation to children, only to the adults caring for them.

Expectations for children in other parts of the world have been shaped by different historical and contemporary influences. The Vietnamese human rights academic Tai (1988) points out that because scholars think of human rights as constitutional rights they tend to consider those rights as originating with the constitutions of the Western world. But he asks whether we should be considering human rights laws only from within a constitutional framework: what of preexisting laws and values? What of preexisting beliefs about the very concept of selfhood that from the Vietnamese standpoint would make the UNCRC redundant or at least at odds with local cultural values? Certainly the very presence of a government-created national law for children raises questions about the Vietnamese government's real level of commitment to the UNCRC. It was only after I had lived in Vietnam for a year that I discovered that there was a Vietnamese National Law for Children: The Law on Child Protection, Care, and Education (August 12, 1991, passed by the National Assembly of the Socialist Republic of Vietnam, 8th Legislation, 9th Session). As far as I could tell it received little general attention. It occurred to me that its mandate may never have been considered or even recognized by UNICEF or its associated NGOs.

The Vietnamese National Law for Children was ratified shortly after the UNCRC, perhaps in an attempt by the government and its advisors to emphasize some of the values that Vietnam but not the UNCRC expect of their children. One of the expectations of Vietnamese children under Article 13.1 of the National Law on Child Protection, Care, and Education is "to show love, respect and piety toward grandparents and parents, politeness toward adults, affection toward younger children and solidarity with friends." The expectations that a child should take responsibility for his or her actions and show respect toward his or her elders is absent from the UNCRC which refers to the individual child as having rights but no responsibilities toward others.

## How Observing the Lives of Vietnamese Children Changed My Research

In Vietnam I focused my fieldwork on children who were considered marginalized and in need of special protection by the child-focused aid organizations that I was also doing fieldwork among. This included children who worked and/or lived on the streets, those who were in a reform school, and children who lived in an orphanage or were at a school for special needs. These were the very children who were most likely to come into contact with organizations that supported child rights. They were also children whose lives were shaped by some very particular and sometimes contradictory influences particular to Vietnam and furthermore were from a segment of society in which child work was the norm. One of the most striking aspects of working with the children I met in Hanoi was that some had left home and were making decisions to work not because they felt abandoned by their families but in order to support another sibling through school, or they were living independently because they and not their parents had made the decision to do so because they felt the financial burden of their own existence. Such decision making by children is not confined to the South, but in the chapter that follows I draw on a body of literature that refers to the more collectivist mentality in particular cultural settings. Some of the most pressing issues for the children I met centered on ambitions that were in opposition to their rights as laid down in the UNCRC. Boys in the reform school were eager to learn a trade so that they could work without the risk of arrest after leaving the school. The NGO I visited the school with supported the boys' intentions by introducing a skills training program for them, something that child rights supporters were deeply opposed to. Children who worked on the streets did not want to be returned to live with their families in the countryside; therefore their wishes clashed with the UNCRC policy on family, in which emphasis is placed on the importance of children growing up in an adult-led family unit.

Recognizing that this international agenda on childhood, and particularly the UNCRC, was being vigorously introduced in Vietnam, I expanded my ethnography to address the following areas. First, I set out to look at the manner in which this globalized, Western-based view of childhood was making its presence felt in Hanoi. It then became necessary as a point of comparison to be able to contrast the approaches and results of two disparate groups of NGOs: those that upheld the UNCRC and those that did not. By understanding ideas about children at the local level, I would be able to discover how (and if) the global perspective was relevant in Hanoi. As Burman points out, "distinctions between local, global and globalized conceptions of childhood are central to the consideration of the success, and limitations, of international policies and programs" (1995, 45).

To do justice to this, I had to adopt two distinctly polarized approaches in my fieldwork. At the local, street level, using techniques of participant observation, I needed to be able to observe the way in which the children played out their lives of survival, noting from their necessarily parochial perspective the impact that authorities (however they were perceived) had on their lives. This required an anthropological perspective. At the other end of the spectrum, I had to become involved with the various agencies to see how the child-intervention policies were being argued and developed into budgets and projects. This required a socioeconomic perspective. Then I had to sit in the middle and try to make sense of the reasons for the disparities that occurred in the gap between the two worlds: the world in which children fought to make a living, often without any understanding that anyone was on their side, and the other world, in which agencies thought they were on the children's side but often had a limited understanding of the children's real problems.

From my observations, it seemed that numerous local and international beliefs about what constituted childhood jostled each other in an uneasy alliance, or appeared to be at complete odds with each other. Meanwhile, the real needs of the children were often lost within the general rhetoric; organizations had different aims and objectives in working with or for children, not always sharing the same ideas about what children needed. As I show in chapter 3, this sometimes resulted in duplication of projects or conflicts of interest between different groups trying to assist the same children. Lack of consensus and understanding among the organizations interested in children led to a situation similar to that observed by anthropologist Mary Douglas in her analysis of institutions: "When individuals disagree on elementary justice, their most insoluble conflict is between institutions based on incompatible principles. The more severe the conflict, the more useful to understand the institutions that are doing most of the thinking" (1986, 125).

It was in a similar conflicting and often competitive environment of the various NGOs active in Hanoi that I found the actual needs of the children could take second place, and sometimes programs intended to help them were either ineffective because of their irrelevance to the local circumstances or even harmful because they were applied without understanding the practical limitations faced by the children.

## Conclusions

When I lived in Hanoi, the child rights–human rights agenda dominated international aid policy, apparently to the exclusion of all other ways of working with children, but as I have noted, I discovered quickly that the internationally upheld United Nations Convention on the Rights of the Child is not universally applicable. Putting one set of values above the rest as being the *right one* creates unrealistic and unattainable expectations. And I came to see that child rights work was often dominated by overzealous expatriate aid professionals who were focused far more on their international objectives than on becoming familiar with the country in which they were living.

Before starting my research in Vietnam I was distrustful of faith-based non-governmental agencies. Once I had lived in Vietnam, my positive findings among such NGOs forced me to rethink some of those prejudices and to simultaneously readdress the true worth of the philosophies informing today's dominant aid organizations. I found that I could only do this by focusing my attention first on children's experiences and only afterward on the organizations that professed to assist them. In the process I realized that the children I knew were ignorant of the more generalized messages about child rights and the rights of the individual child. These children lived and worked in a number of interlinked settings: on the streets, in a reform school (sometimes after being arrested on the streets for illegally working), or an orphanage (some of those children also worked on the streets), or studied at a school for children who were hearing impaired. It is serving their real and actual needs that should dominate aid programs, so this book is largely about those children's lives and aspirations.

In the following chapters, I discuss why children work and then go on to look more closely at the lives of some children who worked on the streets. I then follow some of them by observing life in a reform school, an orphanage, and other institutional settings. Certain aspects of these children's lives were quite striking. Meeting individuals who were categorized as "street children" or "orphans" or as a "girl-child" by social scientists and aid workers working at more of a distance from their subjects than I was able to has made me averse to the use of such terms. The use of such terms inevitably means that children are treated stereotypically, and this in turn reinforces the erroneous argument that international aid is universally applicable.

If my findings demonstrate anything it is that the most successful forms of support to people can come from the least expected sources, that the most visible methods of offering support to people are not necessarily the most useful, and that what works in one area of the world will not work in another. But although I am now quite critical of the manner in which the UNCRC is generally being introduced to Vietnam, there is room for optimism. As I show in the following chapters, as a result of positive intervention by a few of the NGOs some far-reaching changes were occurring in the lives of some children among whom I did fieldwork; there were also a few successful programs drawn from the child rights convention. For me, the most striking observation during my time in Hanoi was that most of the disadvantaged children I knew experienced some kind of positive change in their lives when assisted by an individual or an organization that had direct long-term personal contact with them—people who took the trouble to get to know them and understand their culture.

## Two

# Background to
# Vietnam

---

Most of the children I met during fieldwork were born in the 1980s, a time of great flux for Vietnam: By the mid-1980s Communist-inspired agricultural collectivism was failing, engendering famines and crisis. The crisis was further worsened by the 1991 collapse of the Soviet Union, which resulted in the end of the Soviet Union's financial aid to Vietnam. During the sixth Communist Party Congress in 1986, the Vietnamese government introduced reform under a policy labeled Doi Moi, which means "renovation" or "renewal." This meant that out of pragmatic necessity the Vietnamese government followed its Chinese neighbors in developing a socialist-oriented market economy. This type of mixed market economy held out the best hope for economic growth, and an acceptance of Western economic governance rules, which accompanied this switch in policy, meant that they would be eligible for Western aid and investment.

Vietnam is still a one-party state controlled by the Communist Party. The country is referred to as a socialist republic but has a market-oriented economy. This shift in policy has given Western organizations both in the private and non-government sectors new freedom to enter Vietnam and establish working relationships. But it has also resulted in an unclear future for Vietnam, where, as I show throughout this book, Communist-informed thinking overlaps on the one hand with older belief systems such as Confucianism and on the other with contemporary structural reform influences exerted at an international level, principally from the West. If it were not for a fundamental shift in policy I would never have had such freedom to stay in Vietnam and been able to meet the children who appear on the pages that follow, but neither would I have become engaged in studying the manner in which children's circumstances at the local level are being so readily ignored in the application of Western-driven aid policy.

Vietnam has historically experienced a hard battle with outsiders intent on reshaping and taking over its territory to claim the country as their own. It has been colonized or fought over by the Chinese, the French, the Japanese, and the Americans. A not dissimilar desire for ownership sometimes seems reflected in the work of modern aid workers and academics working in the region. Contemporary Vietnam is being invaded in a more subtle but nevertheless nefarious manner, this time by cultural hijackers intent on, among other objectives, introducing children in the region to a new set of values and expectations, without necessarily first doing the groundwork to find out why they follow their current lifestyles.

In this chapter, to contextualize the experience of the children who appear throughout this book, I discuss some of these historical and cultural influences and explain how they continue to shape the experiences of people living in contemporary Vietnam.

## Geography and Early History

The Socialist Republic of Vietnam lies along the eastern edge of the peninsula of mainland Southeast Asia. The country is more than one thousand miles long, running down from China in the north to the delta of the Mekong River in the south. Vietnam is bordered on the east by the South China Sea; its neighbors to the west are Laos and Cambodia, while to the north lies China. Its land mass totals 329,556 square kilometers (Duiker 1995, 1). Ethnic Vietnamese make up 85 percent of the population, and the remaining 15 percent have had their origins traced back to the Thai, Cham, Khmer, and ethnic Chinese. Today the population is estimated to be about 81 million, and a high growth rate continues. Vietnam's two fertile alluvial deltas—Red River, or Hong-ha, in the north and Mekong in the south—have inspired the image of the typical Vietnamese peasant carrying two rice baskets suspended at the ends of a pole (SarDesai 1992, 1). The capital city, Hanoi, lies to the north in the grain-producing region of the Red River Delta. Ho Chi Minh City (still sometimes locally known as Saigon) is to the south. Between the two lies a thinner, less populated and less productive coastal region. The seventeenth parallel, which from 1954 to 1975 formed a contested political boundary between what were then North Vietnam and South Vietnam, intersects the central portion of Vietnam.

In 1975 North and South Vietnam were united under a Communist government, but significant cultural differences remain between them to this day. A standard generalization is that people from the different regions are suspicious of one another; for example, northerners stereotypically consider themselves modern and efficient and consider southerners to be lazy (Neher 1994, 180). Whatever the reality, the people of the south, many of whom had fought alongside the Americans to ward off Communism, suffered more openly under the Communist leadership after 1975, and a residual resentment exists on both sides.

The ancestral home of the Vietnamese people is in the north of the country. It was originally much smaller in size than present-day Vietnam, and through the centuries it was vulnerable to being conquered from the north by the Chinese. In 206 BC China took over and ruled the north of Vietnam, and for the next thousand years the Chinese considered Vietnam part of their territory; Vietnam was dominated by China until 939 AD (K. Nguyen 1993, 14). An understanding of the effect China had during its rule is key to understanding some of the influences that continue to shape Vietnam.

Although the Vietnamese people acknowledge that China has had some influence over the country, the extent to which this is the case is a hotly debated and quite sensitive issue. My Vietnamese language teacher in Hanoi once explained to me that the Vietnamese have been very good at absorbing and adapting the influences of outsiders such as the Chinese and the French, later producing something that is distinctly different, or at the very least is altered in the Vietnamese context. Hirschman and Loi have gathered evidence suggesting that the Vietnamese adapted the teachings of the Chinese philosopher Confucius so that the philosophy became more closely aligned to their existing social practices (1994).

## *Spiritual Beliefs*

While the teachings of Confucius became more influential, from the fifteenth century the dominant Vietnamese belief system was an amalgamation of four main influences: Confucianism, Taoism, Buddhism, and Christianity. Over the centuries, Confucianism, Taoism, and Buddhism have fused with popular Chinese beliefs and ancient Vietnamese animism to form what is known collectively as Tam Giao ("triple religion"). If asked their religion, the Vietnamese are likely to say they are Buddhist, but when it comes to family or civic duties they are likely to follow Confucianism while turning to Taoist conceptions in their understanding of the cosmos. Perhaps because of this, individual people I spoke to in Hanoi found it difficult to pinpoint what their spiritual beliefs were; one Vietnamese friend with whom I visited a temple (or pagoda) told me she was Buddhist, but the reality was more complex than that because we had already lit incense sticks on her mother's ancestral worship table before leaving the house. On one memorable visit to a pagoda I watched another friend make an offering to Buddha while her aunt made one to the tiger, which as an animistic symbol finds its origins in Taoism and is worshipped because of its associations with business success. In my home in Hanoi a room was set aside by the family I lived with for worship at separate altars for the ancestors, Buddha, and the tiger; although worship of the ancestors took priority in daily prayer, the other two still had offerings of food placed in front of them.

### *Buddhism*

Numerous strands of Buddhism coexist across Asia. The dominant form of Buddhism in Vietnam is Mahayana Buddhism, which was introduced to Vietnam from China in the second century AD. The Mahayana ideal is that of Bodhisattva, who even after attaining perfection in generosity, morality, patience, vigor, concentration, and wisdom, still remained on earth to save others. Also in the second century AD, Theravada Buddhism came to Vietnam from India. This form is only found in southern Vietnam and take its guidance from the earliest Buddhist doctrines. Neither of these strands of Buddhism had any impact upon Vietnam's general populace until the eleventh century. Buddhism's influence has remained ever present, even after the Chinese invasion of 1414, which revived interest in Confucianism. In the 1920s a Buddhist revival took place throughout the country, and during the 1960s South Vietnamese Buddhist monks had a high-profile role in the protest movement in opposition to the regime of Ngo Dinh Diem.

### Taoism

Taoism was developed in the sixth century by Laotse ("the Old One"), who was believed to have cared for the Chinese government's archives. According to Taoist cosmology, Ngoc Hoang, the Emperor of Jade whose abode is heaven, rules over a world of divinities, genies, spirits, and demons, in which the forces of nature are incarnated as supernatural beings. There are very few Taoist temples in Vietnam, but Taoism has been assimilated into Vietnam as a collection of superstitions and animistic beliefs. Taoist influences can be seen in the form of worshipping the tiger, and in the dragon and demon motifs that decorate pagoda rooftops.

Whenever I visited a pagoda I learned to light my incense sticks and to wave them rather than blow out the flames. On one occasion at the One Pillar Pagoda in the center of Hanoi, I was about to give a friend one of the two lit incense that I held in my hand when a soldier rushed to my side because he thought that I intended to use the two together. One may light one, three, five, or seven incense sticks—always an uneven number, and each number has its own symbolic value. The number one represents unity, the whole, the fusion of the male and female principles. The number three suggests mobility of the uneven number, which tends to move toward evenness, stability, and equilibrium. When someone is grappling with difficulties, with something that upsets him or her, he or she offers Buddha three incense sticks; it is customary to light three sticks at Tet (the Vietnamese New Year) and at funerals, but only one stick at ordinary rituals.

### Spiritualism and Children

Whenever I had my photo taken, or took photos, respect for number order and unity had to be adhered to. For example, all my photos among children in the orphanage show odd numbers of children. Before I left Vietnam I had hoped to have a photo taken with Nguyet, who lived at the orphanage, but she would not hear of this and hurriedly picked up a younger child to include in the photo so that there were an odd number of people present when her picture was taken.

While at an orphanage and later on a group vacation with local staff and their families from one of the international aid agencies I was involved with for research purposes, I noticed that some young babies had miniature glass bottle charms tied with string either to their wrists or around their necks; I was told that this would ward off evil spirits. As he jiggled his two-year-old daughter on his hip, one of the trust's workers told me that the bottle on a girl child symbolized her virginity, which would become good with age and better when opened at maturity.

Historically, children have always been protected from spirits by some form of trickery. When a baby is first born, only immediate family members are allowed to meet it for the first thirty days of its life: this is because it is believed that the stronger spirits of adults might harm the fragile soul of newborns. In the south of Vietnam people used to avoid naming their children after dead relatives because when scolding a child one might be disturbing the ancestor who shared that name. To avoid this, children were referred to by the order of their birth. Northerners were happy to have their firstborn be so known. But southerners were more fearful of the devil, who was believed to covet the children who were most cherished by their parents, presumably the firstborn male. So they pretended that the firstborn was only the second child, and the ranking of children began with number two.

In the 1960s it was still possible to see small boys dressed as girls, nails painted and ears pierced, in order to fool the devil. This disguise would last until puberty, when it would no longer be possible to mislead the devil. Some humorous acknowledgment of this dated practice still occasionally takes place. In February 1997, my partner was eating noodles at a stall he regularly visited when the owner's five-year-old son was bustled out of the family house in girl's clothes. The stall owner's friends thought this was hilarious and made witty remarks about his disguise until the boy was so overwhelmed with confusion that he burst into tears. The owner later explained that his son would have had to put up with wearing girls' clothes if he had been born at a time when it was still widely believed that this would protect him from evil spirits. The same logic of fooling the devil led parents to initially give their newborn babies unpleasant or obscene names, such as "pig" or "ugly," in a bid to protect them from being taken away by sprits.

When a child was a month old a feast was held, and on the first birthday parents would try to pinpoint a boy child's future by laying out the tools of trade associated with a scholar, an artisan, a farmer or tradesman for him to then choose by grasping for the associated object (Tai 1988, 118). In Chinese tradition the choice of tradesman was least attractive, while being a farmer was seen as quite respectable.

### Ancestor Worship and Male Dominance

"To be happy after death, the dead person should have children (preferably one father should have at least one son) to correctly comply with funeral rites and then to practice the cult of the parents" (K. Nguyen 1993, 121).

The standard scholarly view is that the Chinese introduced the teachings of Confucius to Vietnam but that it was not until the Le dynasty in the fifteenth century that Confucianism became very influential. Confucius taught that order and peace within each family are prerequisites to a well-run country. Because of this, particular weight has been attached to his teachings about family life. From the Confucian perspective relationships within the family are always hierarchical. The person in the position of superiority should guide, love, and care for inferiors, while those who are inferior should always obey their superiors. The Confucian family works within a hierarchy with particular value attached to the men of the household. The wife obeys her husband, the son and daughter obey their parents, younger siblings obey older ones. Confucianism holds that the firstborn boy has higher status than any boys who follow. The eldest boy is sometimes given a particular name to signify his importance. It is also the eldest son who continues to live with his parents after marriage and who will be expected to take over the practice of maintaining the family ancestral worship table after they die.

Ancestral worship, which finds its roots in the Confucian philosophy, prioritizes male heirs, and the firstborn son has a traditionally higher value placed upon him than is placed upon his siblings, because it is he who will maintain the chief ancestral worship table. The ancestral table is used to worship the last three generations of the paternal family, and some families still follow the worship of ancestors quite strictly. Upon marrying, a woman is expected to honor her husband's family above her own, but if there is no son to honor her parents, she is also able to worship them to ensure that they do not become lost spirits. Each year on the full moon of the seventh lunar month, the Feast of the Wandering Souls is held to ensure that unworshipped spirits are placated. Anniversaries of a relative's death are marked by the preparation of their favorite meal in life, and relatives are often invited to share the food and to observe the burning of votive papers (for example, symbolic money and paper images of worldly goods) in their honor. Alongside votive papers, families burn gifts for the dead. During the first occasion that I was invited to take part in, which honored my landlady's deceased husband, a paper motorbike and symbolic U.S. dollars were burnt for him. The following year he received a paper car among the offerings.

It is likely that Confucian philosophy was adapted to accommodate preexisting lore and values, and it has come to coexist alongside other social practices. Hy Luong found similar levels of familial-based equality among the sexes in the northern village where he did fieldwork: "the affinal ties in the village were by no means insignificant because a married-out woman continued to maintain ritual obligations toward the members of her natal patriline or local patrilineage. She was expected to bring her children to her parents' home to attend the important death anniversaries in her family of birth. At the wedding of any of her children, ancestral offerings were made not only to her husband's ancestors but also to the ancestors of her own father and mother" (1992, 61).

### Catholicism

Catholicism was the last of the most prominent belief systems to be introduced to Vietnam in the sixteenth century by Portuguese, Spanish, and French missionaries. Today only about 10 percent of the population is Catholic, and freedom to practice the faith is still fairly limited. The government does not encourage an expansion of the faith, which means that Catholic international aid agencies (or any other Christian-based aid agencies), while able to work in Vietnam, cannot evangelize.

## Spiritualism in Modern Times

Most of the Vietnamese people adhered to their varied traditional beliefs during the transition from the colonial period, through the time of strict Communism when traditional values and beliefs were firmly suppressed, and on into today's market-oriented socialism. These beliefs and traditions form an integral and important part of Vietnamese society, and some knowledge of their importance is essential if the observer is to gain any sort of understanding of the people's behavior and attitudes. Following the near–Cultural Revolution harshness of the 1950s, ancestor worship became fairly uncommon. But in reality it was Christianity and Buddhism that were more ruthlessly repressed by the Communist ruling government in the North, due to Buddhist anti-Communist agitators. The Communist state put a stop to such religious practices, and particularly harsh laws were enacted during the period of agricultural collectivization in the 1950s when, for example, pagodas were converted into granaries (Hiebert 1995, 92).

Today there is a state-approved Buddhist church and recently a state-approved Catholic church, but all other sects are repressed due to their perceived or actual potential for anti-Communist agitation. This is particularly true of Protestant sects popular among ethnic minorities of the Central Highlands. Traditional festivals and beliefs were also banned at the height of Communism, and it was not until collectivized farming came to an end in the early 1980s that the laws governing such practices became more relaxed. For example, grandmothers have once more resumed the practice of "adopting their children to local deities in the belief that this will afford them protection" (Hiebert 1995, 92).

Newfound awareness of the old traditions is growing among young people who grew up in an environment where such observances were banned. A friend of mine who is in his early twenties was enthralled by the fertility festivals that he had read about in the newspaper. He explained to me and other members of an attentive audience sitting having beer together that in one such festival teenagers on the cusp of adulthood parade around their village with the girls holding clappers with holes in the center and the boys carrying poles with phallus-like sticks on the end. The aim of the parade is for couples to bang the two instruments together ritualistically. Girls who become pregnant during this and other, similar springtime fertility festivals are apparently accepted and not chastised by members of their community. Practices like this probably predate Confucianism, and it is possible that they were retained as a form of lighthearted relief from the introduction of strict rules governing sexual practice.

*Children and Tet*

Celebrations and festivities are marked by the lunar calendar, and the highlight of the year is the lunar new year, Tet, which usually falls in February. This is the one time that everyone takes a holiday and stops working for at least a day. The buildup to the celebrations is enormous, and the holiday offers an opportunity for family reunions and visiting good friends.

During this time all the children who have migrated to Hanoi to work on the streets return to their villages if they still have family there. The number of children attempting to escape from the reform school quadruples and children at the orphanage feel the absence of family more acutely or return for a visit to their extended family. At this time of year the guards and staff at the reform school were far more relaxed with the children. For the duration of Tet they placed a television in each of the children's dormitories as a form of light relief and thus compensation for the boys not being allowed to leave the school and return to their families. During Tet, children at both the reform school and the orphanage voiced concern about my inability to go home to be with my parents. When I explained that Tet is not celebrated in Britain or the United States but that there are other family-oriented holidays such as Christmas and Thanksgiving, they looked baffled: a younger reform-school pupil named Sei asked, "But how could anyone not celebrate Tet?"

At this time of year the Vietnamese believe that they are being judged for the deeds of the previous year. Tet was the only time of year that I did not have to barter for my fruit and vegetables, and it was during my first experience of New Year that I learned how much I'd been overcharged previously! During the week before Tet everyone takes part in the cleaning of their house, and in Hanoi at the end of the week the woman of the household releases a fish, a golden carp, into one of Hanoi's many lakes. It is believed that the kitchen god then flies up to heaven on the back of the carp to report on the state of the family he lives with and to advise the gods about the future that those people deserve. He returns to the family five days later at the start of the New Year.

In the kitchen god's absence there are parties. Modern life in the city has caused some concern over the welfare of the god who traditionally resides in the kitchen fire and not in a modern charcoal burner! I saw this change in the nature of cooking appliances used to good effect in a play for young people that was designed to address the issue of safe sex: On the kitchen god's return to heaven to report on the year's business, he bemoaned the lack of warmth in his fire and asked his heaven-based peers' advice about a new disease called AIDS, which he explained was affecting the young of today, with their more relaxed morals. God responded by acknowledging that indeed times had changed. He then worked out a way to protect the foolish mortals by coming up with the idea of condoms, which were then distributed with much humor to members of the audience by the bemused kitchen god.

When visiting a family's house at Tet, it is common practice to present any children with a small amount of money in an ornate envelope. They are not allowed to open the envelope until New Year's Eve after the "first footer" (the first visitor to step over the threshold once the new year has begun, often a friend of the family who has been invited to arrive at this auspicious moment) has visited the house bringing more of these envelopes to people within the household. After presenting the gifts and offering Happy New Year messages, everyone settles down to drink rice wine, which has been dyed red to symbolize good fortune, and to eat fruits of the same color.

The food delicacy for that time of year is called *banh trung* and consists of a rice cake stuffed with pork and fat. The origin of banh trung is told in a fable to young children and its overriding message is that spiritual wisdom is of greater value than material gain. The story goes that many centuries ago, a king who ruled part of Vietnam sent his younger sons out into the world to live independently. One New Year he asked them to return bearing a gift, by which he would measure their love for him. All except the youngest had bestowed riches upon him, but the youngest son was a poor farmer and owned very little. On hearing of his father's request he had looked around his home and, seeing only his last scraps of rice and pork, created a cake that was cooked and wrapped tightly in banana leaves. The king was insulted and angry on receiving the gift until he realized how thin his son was. Thus he learned that his son had handed over his last morsel out of filial respect and love, and so the Tet festival serves as a reminder that material wealth is of little consequence but that a humble and gracious spirit is of great worth. At the same time, the legend reinforces a child's lowly position in the hierarchical structure of the family.

### The Children's Festival and the Absence of Working Boys on the Streets

The Full Moon Festival, which usually falls in September, is the celebration that focuses on children, and it is a really lighthearted and fun time of year. On the night of the full moon, children and their families in Hanoi congregate around the main lake and older children throw water at each other and at anyone else who happens to get in the way. People wander around holding lit paper lanterns and eating moon cakes, which are a pastry stuffed with sweetened yellow bean paste.

Traditionally, children also don paper masks, and they are encouraged to be outgoing and to play with their friends. Children of all ages really enjoy this festival, and as the celebration of individual birthdays is a new trend, the Full Moon Festival was until recently the only time of year that children had a celebration that focused on them alone. This festival is an adaptation of the Chinese full moon autumn celebration, and evidence of its cultural origins can be seen in the eating of moon cakes and the lighting of red lanterns.

People let go of their inhibitions and become rowdier than normal, becoming the butt of practical jokes: for example, walking by the side of Hoan Kiem Lake, some foreign friends and I constantly had water thrown at us. But it can also be a time of sadness for children who do not live with family or who cannot afford to take part in the festivities, and I noticed during the evening that the street children I knew who normally hung around by the lakeside were not present. Later Hiep and Hai told me they were not interested in children's games. I was saddened by this and guessed that it pained them to see other children out and about having fun with their parents. I also speculated that a stronger police presence during the festival would have made it difficult for them to join in without being arrested or forced to pay a bribe. But when I talked to them they both looked so despondent that I did not probe further to find out whether either of these possibilities was likely. While Chinese influence is very apparent in Tet and the Autumn Festival, which are the two most popular of Vietnam's festivals, the influence of other invaders has been less obvious.

## The Modern Era

Nicholas Nugent writes, "Few countries have had such a miserable twentieth century as Vietnam. For the first half century the French, not the most benevolent of colonial rulers, dominated the country. The next quarter century was spent at war—first against the French and then the Americans—or against each other according to the perspective of many southerners" (1996, 1).

Vietnam was colonized by the French from the seventeenth century to the middle of the twentieth century, when resistance to the Western colonial powers was occurring over much of Southeast Asia. Anticolonialists fought the French in support of the Nguyen dynasty, to restore the independent monarchy. The next stage in the fight for independence was led by members of the Vietnamese middle classes, such as Phan Boi Chau (1867–1940); by the 1900s they were disillusioned with Confucianism and instead looked to the West for new political ideas for overthrowing the French. Phan Boi Chau was captured in 1925 and sentenced to house arrest for life. Afterward younger leaders, both Communist and non-Communist, emerged to replace him as modern nationalists.

Perhaps surprisingly given the Communist-based re-education aspect of the reform school where I did fieldwork, some of the boys in that setting identified strongly with the life of Ho Chi Minh. To them he was a folk hero who had suffered long prison sentences at the hands of colonialists rather than their oppressor. Some of the boys referred to his *Prison Diary* poems for inspiration.

### Socialism

Initially, the transfer to socialism was influenced by China, then led by Mao Tse-tung. But Vietnam's ensuing war with China meant that Vietnam's Communists turned toward the Soviet model of Marxist-Leninism.

According to Nguyen Huy Thiep (Hiebert 1995, 39) Ho Chi Minh remains popular because of the economic improvements he made during the 1950s to alleviate hunger. By the 1990s that era was most frequently referred to as a mistake, to the point of the government deciding to undertake a "Rectification of Errors" campaign. The land reform led to the killing of thousands of landlords and rich peasants, as well as many dubiously accused of being such. It was also a period in which the roles of men and women altered and a different form of austerity in the name of Communism took hold.

For about two decades the policy of collectivization had a big effect on family life. Families were expected to break away from the shackles of the past by abandoning Confucian values, instead treating all members of the household as equal. Differences between the sexes were suppressed by the unilateral wearing of unisex navy workers' suits.

The founder of Vietnamese Communism was born Nguyen Sinh Cuong but later became most commonly known as Ho Chi Minh. He was born in 1890 and received a strongly Confucian upbringing. The well-educated son of a schoolteacher, he was a teacher himself for a short time before leaving Vietnam in 1911 to travel to Europe and the United States, and he was fluent in French, English, Russian, and Chinese. In 1920 he was a founding member of the French Communist Party, and in 1924 he went to Russia where he became a Soviet agent. After a stint in China, he returned to Vietnam and founded the Indochinese Communist Party in 1930. In 1931 Ho Chi Minh was arrested in Hong Kong by the British police and imprisoned there until 1932. On March 22, 1940, as part of its Pacific Theater offensive, Japan invaded Vietnam from the Chinese border to the north and the French resigned themselves to the Japanese taking temporary control of the country. In 1942 Ho Chi Minh was arrested once more, this time by the Chinese nationalist government while he was in training with the Chinese Communists in southern China. This time he was in prison for two years.

On March 2, 1945, Ho Chi declared independence from the French for the north of the country (Karnow 1983, 135). But it was not until August 28, 1945, that the Viet Minh (the Vietnam Revolutionary League), which had been established by Ho Chi Minh while he was in exile in China, announced the formation of the provisional government of the Democratic Republic of Vietnam (DRV), also known in Europe and the United States of America as North Vietnam, with Ho as president and minister of foreign affairs.

At this time the Communists did not have control of the south of Vietnam, which by the end of that year had reverted to French control. But by 1954 Viet Minh resistance to the French was getting much stronger in the north. A peace conference was held in Geneva and a compromise reached: Vietnam would be divided at the seventeenth parallel; all French and South Vietnamese forces were to move south of the demarcation line, while Viet Minh forces were to move to its north. But because of their heavy losses at the battle of Dien Bien Phu, the French quit the country completely. National elections to reunify Vietnam under a single government were to be held in July 1956, but the United States withheld approval. This meant that the country had been effectively divided into a Communist north (governed by the DRV) and a non-Communist south. By then the United States was offering direct aid to South Vietnam.

It was a tense point in the Cold War; the United States felt profoundly threatened by the number of countries aligned with Communism and thus began trying to prevent South Vietnam from being taken over by the Communist north. In 1959 Vietnam slid into the second Indochina, or Vietnam, War. After sixteen years of increasingly futile war with North Vietnam, the United States finally withdrew from Vietnam in 1973, and on April 30, 1975, Saigon fell to DRV troops. On the July 2, 1976, North and South Vietnam were officially reunited as one country, and Saigon, the capital of the south, was renamed Ho Chi Minh City. During this long and bloody war, 58,000 Americans and more than 3,000,000 Vietnamese, 2,000,000 of whom were civilians, lost their lives. Ho Chi Minh, who is still officially referred to as the "uncle of the people," had died in 1969.

### Childhood under Ho

Certainly the severe shortage of food in the 1970s and early 1980s is remembered with clarity. When I asked a group of Vietnamese aid workers taking part in an international NGO workshop on child participation to write a list of childhood games that they had played, they included fighting over food with neighbors and being sent to orchards and ponds in the middle of the night to steal fruit and fish. Some mentioned helping their mothers to cut up meat using scissors so that the neighbors wouldn't hear the sound of chopping and report them to the local political officers.

It is striking that such experiences emerged during a discussion about play, and that those memories had become connected to an aspect of childhood that we most often associate with lighthearted experiences. In fact during the discussion I got the impression that members of the group were using the exercise as an opportunity to share some of the difficulties they had experienced as children; after all, it is self-evident that fighting over food with neighbors and resorting to cutting food with scissors to avoid discovery are not activities that anyone, let alone a malnourished child, would consider "playful" experiences. Perhaps life was too hard for anyone to feel able to truly take part in lighthearted play, which is after all found predominantly among the more privileged societies of the world.

Luong argues that in twentieth-century Vietnam, local traditions played a major role in shaping villagers' responses to capitalist imperialism and socialist policies (1992). So while social commentators such as Hiebert might argue that over the past two decades Vietnam, like other socialist countries, has experienced "rapid transition" toward a Western-informed market economy, the reality of that experience for most Vietnamese is markedly different from anything that "rapid transition" might imply. This is because in reality Vietnam's Communist Party maintains complete control over economic and social change throughout the country, and only an elite section of Vietnamese society has been able to reap the financial rewards created as a result of Western businesses establishing themselves in Vietnam; contrary to what one might expect only a minority of Vietnamese people are members of the Communist Party.

Prior to becoming fully fledged members of the Communist Party, children are given the opportunity to become members of the Young Pioneers movement, a youth organization attached to the party. As children get older, membership in this organization becomes highly selective, and inclusion grants students greater privileges. Children who are part of the movement wear red scarves around their necks to identify themselves; older students wear no emblem but often become leaders of a class of students. From what I understand it is wise to maintain a good relationship with these cadres-in-training because their power within the party is likely to grow as they become adults. One informant told me that during her schooling only a minority of the people in her class were chosen to enter the Young Pioneer movement. She explained that at the start of each school year the numbers were whittled down, so that by the end of high school only two people in her class were still members. Later they were the ones who entered the best colleges and were most likely to become members of the Communist Party.

The Communist Party continues to exert a high level of control over the general population. On every street and in most community settings the government has erected loudspeakers (tannoys) to remind people of their roles within the socialist movement and to disseminate what they consider relevant information to a particular street. On my street, which was in the center of Hanoi, the first report over the tannoy was at 6:30 a.m., and on important days (such as the anniversary of the 1968 Tet Offensive) broadcasting continued all day, reminding people about past brutalities suffered at the hands of imperialist American soldiers. Sometimes households were publicly chastised for social misdemeanors, for example, local residents who violated the two-child policy. People rarely talk of these experiences, but one girl I knew who had always lived in Hanoi quietly said that "you could never know and understand what it was like, and how much better life is now."

## Reforms

When the Soviet bloc collapsed, Vietnam lost some of its closest allies and aid support. Keen to avoid similar socioeconomic chaos and loss of one-party control, Vietnam shrewdly followed the reform pattern that China has taken by concentrating its policy change on economic liberalization, growth, and structural change. Until the 1980s economic policy centered on the state and collective sectors, which were highly subsidized by the state budget. The central aim had been to move toward industrialization, but this effort is an acknowledged failure. Collective communal farming led to low productivity and production, which meant that Vietnam was unable to produce enough food to support its population. The reduction of foreign aid from the Soviet Union in 1979–80 created a food crisis and mass famine, which triggered land use reforms.

The promotion of the private-sector economy under Doi Moi has led to a reduction in sectors and branches within the state economy, the shutting down of uncompetitive state-owned enterprises, and the privatization of all nonessential economic activities. This shift in policy signifies a "virtual revolution" according to Stefan de Vylder (Hiebert 1995, 49), because state control over the allocation of resources had been so pervasive.

The Vietnamese were originally very optimistic about Doi Moi and believed that they were going to follow closely behind China in terms of economic success. The Japanese invested heavily, as did the Australians, Koreans, and Americans. But growth has not escalated in the way that was once hoped, partly because foreign investors have quickly become frustrated by the bureaucratic nature of doing business in Vietnam, and also because of the 1997 Asian financial crisis that most greatly affected Indonesia and Thailand. The optimism that existed when I first arrived dwindled and the government is now artificially propping the dong (the Vietnamese unit of currency) up against the U.S. dollar.

### Economic Reforms

The first Western organizations of any significance to enter Vietnam were the World Bank and the International Monetary Fund (IMF). The World Bank has directly influenced the Vietnamese government's development policies since 1987. The World Bank is a lending bank and is primarily interested in offering loans to countries on the proviso that those countries adhere to its guidelines as they begin the transition toward becoming capitalist market economies. The key objective of the World Bank is to involve countries in economic expansion within the free market. In April 2004 Amy Kazmin, writing for the *Financial Times*, reported that "Hanoi receives up to two billion dollars in assistance each year from the World Bank, the Asian Development Bank and other bilateral donors" (Kazmin 2004, 17).

Prior to 1987 the Soviet Union had subsidized Vietnam's health care and education. It was the World Bank that advised the Vietnamese to privatize education and health care. These policies (from which the bank has more recently backtracked because of pressure from within the NGO community) are undoubtedly having a negative effect on the lives of children and particularly those whose families exist at subsistence level. John Pilger writes critically about the application of these measures in Vietnam:

The World Bank now offers loans conditional on the sacking of tens of thousands of workers from public enterprises and the scrapping of public services that were once the envy of other poor countries. Even during the long years of war, primary care where people lived and worked had raised life expectancy to among the highest in the developing world. More babies had survived birth and their first precarious years than in most Asian countries. Now, under the tutelage of the foreign "donor community," the government was forced to abandon support for health services; diseases, such as malaria, dengue and cholera, returned. It was as if the Vietnamese were finally being granted membership of the international community as long as they created a society based on divisions of wealth and poverty and exploited labor, in which social achievements were no longer valued: the kind of foreign-imposed system they had sacrificed so much to escape. (Pilger 2000, 17)

### Consequences for Children

Most of the children I met during fieldwork did not have access to health care. In addition, few had finished primary school because it was too costly to do so and because everyday costs of living necessitated that they work.

For all its recent industrialization, Vietnam is still predominantly an agrarian society, and most of its people live and work in the countryside on small agricultural units. The children I met who worked in Hanoi most often had parents and certainly extended family who worked on the land. Changes in the structure of agriculture have had an impact on children's lives, and while children have always worked the land alongside adult family members, some, as I show in chapters 4 and 5, feel a need to contribute in some other way to the family economy.

As part of the move away from the collectivism of strict communism families today run their own self-governing farm units. This means that buying and selling between farmers and state and cooperative businesses are no longer administratively and vertically determined but are based instead on market conditions.

There has been an increase in complaints among farmers because of unfair allocation of land to the well connected in a number of provinces. Nevertheless, productivity rose sharply in the 1980s, and as a result of individual incentives and a move away from collectivism Vietnam is not only self-supporting but has become a world exporter of rice. In 1992 output was 1.97 million tons greater than 1991's crop (Heiburt 1995, 29). This success has not always benefited farmers, however; "recent surveys show 20 percent of farming households are still at or below the poverty level . . . and average capita income is only half of the income in urban areas" (Nguyen Cong Tan, Minister for Rural Development, interview by the *Vietnam Investment Review*, December 27, 1997). This divide continues to this day.

The transfer of farming rights has created other problems, including some for children. Education Minister Tran Hong Quan says that "the country's economic difficulties coupled with the government reforms giving people greater freedom to make money had increased the school drop out rate . . . we're entering a market economy. . . so many families want their children to work at an early age" (Duiker 1995, 170). Historically, most of Vietnam's children have always had to work the land, but even so the competitive nature of contemporary life for the Vietnamese farmers has placed a new type of pressure on their families. For example, most of the boys who worked on the streets of Hanoi selling postcards or cleaning shoes for a living had moved to the city from rural areas; a significant number of them sent money back to help support their families, who remained in the countryside.

### Education Reform

One of the central aims of Communism was to create free education for all. Schooling was heavily subsidized by the state, and literacy rates were reported to have improved dramatically. In fact, in the late 1990s Vietnam claimed a literacy rate of 92 percent, which is one of the highest in Asia (*Vietnam News,* April 4, 1998). However since Doi Moi there have been problems raising the money needed to maintain a satisfactory system, and every week the national newspapers bemoan the decline in education standards. Teachers are paid poorly and as a result rely on private tutoring to supplement their salaries. Because of lack of funds the government began to comply with the dictums of the World Bank and decided to start charging compulsory fees in all schools. This, alongside the pressure that people now put themselves under to make money within a freer market, has resulted in a high drop-out rate among pupils: "the ministry of education survey showed that in 1990 more than 2 million people aged between 15 and 35 were illiterate in Vietnam and that 2.1 million children aged 6–11 had no access to schooling or dropped out of school" (Thu Hanh May, *Vietnam Courier,* May 25–31, 1997). Exactly how many children are receiving a formal education is unclear with conflicting opinions regarding the actual situation. Thus, in the same issue of the same periodical that the preceding quote appeared in, the journalist Vuong Thanh May wrote, "Vietnam's fast economic growth has improved living standards, particularly for children. Millions of children have gained access to better health care and schooling" (*Vietnam Courier,* May 25–31, 1997).

A large proportion of the children with whom I came into contact at the reform school, at the orphanage, and on the streets had received very inadequate education. One result of mainstream education becoming fee-paying has been that a large group of children is excluded from receiving any schooling because their parents cannot afford the fees. At present only primary school up to grade three is free, but expenses may include a bag of rice for the teacher, and children might receive less attention in class if they do not provide the teacher with the little extras that supplement his or her income. Teachers' salaries are so low that they are frequently unable to survive unless their incomes are subsidized by money given to them by children's families.

*Compassion Schools and Unequal Schooling.* Awareness of this trend toward exclusion has led to the development of "compassion schools," which cater to children who cannot afford fees, or who have hitherto received sporadic schooling. The syllabus is different to that found within the mainstream schools, setting the children at a further disadvantage because any results they achieve are viewed as second-rate. Based on these results they would not get into college and even if they could get in they would again be unable to afford the fees.

Thus a three-tier education system has developed, in which there is an elite whose children receive fee-paid education in top schools that virtually guarantee later university entrance. Then there are children who continue to study at state schools but who nevertheless can afford to pay informal fees (or bribes) to individual teachers to keep them there. Lastly, there are the children who may have had some education but who dropped out of school for various reasons and who now sometimes attend compassion classes. The majority of the children I came into contact with for research purposes fell into the last category. But there were also a significant number who had dropped out of school altogether. Over the two-year period that I was visiting the reform school, there was a noticeable increase in the number of boys who did not attend classes because they were illiterate. From my observations, most of the children who attended compassion school felt frustrated by its limitations and lacked confidence in their learning, indicating that the education system that now exists was not addressing their real needs.

*Health Care Reform*

The provision of health care has followed the same route as education and has become fee paying, again in accordance with World Bank policies adopted in order to obtain crucial international loans. According to a report published by UNICEF and the World Health Organization (WHO) in 1990, Vietnam's health care was not based on reliable research. As a rough estimate according to the Institute for Protection of Child Health in Hanoi, child mortality stands at sixty per thousand in the north of the country. When children die it is as a result of catching preventable diseases that take a hold partly as a result of poor diet, since: "the national diet is severely lacking both in calories and variety" (UNICEF/WHO 1990, 73). UNICEF estimates that "53–56 percent of children will not reach their full genetic potential because of malnutrition and poor health" (ibid., 108).

The children that I met, particularly those in the reform school, were small in stature in comparison with their peers in the West. Often I would estimate that a child was two to three years younger than he actually was, and getting ages right took adjustment on my part. The diet in the school was very poor, usually sticky rice for breakfast, a bowl of rice with a few bits of vegetable or meat for lunch, and rice again in the evenings. Children often had chronic skin conditions, and at one point in the winter months when fresh vegetables were scarce the whole reform school population seemed to have an itchy, blistered rash. The children were more likely to put saliva on scabs and spots than to use a cream because medical supplies were scarce and therefore expensive: "Vietnam's health system is great on paper—there are health systems in most communes . . . but there's a lack of basic medical supplies. If clinics have nothing to offer, people don't expect anything and stop coming" (Hiebert 1995, 166).

Concern about the growing population and the poor health of people who do not receive a balanced diet led to the introduction of the Family Planning Law of 1988, which set two children as the family limit. People have been advised to space births three to five years apart, but minority groups have been given freedom to have more children. Obviously this has changed the expected shape of the family. In general Vietnamese people enjoy their children, and the more children the better. Not everyone follows the policy, but those who do not run the risk of losing benefits and of being asked to leave the Communist Party. A young woman I met in Ha Long, a town northeast of Hanoi, told me that because her parents had had three children (the last of whom was unplanned) they had been made to leave the local Communist Party. Party privileges, which had included cheaper schooling and accessibility to high-quality farmland, were subsequently taken away from her parents, and they had been reduced to selling wares on the streets, while she had to reduce her school hours. Even after her little brother was killed at the age of two in a tragic accident when a wall fell on top of him, her family was not allowed to rejoin the local Party.

A shortage of contraceptives means that abortion is an obvious option for population control, and a UNICEF report (1990, 162) estimates that one in three pregnancies are terminated. Pressure to have only two children can become a big issue where one or both parents of a family split up or a spouse dies and finds a new partner. Girls at the state-run orphanage where I also did fieldwork told me that they had entered the institution when their mothers became pregnant in a new marriage, presumably so that the new family would be seen to adhere to government policy concerning size of family. I also discovered during these conversations that a large number of the children had one living parent but that in Vietnamese terms this would no longer be seen as a family unit and that these children were therefore viewed as orphans.

The two-child policy also puts female babies at risk of rejection or death by infanticide. According to one doctor I talked to at a Hanoi hospital, unmarried girls are likely to abandon their babies after birth, and these children are often adopted overseas. The policy also puts strain on families because they have fewer chances to produce favored male heirs, the preference for whom is still a firmly followed part of the Confucian tradition. Among the families I knew in Hanoi were two in which two girls had been born to first-born sons. This meant that in the eyes of the girls' paternal grandparents, their sons and daughters-in-law had failed them. In both families the parents held high-ranking government jobs and their daughters were being brought up to expect that they would have successful careers. Nevertheless, both families voiced disappointment over the absence of a son. In the first it was the mother who one day told me that if her second daughter had been a boy she would have taken a name that, translated, means "dragon." Her daughter then explained to me that it would have been far better if she had been a boy, and that the possibility that she would be a girl was so unexpected that for a while her parents had had no name to give her. In the second family, one of the girls had won a number of national scholarships. She explained to me that the motivation for her successes lay with her grandmother, who had always lavished affection on her male cousin because he was a boy.

While I was in Vietnam I heard that methods to ensure a male heir included eating particular foods prior to conception, going to the priest for guidance, or even abandoning girl babies after birth. Wealthier Vietnamese could afford to have ultrasound scans to determine the sex of the fetus before deciding whether to have an abortion if it was female, or in some cases placing a girl child in an orphanage. Goodkind describes the Vietnamese two-child policy as "another blow to gender equality" (1995, 338). In his extensive study of gender inequality in Vietnam he found that the sex ratios of death probabilities at ages one to fourteen shifted strongly between 1979 and 1989 from a surplus of male deaths to a surplus of female deaths, pointing to decreasing survival probabilities for female children compared to male children (ibid., 342–359).

Women, like myself, who have two boys are seen as very fortunate. The extra value of the male child was demonstrated to me and my partner quite forcibly when six months after our twin boys were born we visited the Vietnamese community center in London where we had both worked. I remember being overwhelmed by the emphasis placed on our babies' genders. On arrival at the center we were welcomed with enormous enthusiasm as over and over again men and women alike clasped our hands or whisked a baby away from one us for a long cuddle while repeating what great fortune it was to have not one but two boys. This preference for male children is by no means universal in Vietnam but the fact that it exists at all raises some unsettling questions about how women might be treated as a result of failing to produce a male child.

### Human Rights

One only has to take a brief glance at Vietnam's human rights record to recognize the precarious nature of any type of human rights objectives in that context and the piecemeal improvements that the post–Doi Moi reforms have brought to the country. Since 1986 and Doi Moi, legislation has been introduced that the authorities say is intended to guarantee the legal rights of citizens and to protect human rights (Amnesty International 1991, 67). New legislation provides for the development of an independent judiciary. New judicial procedures have introduced the principles of the presumption of innocence, the right not to be detained without a court order, the right to have a legal defense, and the right to choose an independent lawyer. Amnesty International also reports that the "renovation" policies have resulted in the release of thousands of people held without charge or trial in re-education camps, although an unknown number of political prisoners continue to be held without trial (Human Rights Watch 2005).

In December 2003 Brad Adams, executive director of the Asia Division of Human Rights Watch, reported that "Vietnam's already dismal human rights record has sunk to new depths this year" and that as in the past, "the Vietnamese government has spent the year arresting and imprisoning dozens of Buddhists, political dissidents, 'cyber-dissidents' and ethnic minority Christians." In the same report he asks that Vietnam's donors insist on human rights progress before releasing further funds (Human Rights Watch 2003). Also in 2003, Amnesty International was denied access to Vietnam and did not receive a direct response from the government to any of the concerns it raised with the authorities regarding the human rights situation. On January 5, 2004, Amnesty International reported:

> Domestic human rights monitoring was not permitted and access continued to be denied to independent international human rights monitors. Amnesty International is shocked by the news that the Vietnamese government, in a decision signed by the Prime Minister on 5 January, has made the reporting and dissemination of statistics on the use of the death penalty a state secret and are hiding behind draconian decrees protecting so-called "state secrets." The Vietnamese authorities are flouting international human rights standards and basic rights surrounding freedom of expression and freedom of access to information.
>
> According to official Vietnamese media sources, more than one hundred people were given the death sentence and more than sixty were executed in 2003. Amnesty International believes these figures understate the true picture, and that the true number of those put to death by the Vietnamese state is far higher. Both figures represent an increase of at least 100 percent over the previous year.

The 2004 report went on to say, "The dramatic rise in the reported use of the death penalty in 2003 for crimes including economic offences is of grave concern and unjustified. . . . In just the first week of 2004, six people have already been executed and three sentenced to death" (Amnesty International 2004). In 2004 Amnesty International also discovered that the Vietnamese government had directly criticized the organization for alleged "interference in internal affairs."

### Restrictions on Movement

It is still difficult for members of the population to move around the country freely because Vietnam is divided into residency zones and in general people are required to stay in their allocated zone, which is often determined by their place of birth. Failure to adhere to such conditions can result in people being penalized or becoming ineligible to receive basic services. As Susan Hopkins states in her report on the state of Vietnamese children's lives, "Children without sufficient identification, including registration permits and especially birth certificates, are often denied permission to attend public schools: claims to the contrary at higher levels not with standing, this is a fairly well documented problem" (1996, xi).

In spite of the moves toward a market-oriented socialist economy and a generally more relaxed attitude toward individual liberties, the apparatus of centralized Communist state control clearly remains in place, and this extends to the patronage of privileged elites. The powerful and their extended families who run the country are members of the Communist Party. Being a member of the Communist Party is still considered advantageous, and membership is by no means an automatic right. Kelly McEven reports that only 3 percent of the Vietnamese population are members of the Communist Party (2000, 2).

Corruption is such a normal part of life that its existence is rarely questioned. This is partly because at every social level, people are likely to have connections to enable them to reap some benefit. Templar reports that now that there is widespread belief in personal ownership of property corruption is more visible. Where bribes and taxes have become unmanageable, there has been protest. In the 1990s Hanoians began to demonstrate noisily when they were removed from their homes to make way for new office buildings, hotels, golf courses, or roads. When villagers in Kim Po tried to hold out for more compensation they sent their children out with posters of Ho Chi Minh to march in front of the police. One of the police told the villagers, "This isn't Ho Chi Minh's time anymore" as the police smashed the placards and physically removed the resistant residents (Templar 1999, 225).

The high level of corruption among members of the establishment and the bribe system they support undermines general respect for law enforcement. The boys at the reform school recognized that if they or their family had had enough money to give to the police they would not have been locked up. Boys who made their money on the streets were constantly required to share some of their profits with the police, and if they did not do so their means of making a livelihood was confiscated. Sometimes boys would become beggars until they had collected enough money to reclaim their tools of trade, such as their shoe-cleaning equipment, from the police. At other times the police would send the children to a detention center or reform school, where after being locked up they could be freed if they were able to raise the money to pay off their custodial guards.

Such is the secrecy that surrounds detention and imprisonment that as a foreigner I was never able to gain access to the police departments or legal systems that the children passed through before being sent to the reform school. However, the reform school director told us that the reform school was the most lenient center within the juvenile system, whereas children who had committed more serious crimes, such as those involving drug taking, were sent to a reform center in a more remote northern province, where they were expected to perform manual labor. But no one outside of the Ministry of Interior could gain access and so I could not validate these claims.

A great deal of secrecy still surrounds the use of detention centers and reform schools by the Vietnamese government, but as Robert Templar indicates and I was to discover through fieldwork these institutions are still in operation: "The fear in the leadership and its undue obsession with stability had led to a massive exaggeration of the dangers of subversion from outside and from within the country. For this reason there are still unnecessary arrests, deportations and confinements of some people, even religious leaders" (1999, 121). Imprisonment and house arrest of dissidents, writers, religious leaders, and even actors appearing in American war films are well documented and remain a sticking point for Vietnam's foreign relations with the West.

### Control over Foreigners

Given Vietnam's history of colonial domination and wars with Western powers, it remains understandably wary of the West. Yet it is also a recipient of Western-driven aid and business investments. The government's response to the tension wrought by being both beholden to and suspicious of foreign investors has been to try to maintain as much control as possible over domestic operations. This means foreigners are likely to be reprimanded or asked to leave the country if they ask difficult questions that are considered to be generally subversive. Thus, as with the Communists of old, the Vietnamese government continues to observe and monitor the activities of foreign organizations and individuals. I always tried to keep a low profile during fieldwork and did not speak openly, particularly among Vietnamese friends, about what I was doing. After I had been in Vietnam for eight months and had established myself as a regular fixture on the streets of Hanoi, I was unexpectedly warned by one of my Vietnamese teachers to loosen my ties with "street children." She explained that the police had been on campus asking about me and did not want me getting involved in things that were of no concern to me. Then with a knowing smile she laughed and said, "After all, Rachel, you would not want to have your notes confiscated or be accused of doing anything silly like writing about children's lives."

Expatriates who worked for international NGOs sometimes confided in me that they thought particular local staff members of their organization were placed there purely to monitor their work and influence the organization's decision making. While this may seem far-fetched, most expatriates I knew had similar stories of having their actions reported back to them or questioned at a later time. Indeed, all NGOs had to hire their staff through the Ministry of Labor, Industry, and Social Affairs (MOLISA), the state-run organization that controlled them. If a potential staff member was not approved by the state then he or she could not work for the NGO. Some expatriates thought that this process was in place so that only Vietnamese who were loyal to the Communist Party would have regular contact with foreigners.

This approach had obvious repercussions for NGOs because it meant that in reality the type of work they did was influenced by government policy, and international objectives could not be introduced with the independence that was originally intended. Such was the paranoia and suspicion that few people felt able to talk openly about the manner in which the state apparatus seemed to maintain control over their everyday actions. One NGO director I met resigned and left the country to protest being "unofficially" told that the state would not allow his organization to pursue its interest in working with street children. In view of such limitations any improvements to people's lives are bound to appear piecemeal to the uninformed or ill-informed outsider, and small successes such as I witnessed in the reform school tended to be overlooked by expatriate NGO workers who were not well versed in the strict controls on changes imposed at the domestic level.

### Child-Focused Influences from the West

I have described how Vietnam is still in essence a collectivist rather than an individualistic society. Filial piety and respect for one's elders still dominate and are informed by traditional Southeast Asian values. Moreover, the Vietnamese still live in a one-party state that is wary of overtly embracing Western influences and has not embraced an understanding of individually based human rights. Yet, in 1990, Vietnam became the first country in Asia and the second country in the world to ratify the United Nations Convention on the Rights of the Child (UNCRC). As I show later in this book, this embracing of Western policies in conflict with local traditions has caused misunderstandings both at the local level and among members of the international aid community.

In this chapter I have provided only a cursory examination of Vietnam's general human rights record and the limitations imposed by the state upon organizations working in the country. I have done this partly to highlight that for the children I knew there was room for optimism, even though on first meeting their circumstances appear so bleak. But more importantly, I have done this to provide a context for understanding why supporters of child rights meet such baffled resistance. Vietnam's current human rights record is a sure indicator that the individually oriented rights-based approach supported through the UNCRC and upheld by child rights supporters holds objectives that are very unrealistic and as a result far removed from local needs and current experiences.

# Child Rights and the
# International Aid Community

In February 1997 the director of an international NGO that worked with children but had no interest in working in the field of child rights invited me to join him and his Vietnamese staff to watch a short film produced by members of an international child rights NGO working in Hanoi. When we saw the film it was still a rough cut of the final version and did not at that point have a title. As far as I know the film was never completed, because its contents meant that it was most unlikely to meet government approval. The film set out to explore the extent to which the child rights movement was having any positive influences over the lives of children living in difficult circumstances in Vietnam. Most of the filming had taken place on the streets of Hanoi among "street children" who lived in makeshift housing down by the river and who spent their days working long hours doing street-based work.

In the film individual children spoke directly to the camera about the difficulties they experienced while working: the long hours they kept, how much they missed their families, and being vulnerable to arrest by the police. As each interview drew to a close, the commentator interjected with a child rights–linked assessment of the situation; for example, after a child had spoken of having to work long hours the commentator pointed out "Article 32 of the UNCRC recognizes the right of a child to be protected from economic exploitation, and this example shows that the Vietnamese are not doing enough to adhere to this objective."

Throughout the film I do not recall the commentator having anything positive to say about Vietnamese people's treatment of their children. The film drew to a close with the camera panning in on a young boy who started to cry as he told his story of working long hours. Rather than pull away at this moment the camera was focused in on the boy's face, and the interviewer asked him if he was aware that he had the right to change his circumstances because Vietnam had ratified the UNCRC. The boy looked a little lost and confused as he shook his head. He had never heard of the UNCRC. As the film faded and the screen turned blank the commentator concluded that "It is an outrage that children are living and working in such appalling conditions, although Vietnam has ratified the UNCRC it is doing nothing to help these children improve their lives."

Once the television was turned off there was silence in the room. There was a reason for this. The film was openly critical of the Vietnamese government's apparent failings to adhere to the UNCRC in a way that we all knew to be risky for the people involved in making the film. As a result nobody felt comfortable or particularly interested in talking about the film, and everybody, including Chinh and Tung, two of the Vietnamese staff members of the NGO with whom I visited the reform school, quickly left to get on with the business of the day.

While it was easy to empathize with the experiences of the children in the film, none of their experiences were new to us, and I wondered what type of audience the filmmakers had in mind. The film was unsettling, but as far as I was concerned not for the reasons that the filmmakers were hoping. At that time the film had not been approved by the government and was still only making the internal rounds of various international NGOs. Eighteen months later, when I left Vietnam, the film had still not been given the government's seal of approval and instead had become a costly white elephant project for the NGOs that had developed and funded it.

This chapter examines a number of questions that I first began to think about after watching the film. First, is it appropriate for the UNCRC—which Vietnam only signed in 1989 and ratified in 1990—to be used as a critical yardstick against which to measure the daily experiences of Vietnamese children? In addition, should responsibility for the conditions under which certain people live reside with the immediate community and country, as the commentator of the film indicated that they should? Or should conditions also be examined in relation to some of the internationally driven economic, social, and political influences at work in a specific country, in this case Vietnam? With this last point in mind, what pressures are at play for the different types of NGOs working in Vietnam?

## International Aid Agencies

International aid works on a number of levels and involves players with different philosophies, different levels of influence, and different sources of funding. It is still generally the case that more affluent countries offer aid to less well off countries and that aid is often conditional on the acceptance of political or economic reforms. It is no coincidence that the majority of donor countries once colonized the countries that are today the recipients of their aid. Aid is usually given with a particular development project in mind, and often with clear objectives from the donors. Recipients of aid are not given free reign to use the money as they see fit; external advisors become involved and international workers oversee projects. Above the level of individual governments, there are a number of international supragovernmental agencies whose work is funded directly by member states.

### The United Nations

The United Nations (UN) is chief among these agencies. Member countries subscribe to the funding of the UN according to their ability to pay; hence the biggest contributor is the United States. Many developing countries receive direct support from the UN or one of its many agencies, such as UNICEF. The UN is also highly influential at both the international and local level of aid provision. As a body it is meant to represent the common will of countries across the globe, and through its many programs it is the dominant international organization on the issue of human rights.

The United Nations International Children Education Fund (UNICEF) is the UN agency that works on behalf of children and is the umbrella organization that exists to provide educational aid to developing countries like Vietnam. It also oversees the introduction of the UNCRC around the world. When countries ratify the UNCRC they agree to adhere to the child rights doctrine; in principle the UNCRC is legally binding and governments can be held to account for failing to adhere to it. Countries are able to opt out of signing every article of the UNCRC, but this is with the view that all articles will eventually be implemented. Adoption of the UNCRC by a member state opens the way to a number of forms of aid, and signatory countries have to report every five years to the UN Committee on the Rights of the Child on the progress made in order to receive further aid. On January 22, 2003, Vietnam reported to the committee and was advised in very general terms that still more needed to be done to make child rights a reality for Vietnamese children (Committee on the Rights of the Child 2003).

### The World Bank

At the macroeconomic level, the World Bank is the most influential body in existence today. It was set up in 1944 to loan money to less developed countries so that they could compete on the global market. At its inception, it was seen as a way to bring prosperity to a world that had recently been shaken by war. It was believed that by contributing to a world central bank, governments would enable poor countries to borrow in an orderly way, avoiding the boom and bust cycles of the past. Such ideals appear to be very straightforward and well intentioned, yet the work of the World Bank and its sister organization, the International Monetary Fund (IMF), remains controversial.

In order to qualify for loans from the World Bank, countries have to agree to implement particular economic policies, implemented through Structural Adjustment Programs (SAPs). Policies imposed by these programs focus on the repayment of foreign debt, the balancing of national budgets (so that governments do not spend more than they produce), and promotion of a free market economy. In practice, acceptance of these policies often means that governments have to agree to implement tough reforms. These include a requirement to balance the national budget by cutting social spending or devaluing the currency so that exports are cheaper for other countries to buy, or selling off publicly owned assets, often through privatization (using foreign companies) of public services. It has been pointed out that such Western-driven reforms have to be carefully designed and implemented if they are not to further damage the economy of the recipient country, which may not have in place the democratic or governmental processes needed to effectively manage the reforms demanded (Burr 1995, 240). For people living at subsistence levels, the structural reforms can have devastating economic consequences, and as John Madeley asserts, "the development projects drawn up and implemented in a World Bank project are usually poles apart from local realities" (1991, 5).

### Non-Governmental Organizations

Non-governmental organizations (NGOs) are independent organizations that provide a wide range of humanitarian services. They can take many forms according to their terms of reference. Many of them run aid programs on behalf of international aid agencies and hence are recipients of large amounts of funds from the World Bank and its subsidiary agencies. They also raise sums from the general public and normally have tax-exempt (charitable) status. Some are founded by religious groups, and thus their primary underlying goal is to spread the word of their particular creed. Major international NGOs include the Red Cross, widely applauded for its work in health care, and Medicin Sans Frontières, equally respected for providing front-line medical care to countries suffering from war or famine. Other NGOs such as Oxfam have a reputation for helping with famine relief, while Save the Children Fund concentrates on humanitarian support to children worldwide. This last NGO is one of a number that are heavily involved in helping to spread the work of the UNCRC.

### Government Constraints on International NGOs in Vietnam

If they wish to work in Vietnam, international NGOs have to obtain approval from the Peoples' Aid Coordinating Committee (PACCOM). PACCOM is the government's coordinating body for NGOs in Vietnam. According to its deputy director, "PACCOM works to facilitate relations between INGOs [International NGOs] and local officials and recommends activities. INGOs must work through government officials, which may appear at first to hinder them, but in the long run it allows them to do more" (V. K. Nguyen, 1999). In reality, a number of restrictions are placed on the type of work that NGOs can do, one of which is that the religious organizations are not allowed to practice their faith in public or attempt to convert local people. NGO work is monitored closely and aid workers, like the majority of expatriates, are placed on six-month visas. It was very common during the time that I was in Hanoi for people to have visa extensions refused and for groups to be expelled from the country.

All projects must obtain prior approval from PACCOM, and conflicts of interest between Vietnamese and international interests undoubtedly exist. Gray has written about the circumstances under which NGOs work in Vietnam: "Research to date indicates that the NGO sector in Vietnam is in many ways a construct of the State. . . . The State has created the frame within which NGOs operate, and control over the 'political space' available to NGOs remains firmly in its hands" (1998, 12).

Expatriate workers of a number of NGOs voiced their frustrations to me over limitations placed upon the work they did with children. Once child-focused NGOs are approved by PACCOM they may be encouraged to do joint work with government organizations such as the Ministry of Labor, Industry, and Social Affairs (MOLISA) and with one of its specialist sections, the Committee for the Protection and Care of Children (CPCC). For example, one expatriate director told me that he wanted his organization to concentrate on working with street children, but he could not gain permission to do so. He made it known that he did not agree with the government's practice of reuniting street children with their families by sending the children back to the rural areas from which they had originally come. "I would like to specialize in street children. The problem will grow, and right now MOLISA and CPCC want reunification with families. But reality is the children will keep coming, and setting up a social net would be more appropriate. You want to give people a chance but what can you really offer?" (interview with Rachel Burr, January 1998, source withheld).

While this director believed that the enforced repatriation program was misguided, members of other child rights NGOs took a different stance. One of the large NGOs that supported the UNCRC completed a study conducted in partnership with the government's Youth Research Institute in which they looked at why the program was not working. The report made a number of suggestions that included creating new work opportunities and setting up research programs to assist rural economic development. While these are commendable suggestions, the possibilities that children might be happier away from home, or that they were doing better than their counterparts in the countryside (in terms of being able to afford to pay for an education or help their families financially) were not discussed. In the draft report, children were portrayed as weak and helpless. The possibility that some of them might be enjoying aspects of their lifestyle or that they were confident and able to care for themselves was given little consideration. "We also know that their lives are full of difficulties: hard work, illness/disease, illiteracy and a total lack of opportunity to develop as normal children. . . . They all however have a common desire and that is to be helped . . . our aim is to help them reunite with their families and communities" (Ha 1996, 6)

One of the report's Vietnamese authors told me in an interview that it had not been possible to acknowledge the benefits for children of leaving home. The government was so concerned about limiting rural-urban migration that it chose to ignore the problem entirely rather than acknowledge its positive aspects in any way. From everything that the boys who worked on the streets told me about their reasons for coming to the city, this was a glaring omission, one that greatly compromised the quality of work that the NGO involved was producing, because it meant that some of the problems facing rural families were still left unexplained and thus unknown to the organizations trying to work with such children. During my final year in Hanoi, one child rights NGO did some research in a rural community to find out why children were leaving home. I worked on the report with the Vietnamese staff who had done the interviews. They reported that 70 percent of the parents interviewed said that poverty was the driving force behind children's departure to the city. While this was a useful finding, this NGO was already heavily involved in the government-supported program to send children home from the city. One of the staff members I worked with was particularly cynical about the usefulness of the findings and argued that the desire to reunited families far outweighed the government's interest in easing the levels of poverty experienced in rural areas.

## *Development Aid*

The main objective of providing aid is to allow a country to become more developed, or to be redeveloped after war (for the purposes of this book I exclude humanitarian aid for the alleviation of the consequences of natural disasters such as earthquake or famine). The term "development" can be interpreted differently depending on, among other influences, the political stand taken and the type of agency offering support. The term implies that a country needs to better its citizens' existing circumstances.

Implicit in the term is the assumption that support is required from outside the region, from postindustrial societies: "The idea of under development itself and the means to alleviate the perceived problem are formulated in the dominant powers' account of how the world is" (Hobart 1993, 2). Some critics of the international aid process ascribe neocolonial intentions to it, because as a condition of aid, recipient countries often have to take economic and social policy in a direction dictated by the donor. Therefore, those donors have an advantageous stake hold in how a country is run.

Development aid falls into three broad categories. *Bilateral* aid refers to one government giving funding directly to another. This form of support was more commonly used in the more immediate aftermath of the colonial period. Bilateral aid may take the form of a direct budgetary donation from one government to another, a government providing grants aimed at a particular project, or funding directed through an NGO. Japan is Vietnam's biggest bilateral funder; in 1999 it gave eighty-eight billion yen in aid. It is perhaps no coincidence that Japan has also cornered the Vietnamese market in developing light industries and privatizing previously state-owned companies. The profits that the Japanese are making in Vietnam far outweigh the aid they are giving to the country. This is not a practice unique to Japan, and because it is so widespread this form of funding—which in reality is of most benefit to the donor country—has come under attack in some arenas for political and commercial motives for aid. *Multilateral* aid comes from a number of funders from different countries, providing collective support to a recipient country. This form of aid was to some degree a response to the criticisms attached to the political motivations associated with bilateral aid. By drawing funding from a number of sources, such as the European Commission, World Bank, the United Nations and national governments, the organizers intend that aid would be offered more objectively.

The third category of aid relates to NGOs, which are recipients of *financial support from private donors*, which may be charities, private trusts, or individuals. Private donations are sometimes offered with a general benevolent spirit rather than for the expressed fulfillment of any particular type of aid project, but members of the public often respond to calls to support particular projects, such as famine relief or flood-disaster alleviation. Under some circumstances, religious-based NGOs have been criticized for using funds from their aid contacts such as church congregations to evangelize and convert people from existing belief systems. This criticism has little if any weight in Vietnam because the government only allows religious-based organizations to work in the country as long as they do not evangelize. Anyone who is suspected of evangelizing has his or her right to live in Vietnam revoked.

### The Practice of Giving International Aid via NGOs

The practice of giving international aid via NGOs became more prevalent as the colonial period was coming to an end. NGOs provide an essential source of expertise and additional resources to help their aid-agency masters implement aid programs. Their work is diverse and they respond to perceived needs in what are often unfamiliar cultural settings for both the NGOs and their workers. NGOs rely to varying degrees on funding from bilateral and multilateral sources for their continued existence, so they need to show willingness to go along with the latest funding interest of those sources. Thus, NGOs may need to demonstrate that a project will address the needs of a particular group of people, such as of ethnic minorities, even if they would like to do work in other areas and do not have expertise in the current favored funding area. As Robert Cassen points out, "There is aid fashion: a type of 'herd behavior' can be seen, as the swings of intellectual analysis bring one or another type of investment to the fore as desirable" (1994, 177). One expatriate director, newly arrived in Vietnam, told me during an interview in May 1998 that he felt the most pressing need was to work among children who lived on the streets in cities other than Hanoi, but he was unlikely to get funding for that type of project:

> We are a small NGO and it is difficult to collect funds, leaving us with no area we are specialists in. We are always looking towards finding funds, so that we do projects which answer to the wish of donors. We don't have advertising and money from the public. We rely on grants from the European Community donors, and [because of their current funding interests] are now under pressure to write a project in Lao Cai . . . the project will not be based on my experiences. Probably it will be something to do with education among the Hmong (an ethnic minority of hill tribes who live in the mountains on the Vietnam-China border) because the European Community is interested in helping ethnic minorities. While they

may need support I think that the needs of street children are more pressing.

This aid worker was voicing a weary acceptance of the reality that in order to gain funding he had to meet the requirements of funders who were not necessarily aware of what was happening in Vietnam on a daily basis. This is problematic for a number of reasons.

First, under such circumstances funding is allocated for particular causes at the international and not the local level. Thus money may be invested without due regard to the peculiarities of the recipient country's local needs or without acknowledging cultural specificity. Because the most significant international funding bodies are most likely to show continued support if money is spent in the ways they originally stipulated, NGOs that rely on bilateral and multilateral aid are more likely to be beholden to the interests and concerns of those organizations. This limits creativity at the local level and results in the pursuit of financially driven, rather than needs-led, work.

Second, these forms of funding are rarely guaranteed for extended periods of time, and lack of sustained support means that NGO workers are under pressure to get positive results quickly and in ways which are easily demonstrated to their funders, such as the film I discussed earlier in this chapter, or in setting up out-of-hours schooling for working children. In view of these external pressures it is perhaps understandable that some international NGO workers focus on international rather than locally articulated objectives. It is clear that some organizations have little scope to do otherwise if they wish to continue to have any presence.

The decisions about the direction that aid will take are not entirely the prerogative of aid agencies; as field operatives, the NGO sector has some sway over the work of the multilateral and bilateral funders. In the year I arrived in Vietnam some of the most significant funders of NGOs at government and international levels were showing a growing interest in directing funds toward projects that focused on the girl child. This new interest was partly a response to pressure exerted by NGO representatives at the Women's Conference held in Beijing in 1995, when they had argued that girl children rarely got any attention and aid support. This type of child-centered assistance becomes shaped by factors that have little to do with local opinion or actual need but rather with a very generally perceived idea that a new and hitherto unrecognized social issue needs some attention. It is important that bilateral and multilateral funders respond to NGOs: in principle NGOs have closer dealings with the people who are aid recipients, and know which people are in need of assistance. While there is valid concern about, for example, girl children, some of whom might benefit from internationally led support, one of the problems with this funding approach is that it centers on one group at a time, and through such groupings categorizes people in ways that do not reflect the diverse patterns of real life. Moreover, it cuts across any objective assessment process for prioritizing aid, so that it is aimed at the programs perceived for that moment to be the most deserving; thus, when one "group" such as a "girl child" or "street child" becomes a focus of funding it is done to the exclusion of other groups.

In this ethnographic study of children's lives, I have sought to show that referring to particular children as, for example, only "working children" or only "street children" fails individual children because such terms are too general and overlook the particular circumstances that inform each child's life. I extend this argument here to argue that the NGOs and individual professionals who come into contact with children, and the children themselves, each have their own agendas and expectations. These may at times match, but at other times they contradict and conflict with each other.

### International Aid: A Critique

The World Bank's methods of providing support have not escaped criticism. Susan George is probably most famous for her damnation of the influence of the World Bank because of its financial power, exercised through its associate organization the International Monetary Fund: "I do believe that most authentic development is what people manage to do against official "developers" like the World Bank" (1988, 4). In her book *A Fate Worse Than Debt* she blames the World Bank for the level of debt that recipient countries fall into, accusing the bank of creating adjustment programs that take little account of the specific needs of the country and "are carbon copies of each other" (ibid). Susan George is not alone; there has been growing resistance from recipient countries of aid to the expectations laid out by the World Bank and IMF. For example, in July 2000, the Argentine federal court sent down a landmark ruling that a substantial portion of Argentina's foreign debt is rooted in illegitimate loans amassed during the country's military period. In his decision, Judge Jorge Ballestero directed criticism at international financial institutions such as the IMF and World Bank for refinancing debts that have already been declared illicit and introducing "a damaging economic policy that forced [Argentina] on its knees and which tended to benefit and support private companies and foreign investors—to the detriment of society and state companies" (Global Policy Forum, 2000)

Likewise, Jeffrey Winters (1996) argues that Indonesia can demand debt reduction because of the illegal behavior of its creditors, particularly the World Bank. He presents overwhelming evidence that the bank granted loans that it knew would be used for corrupt purposes. The most damning evidence comes from a leaked World Bank memorandum titled "Summary of RSI staff views regarding the proposed "leakage" from World Bank project budgets" in which it is estimated that "20–30 percent of government of Indonesia development budget funds were diverted through informal payments to GOI staff and politicians" (Winters 1996).

Ironically, and perhaps cynically, in June 2004 U.S. President George W. Bush agreed in principle to the long-standing calls for international debt relief—capitulating solely so that occupied Iraq would be free of the mass of debt accrued by the Saddam Hussein regime. Thus, when international debt hinders a neocolonial project, the rules are liable to be changed by those who make them. Equally ironic is that the United States and other international creditors demanded that the Vietnamese government repay debts accrued prior to reunification—that is, accrued by the now wholly nonexistent South Vietnam regime supported by the United States. Sohan Sharma and Surindar Kumar state,

When the US signed a peace treaty with Vietnam in 1973, it promised $3.2 billion in grant aid for reconstruction. A few years later, the US reneged. In 1995, it demanded that, before Vietnam could receive any assistance, it had to pay off the debt owed by the defeated South Vietnamese government of General Thieu (a puppet of the US who fought alongside the invading US army) for American food and infrastructural aid. If Vietnam did not pay, it would become subject to "economic sanctions." The enforcers of the sanctions would be the World Bank, the IMF, the Export-Import

Bank, the Paris Club and others. In 1997, Vietnam began to pay off its $145 million debt. (2002, 12)

## Internationally Guided Reforms

Free market reforms were launched in Vietnam in 1986 under the guidance of the World Bank and IMF. Vietnam was directed to carry out the same structural reforms as any other country that accepts loans from those two bodies: devalue its currency; liquidate failing state enterprises; downsize the civil service; remove tariff barriers and subsidies; deregulate; and restructure the nation's central bank. In the mid-1980s the Vietnamese people were struggling to get by. Vietnam did not produce enough to support its people, and there was not enough food to go around. The Soviet Union, which had been Vietnam's main source of aid, was unable to assist Vietnam because it was experiencing its own difficulties. The Soviet Union dissolved in 1991, but in the mid-1980s it was also undergoing economic crisis. Vietnam had no choice but to go along with the World Bank's offer of assistance: it was the only offer of help it had. Additionally, the United States trade embargo prevented Vietnam from profiting substantially from international trade, as well as from importing much-needed goods from the majority of industrialized countries.

Evelyn Hong has argued that there was a hidden agenda to the World Bank–directed economic reforms in Vietnam, namely to destabilize the country's industrial base so that all heavy industry, oil and gas, natural resources and mining, cement, and steel production were restructured and taken over by foreign capital to the benefit of the Japanese conglomerates that took the lead role. Similarly, in the agriculture sector, Vietnamese farmers were encouraged to switch to "high value" cash crops for export, at the expense of locally needed production (Hong 2000).

### World Bank Reforms

The reforms that the World Bank required of Vietnam clashed directly with those that Vietnam had separately agreed to when it ratified the UNCRC. Article 28 of the UNCRC stipulates that primary education should be free for all. When Vietnam agreed to the World Bank's structural adjustment program, Vietnam's children, like the rest of the Vietnamese population, were not given the opportunity to voice their opinion about whether this was a good idea. Stefan De Vylder points out that structural adjustment programs and foreign debt are good examples of how macro-economic policies can neglect children's rights. He notes out that the introduction of school fees, which often accompanies structural adjustment, is simply incompatible with the UNCRC (De Vylder 2000, 12). Nancy Scheper-Hughes and Carolyn Sargent have observed that children who once "worked" in the context of home communities now "labor" in industrial and global capitalism (1998, 12). At the same time, they and others point to the impact of structural adjustment policies: while designed to stabilize state economies, they often seriously burden the poorest populations, especially women and children, as the following examples demonstrate.

### Privatization of Education

Prior to 1987 the Soviet Union had subsidized Vietnam's health care and education to help fulfill the socialist principle that both these basic services should be available free to all. When the World Bank offered to give Vietnam crucial loans without which it could not have continued to function adequately, it did so on condition that Vietnam privatize education and health care. Evelyn Hong quotes a commonly accepted statistic that before the World Bank introduced privatization reforms, Vietnam had a 90 percent literacy rate and school enrollments were among the highest in Southeast Asia. The proportion of graduates from primary school who entered the four-year lower secondary education system declined from 92 percent in 1986–87 to 72 percent in 1989–90. A total of nearly three-quarters of a million children were pushed out of the secondary school system during the first three years of the reforms (Hong 2000). Hong argues that economic reforms in Vietnam have resulted in shrinking the educational budget, depressing teachers' salaries, and commercializing secondary, vocational, and higher education through the introduction of tuition fees. Even before the effects of these reforms took hold, parents were unofficially expected to prop up the low salaries of teachers with gifts in kind or of money, and this expectation has been heightened by the economic reforms.

Land reforms have further added to these problems. These reforms have placed land back in the hands of individual farmers, who have found it increasingly difficult to make a decent living as the cost of living has gone up. In turn this has made it more difficult for families to allow their children to attend school, because the children are needed to work the land. By 2003 the World Bank had come under enough pressure from within the NGO community to backtrack on the privatization of primary school education. A new poverty adjustment program initiated by the World Bank and some NGOs now supports free education throughout the primary school level, but contradictions still exist. The World Bank is still doing research into the profits to be made if it were to support further development of private higher education establishments in Vietnam. Secondary schooling is also not free, and this too conflicts with the education ideals written into Article 28 of the UNCRC.

### Urban Education

An additional problem exists for Vietnamese children who have migrated from the countryside to live in the city. Although they may now qualify for free primary schooling in their place of birth, they need permits to live legally in the city. When staff in a reform school I visited learned that the majority of children in their care did not have official documents giving them permission to stay in the city, they advised them to register on return to their local commune where they and their families lived. To their surprise this idea was met with resistance and fear. Most of the children came from families who had illegally migrated to the city perimeters without having received official approval to live in their current commune. From their perspective it was preferable to remain anonymous, because official recognition would lead to their forced return to the town or village of birth, and away from the new life that they had created for themselves.

Two expatriate NGO field directors expressed surprise when I discussed this problem with them. One of the directors, who was a strong advocate of the UNCRC, told me that one of her future project ideas was inspired by Article 7 of the UNCRC, which states that "the child shall be registered immediately after birth and shall have the right from birth to a name, the right to acquire a nationality." She intended to organize registration of children who worked on the street so that they could go to school, but in reality this was something all children living under such circumstances were likely to avoid. If children do not have permits, access to any type of health care or mainstream schooling is denied them. Until the World Bank and advocates for child rights address the government's policy of distributing settlement permits, none of the international rights or poverty alleviation programs linked to free education can be properly put into practice.

### The UNCRC: A Key Symbol

When I interviewed local people and expatriates who worked for NGOs, I asked about the local relevance of the UNCRC. Those respondents who supported the UNCRC were very positive about it; as one expatriate director said, "The convention is necessary, of course it is; we need to protect children and this is the way to do it."

One of the expectations written into the UNCRC is that children will automatically have the right to "participate" in decision making about their lives. UNCRC 1989 Article 12 states: "States parties shall assure to the child who is capable of forming his or her own views the right to express those views freely in all matters affecting the child, the views of the child being given due weight in accordance with the age and maturity of the child." Kirby and Woodhead explain that "participation is a multifaceted concept. It is about children's activity and agency being recognized; about children being treated with dignity and respect, about them being entitled to express their feelings, beliefs and ideas; about being listened to and about their voices being heard"( 2003, 236).

It is the participatory element of the UNCRC that has caused the most contention and confusion across the globe, and this is particularly the case in Vietnam's hierarchical society, where respect toward one's elders and compliance with their wishes is even built into the language's personal pronouns. In two of the interviews that I conducted with expatriate NGO staff who were in favor of the UNCRC, the staff members complained about the lack of understanding local staff had about the work that they were doing; in the process the expatriate NGO staffers ignored the large cultural gulf that existed between them and the local staff. Moreover, as Judith Justice argues, and my examples show, the reality may be more complicated than that: "International planners often attribute failures to the fact that cultural influences can lead people to reject programs, but the bureaucrats have their own culture too. One that may obstruct their views of other cultures, resulting in programs that are destined to fail" (Justice 1989, 151).

## Cultural Differences

NGOs in Hanoi that support the UNCRC have paid particular attention to the aspect supporting child participation in decision making. In January 1998 I was invited to attend a training session for Vietnamese NGO staff on child participation. The objective of the program was to train local NGO staff in ways of encouraging children to take part in village "development" projects. The expatriate leader of the workshop was very eager to teach those in attendance about the child-to-child program, and to train Vietnamese staff to adopt this method of communicating with children. Having had this explained to me, I suggested that his training outline could be developed to acknowledge local opinions and ideas; before the training started I proposed that before talking about Western-grounded understanding of child participation, we could first ask the participants to discuss whether they thought local children already took part in project design, and what they themselves had done for the community as children. We could then move effectively away from looking at childhood as an abstract concept and instead concentrate on adjusting knowledge to the local setting. My ideas were turned down because the organizer did not see the relevance of asking participants about their own childhood experiences, presuming from the outset that Vietnamese staff were unaware of how children communicated with each other and with adults. From the beginning of the workshop the trainer used Western-based child intervention approaches, and Vietnamese methods were either overlooked or unwelcome. He had "prejudiced the problem" by immediately introducing a theoretical discourse on childhood that was not relevant to the specific culture and circumstances.

As the workshop unfolded over the following week, the Vietnamese people that I knew in the audience discussed their concerns with me. One told me that at work she felt under pressure to support the child participatory approach, even though it was not something she felt comfortable with. In her view children should respect and follow their parents' line of argument, rather than develop an independent viewpoint. "We use child participation at work but I do not use it with my own children. I am not comfortable with going outside the Vietnamese way." We encouraged her to speak about this more openly with the whole group, and subsequently the organizers decided to introduce the ideas I had originally proposed; halfway through the week a session was introduced in which participants talked about what they understood child participation to mean. A number of local NGO staff talked about their concern that child-to-child training conflicted with Vietnamese expectations, as the following example illustrates: "After we had done child-to-child training in a village school, a mother of a young girl came to us and recounted her conversation with her daughter on her return home. The girl had said, "It's my right to have an education and to have food," and the mother had laughed with us and said how silly this was and that if this was so, her daughter could go and live with the foreigners in a foreign land, because this was their idea and not hers."

When we discussed what child participation meant there were some muddled responses. One local NGO worker felt that children's ideas had been introduced to fulfill adults' expectations, and because it was a current trend, rather than to give children any real voice: "We involve children for the purpose of adults." There was confusion about how involved an adult should be when encouraging children to be more independent: "If a child is to be self-reliant he should be taught and be told how to participate." Two members of the audience responded with weary amusement. The first said, "We use it because it is a new policy within our organizations," and the second said, "So that development agencies [NGOs] can have more work to do, to justify funding, to write up reports."

It is striking that the responses referring to participation of children still place an emphasis on adult leadership and responsibility. The last two quotes were a surprise to the group facilitator and demonstrate that particular methods hold different meaning for people within the same organization; such ideas are rarely shared, however. Justice found that local staff in Nepal had concerns that went unrecognized by their expatriate bosses but that clearly demonstrated why they might view projects in a different light. "A Nepali may agree to a program that he knows is inappropriate for Nepal in order to ensure his own job security" (1989, 44).

The local staff became more open once they realized they were in an environment in which their opinions were being heard confidentially. The fact that their employers were not present probably increased their willingness to have such a frank discussion, but this was also limiting. It may have been that some of the NGO's expatriate managers would have welcomed this form of debate. Perhaps they too had their doubts about the relevance of some projects but presumed that their Vietnamese colleagues would raise any concerns with them. Directors of organizations may not have visited project sites as often as their employees and would therefore probably be shielded from everyday concerns. Where the director was new to Vietnam and was unfamiliar with local methods of communicating, he or she might also have missed problems that were just hinted at. Whatever the reasons, in my experience local and expatriate staff rarely spoke so openly with each other, and in general Vietnamese staff colluded in praising project ideas that they privately had reservations about.

A similar point was made on a separate occasion during an interview I conducted with a local woman who worked for a children-focused international NGO. "But for us we have many customs which prevent us raising children . . . social, economic situation . . . they say children should not work . . . but for many this is an impossibility. Many of us aid workers know this and there is a difference between the foreigners' approach and ours but we do not voice this. Rather we prefer to do as much as we can. We know our country is not ready for many of these changes."

### Children's Voices?

Child participation means recognizing children as experts in their own lives. Here lies the biggest problem for child rights workers. Most adults feel a need to protect children as well as develop respect for them. Recognizing children as experts in their own lives means properly paying attention to them, and if we genuinely believe that they should be able to participate in decision making about their lives this sometimes necessitates putting one's own expectations to one side. For example, when children told me that by working on the streets and living away from their families they had created opportunities for themselves, this possibility needed to be properly respected. Respecting these children's decisions also meant supporting their decision to work. These children were not misguided in making their claims (as one Vietnamese aid worker told me they were), nor were they leading perpetually sad and difficult lives as she also explained to me was the case. Most of the children I met during fieldwork worked, and their opportunities to enter full-time education or to afford to stop working were minimal. The opportunity to enter education was also not going to improve any time soon, because the mechanisms were not in place to create this possibility, regardless of what child rights legislation might intend to be the case.

Jack, who ran the Butterfly Trust (the NGO that regularly visited the reform school), appreciated this. He also recognized that improving children's work skills would do the most to improve their lifestyles once they returned to the wider community. When children at the reform school came to Jack and told him they wanted to join a skill training program in motorbike mechanics or in computers, he organized classes and paid for children to continue their training once they returned to work on the streets or went back to live with their families. This was useful and practical. It is also an approach adopted by some other NGOs, some of which are also based in Hanoi, such as Hoa Sua, an NGO offering cooking and catering training to children who were previously working on the streets.

The "educate for work" approach was not one that child rights activists could acknowledge or support openly, because to do so would clash with the basic tenets of the UNCRC that children should not prioritize work over receiving a primary education. In fact, many of the ideals laid out in the UNCRC did not hold up at the local level. Of course, in an ideal world most people—including myself—do not want children to enter the workplace and grow up isolated from family support. Before I moved to Vietnam, I did not expect the children I would meet to tell me that street life benefited them or that living in the reform school provided them with a structure and an education that they would otherwise not have been able to afford. But this was the case. Furthermore, it turned out that few of the children I met during my fieldwork were familiar with the UNCRC and the rights the document gave them. Even if they had known about the UNCRC they could not access any type of legal services to do something about their inability to exercise these rights because no such service existed. The bottom line is that children are working because their families need the money. Children's income is needed because parents cannot support themselves and their family without their contribution.

### Should Children Work?

At the end of 2001 the Vietnam News Agency, citing a survey from the General Statistics Office, reported that average incomes in the country had risen 12.2 percent from 1999 to 2001, to around twenty-two dollars a month. The statistics report showed that in a country where about one-third of the population of 80 million lives in poverty, the rich earned 12.5 times more than the worst off, a figure that nearly doubled from 1999 to 2001. So the divide between the richest and poorest members of Vietnamese society is widening.

Addressing the underlying reasons that children need to work requires acknowledgment of complex and diverse factors. It requires acknowledgment of international influences that have contributed to Vietnam's present economic growth and of the growing disparity in the distribution of wealth. By embracing the World Bank Structural Adjustment Program (SAP), Vietnam may well increase poverty among the poorest members of its population. The World Bank advocates privatization of health care, water services, and schooling beyond primary age, and the imposition of charges for these services. But the poorest members of the recipient population will suffer the most because they can least afford the new costs involved for paying for them, and hence will forgo them.

Under the same SAP initiative, foreign investors are encouraged to build their own factory sites in Vietnam, manufacturing goods cheaply by employing local labor whose wages remain at near-subsistence levels. Thus, manufacturers and their customers, not the Vietnamese, profit from turning Vietnam's raw materials and labor into consumer products, since the low wages do not allow the workers to buy these products. The evidence of growth in export manufacturing in Vietnam is all around us: in the 1980s and early 1990s very few products bought in the West were made in Vietnam. This is no longer the case. You, the reader, probably own something that was made in Vietnam. It is also very likely that this product was not made by a Vietnamese company but by a foreign company with a factory in Vietnam, employing local labor and often paying at near-subsistence levels. This means that as Vietnam enters the global market it is doing so to the continuing advantage of previous colonial powers, alongside Japan and the United States, and their commercial interests. And while the economy may be benefiting at a national level, it is still not doing so to the extent that it could if Vietnam were developing its manufacturing and service industries without foreign investment, because much of the profit goes back to the Western-owned companies.

These negative effects of globalization, which further add to the disparity of wealth between ex-colonies and their past colonizers, make any genuine commitment to the UNCRC virtually impossible. The NGOs that support the UNCRC are also those that rely on funding from the World Bank, so they too are in league with the very organizations that are perpetuating the disparities of wealth and increasing the likelihood that the poorest children in Vietnam will have to continue to work. Why was this issue not raised by any of the child rights NGO workers I met in Vietnam? Possibly because individual workers had not made the link, or because they believed in the dominant international development philosophy, or because they were understandably heavily occupied in their work and felt they had little choice but to accept funding from any source.

If we return to the child rights video that depicted a crying boy, it is now easy to see why the film commentator might have concluded that a child is unhappy because he had to work and that this is simply because Vietnam is failing to adhere to the UNCRC. That Vietnam cannot at present afford to adhere to the UNCRC, or that some of the UNCRC objectives are culturally alien, was not acknowledged anywhere in the film. If child rights were discussed from the starting point of its present limitations, with the intention of making changes from the local level up, it would have more meaning and perhaps in the long term some sustained influence. Instead, child rights advocates tend to follow global dictates and ignore local realities.

### Responses to Child Rights within the NGO Community

Some expatriate directors of child-focused NGOs I interviewed were aware of these limitations, but these directors did not work within the field of child rights. A director of a small religious organization working with children in local orphanages told me that the UNCRC was of no relevance. He took the position that "the ratification of the UNCRC can allow the Vietnamese to be praised but their attitude towards children is the same as it was before: children should still show filial piety." As a neutral observer whose agency did not use the UNCRC, he went on to explain that "it will continue to have no impact in Vietnam but the agency take on this will be, it is likely that the UNCRC has been taken into account." Both he and his colleague were surprised that the Vietnamese government had been given a prize for its work in connection with the UNCRC's ratification. As we closed the interview, he said that they felt that "the UN allotted money without having an understanding of where that money was to go . . . thus they had no recognition of the level of corruption, or that children are used as a fund raising tool . . . and that public opinion in the West is of paramount importance."

A local woman who worked for one of the NGOs that placed a central focus on the UNCRC felt that the "UNCRC is useful in so far as it lays out what a child could have, but it should then be up to a country to redefine its intentions. We can't apply all articles." In fact, Vietnam has tried to develop some of the ideals of the UNCRC in its program to return "street children" to their families. But in the aftermath of signing the UNCRC, Vietnam developed a National Law on Child Protection, Care, and Education, moving the emphasis away from the rights of the individual autonomous child and placing child rights within the larger family context.

### Differences of Approach

From my observations, it seemed that numerous local and international beliefs about what constituted childhood jostled together in an uneasy alliance and at times were completely at odds with each other. The children's interests, despite good intentions, were often lost in the general rhetoric. I found organizations had different aims and objectives in working with or for children and did not always share the same ideas about what children needed. This sometimes resulted in duplication of projects or conflicts of interest between different groups trying to assist the same children. It also created a situation in which people often had a vague or inaccurate understanding of the roles of other organizations and the people in them. This lack of consensus and understanding among the organizations interested in children led to a situation similar to the one Douglas refers to in her analysis of institutions: "When individuals disagree on elementary justice, their most insoluble conflict is between institutions based on incompatible principles. The more severe the conflict, the more useful to understand the institutions that are doing most of the thinking" (1986, 125).

Additionally, NGOs that held conflicting philosophies were unlikely to associate with each other, remaining only partly aware of the activities that they were all involved in and with differently held understandings of the local culture. Some NGO workers considered Vietnamese children passive, while others referred to the children as independent and strong. It is clear from such accounts that whatever children might be, opinions concerning them are certainly not founded on a common set of criteria: "A consequence of apotheosizing Western knowledge is the dismissal of existing knowledge. One person's claim to knowledge is all too often another's condemnation to ignorance. Whatever knowledge is it is not neutral" (Fardon 1995, 51).

I have already referred to the distinction I had begun to make between NGOs working in concert with the UNCRC guidelines and those that showed no interest in the document. I concluded that there were three quite distinct forms of NGO that worked with children: first, those that upheld the international UNCRC agenda; second, a group of smaller international NGOs that received money from private (sometimes religious) sources; and, finally, Vietnamese-run and-funded NGOs. The three groups rarely came into contact with each other, had very different agendas and working practices, and had different issues regarding funding.

The organizations in the first group were international and more likely to apply for financial assistance through multilateral and bilateral funders (Atkinson and Gaskell 1999, 5). For the UNCRC adherents, UNICEF headquarters were regularly used for meetings on various topics. The other forum from which they could operate was the NGO Resource Center.

The second group encompassed agencies that worked independently of the others and did not adhere to the UNCRC. Two expatriate directors of small religious NGOs told me on separate occasions that the agencies that were not using the UNCRC as part of their mission statement did not get invited to UNICEF-sponsored meetings. They also received funding from quite different sources. One group of international NGOs that did not uphold the UNCRC received the bulk of its funding from religious groups outside Vietnam and from small independent charity organizations that did not demand particular policies to be followed.

The third group of NGOs were solely Vietnamese run, receiving funds from the Vietnamese government. They seemed to be altogether separate and never attended the meetings that other NGOs held. They were as tightly controlled as the international NGOs, and in some respects more so because they were unable to refer to internationally driven directives as a means of gaining some freedom to deviate from government policy. Because I was unable to gain access to any of the groups in this category, the closest I got was through my work with the orphanage, which was run by local staff who worked quite independently of international NGOs and resisted pressure to associate themselves with any of them. I had heard of the orphan-age a long time before I went there, because it was a government institution that did not have any NGOs permanently attached to it: this in itself interested me and I was intrigued to understand the reasons. I found that a number of NGO directors wanted to develop permanent ties to it; for example one NGO director I met at a workshop on social work told me she was keen to introduce the children and staff to the UNCRC, and another wanted to set up a counseling center for street children in its grounds. Mrs. Ha, the director of the orphanage, was not enthusiastic about any of these proposals. Huong, one of my Vietnamese friends, who had once worked there and now worked for an international child rights NGO, told me that Mrs. Ha was wary of any type of NGO intervention because previous interactions had resulted in her vision for the orphanage being subsumed to the will of outsiders.

### Competition and Cooperation

There are about five hundred NGOs operating in Vietnam (V. K. Nguyen 1999), many of them in Hanoi. They often communicate poorly with each other, and some are in competition for funds and the right to work on certain projects. Aid projects are often duplicated among different NGOs working in the same area because it is the policy of the funding agencies to employ a number of NGOs, often needing different skills for different aspects of the same program; some of the projects are large enough to need more resources than are available from a single NGO. Also, when NGOs make funding applications their sponsors are likely to require that they spend money in a certain way, thus increasing the possibility of duplication among themselves and the other NGOs that also submitted successful applications.

While conducting some of my interviews I asked people how they felt about the other types of agencies. A director of an international NGO who had been based in Hanoi for six years told me that "the NGOs that work with children often aim their message at fund-raisers rather than the recipients of aid. Last year UNICEF ran a campaign here with the opening gambit 'every child has the right to clean water' . . . what the hell does that mean?" He went on to tell me that "relationships in Hanoi between the agencies are based on the personalities of the individuals involved, and at this level they shape how work will be done and greatly influence interpretation of their agency policy."

I found that the groups that were most likely to collaborate and be accurately aware of other agencies' work were those that had a religious base. I concluded from this that one of the differences between the religious-based organizations and the secular-based ones was that the religious-based groups were rarely competing for money—their incomes were reliably received from organizations that shared the same religious faith and whose consistent support they could count on. Although they sometimes received money from international aid funders, such funders were not their only source of income and they therefore had more freedom to follow their own agendas. These groups also often had very different motivations for carrying out their work.

### Religious-Based NGOs: Relative Success

In describing their operations I am not arguing that missionary groups are superior in quality to other types of organizations (far from it), nor do I wish to ignore the complex, sometimes hypocritical, pasts of some such groups. But it was certainly the case that during my stay in Hanoi they provided more consistent long-term support that came closer to meeting real humanitarian and local needs than did their nonreligious counterparts. To understand why this might be so, and to see if the secular NGOs could improve their sensitivity, we need to look briefly at the history of religious-based groups.

Even in the colonial period, religious-based organizations had many quite varied reasons and differing ethical motivations for working in foreign lands. For example, when writing about the Nyasaland rising of 1915, Shepperson (1958) showed that in that situation Catholic missionaries were opposed to what they perceived as too rapid education of the locals because they feared the Africans might subsequently become less manageable and thus a threat to the colonial regime. Conversely, the Scottish Blantyre missionaries held to the policy that Africa was for the Africans and that missionaries were there so that "they may train its people to develop its marvelous resources for themselves" (ibid., 361). Perhaps it is from this relatively long history, in Africa and elsewhere, and the hard lessons learned through working in both colonial and postcolonial times, that the missionary organizations (now called NGOs) show more willingness to understand local practices than other international NGO groups, and are less likely to presume that their methods for bettering people's lot would be applicable in the Vietnamese context. It is certainly the case that expatriate missionary workers, often priests or nuns, regarded their stay in a country as a long-term vocation, often for their entire life, so that they came to know the local people, language, and customs very well. It may also have been that expatriates working for religious-based organizations developed a level of accountability and a sensitivity informed by earlier mistakes and external criticisms of their organizations. It is significant that today's international secular NGOs have not escaped their critics, but they have also not received the same types of blanket criticisms that religious organizations have. Perhaps therein lies the general difference in attitude and approach.

I discovered that in Vietnam religious-based organizations are generally run differently from those that uphold the UNCRC agenda. As well as being smaller in size they also tend to distribute manageable projects to separate teams, each of which is most likely to be run by an expatriate and his or her team of Vietnamese contemporaries. This means that expatriate team leaders are immediately involved at the local level and are more likely to learn firsthand about Vietnamese reaction to project ideas.

There was another significant difference for NGOs with religious backgrounds. Because they are banned from evangelizing, their work arguably takes on a unique dimension because the fundamental reasons individual employees have for joining that type of NGO (for example, a desire to promulgate their faith) have to be set aside. While in Vietnam, workers in religious-based NGOs have to redefine the direction of their work and focus on humanitarian, rather than spiritual, objectives. This has a profound effect on how they adapt to Vietnam; it also raises the question of whether the same religious-based NGOs would be as positive a role model in contexts where they are allowed to openly practice their faith and evangelize. Everyone I interviewed in Hanoi who worked for an NGO with a religious background spoke of showing caution and being mindful that Vietnamese thinking was different from their own. Barley found something similar during fieldwork in the Cameroons: "Far from being cultural imperialists, I found the missionaries . . . to be extremely diffident about imposing their own views" (1986, 28).

It was common knowledge that the Vietnamese government would ask people found evangelizing to leave the country, and I think this partly informs the more respectful and reflective stance that people working for these types of NGOs are forced to take. Jack, an NGO worker with whom I spent time in the reform school, worked for a religious-based agency. He often referred to what he did as a lifetime vocation: he had spent extended periods during most of his adult life living overseas, and he planned to stay in Vietnam for at least fifteen years. He told me that this length of time was necessary if he were really going to understand the language and culture of the people he hoped to work with and assist. Anything less would not provide him with the right sort of time scale in which to launch projects that would have a long-term impact. In contrast, staff of the larger and more prominent NGOs were usually in Vietnam on short-term contracts lasting on average about three years, and with little advance preparation: "Advisors [are] usually posted to a country mission for two to four years . . . most do not receive language training or any other form of cultural preparation" (Justice 1989, 42).

A couple I interviewed who were not members of the prominent agencies but instead ran very small programs funded by religious groups, told me, "We feel that we have different priorities: that we are more humanitarian and spend less money on bureaucracy. We are cynical of UN results and statistics, and the fashion changes in the focus of the international agencies. Our own budget comes from the churches which are a reliable and stabilizing income."

### Perceptions of Children

In formal but open-ended interviews with directors of aid agencies working with children, I asked how they understood children in Vietnam and children in their home country. There was a tendency among most of the foreigners to view children differently depending on whether they lived in the West or in Vietnam. Such responses were in contrast to the universal view of childhood that informs the UNCRC. On the question of childhood in his country of origin, one Australian director told me in May 1998 that "children are rich, overindulged, wealthy, privileged, have no discipline, . . . are bought up by single parents, [are] dysfunctional, and have no boundaries." About childhood he told me that in Vietnam it is "based on rights going as far as the society can afford; children are bred to work and in the countryside are weaned from their mother's milk within a week of birth so that the mother can return to the fields. This results in children being bought up by grandparents and then being reunited with their parents when they are old enough to work in the fields. Over half the population was born after the U.S. war and this generation have a hardness and bitterness which creates a tough 'me first' society."

Both of these responses may describe the lives of some children, but they are extreme interpretations of childhood experience. They ignore the many other lifestyles that children experience in either country. Why should a Western child be assumed to be indulged and spoiled? Is it always the case that a Vietnamese child is bred to work, or that, as the interviewee said, "working with buffaloes numbs the mind"? Such generalizations can be easily challenged. However, this director was not alone in his views; during the same week I interviewed an expatriate who worked for a small, independently funded NGO, and he made a similar distinction. "If children at home knew how these kids live they would not complain. Life is far tougher here, and at home the lifestyles are incredibly rich and materialistic." These perceptions overly romanticize and exaggerate the distribution of wealth in the West while also stereotyping and generalizing the form that childhood can take in the South.

Toward the end of the fiscal year, NGO employees usually become preoccupied with writing reports at their organizations' headquarters, because reports are required as a summary of the year's work and justification of their funding. "Report writing is often a highly contested business, having as much to do with internal power relations as a hegemonic representation of the third world 'other'"(Gardner and Lewis 1996, 76). A couple of the large NGOs also wrote regular reports in which they presented research findings.

On first reading NGO reports, I was struck by the consistent style of describing children in the abstract. Although there has been a recent fashion for NGOs that focus on the UNCRC to "give children a voice," this intent was not apparent in the reports that I read. For example, in the final year of my stay, a large proportion of NGOs that worked primarily with children were focusing their work on the area of integrated education for children with disabilities (that is, placement in mainstream schools). That year, funding for such work was available, and at least four of the dominant aid agencies were addressing the issue. While I was teaching Vietnamese NGO staff about participatory observation methodology, I spent time at the Hanoi school for deaf children and the integrated school for visually impaired and visually able children. The teachers told us that we were the sixth such group in two months to come through the school. Our interests thus reflected current priorities and a willingness to duplicate focus and effort.

When reading the report by the Catholic Relief Services (a religious-based NGO that nonetheless and atypically appeared to align itself with the mainstream international bodies and their policies) on inclusive education, I found that the views of the children and their parents were either out of context and placed after the main text as case studies, or were completely absent. Children's ideas were not referred to directly and instead appeared in isolation, perhaps serving only to demonstrate that the agency had little awareness of how children lived their lives both outside and inside school. This approach is underlined by the following quotation: "The fundamental principle of the inclusive school is that all children should learn together. Countries with few or no special schools should establish inclusive, not special schools" (internal NGO report 1997). The organizations following this line of reasoning had decided that children with disabilities would want to be in school with their contemporaries. I later became quite friendly with one of the girls with impaired vision who attended the school, who told me, "We don't mix, and because the school does not have enough Braille books it is very difficult to keep up. This means that we are always in classes with children who are a couple of years younger than us." Thus what sounded like an excellent concept when described formally in the NGO reports did not necessarily reflect children's real experiences. "The social worlds of developers, whether foreigners or nationals, are almost always far apart from those being developed, as is the nature of their involvement" (Hobart 1993, 7).

In another case, I accidentally discovered that one of the most prominent child rights NGOs had been taking photographs of children in the reform school with the sole purpose of using the images in the annual report that was to be sent to prominent funders in their home country. I remember being both surprised and shocked that the faces of children I was doing fieldwork among were sitting on the director's desk. I was well aware that this NGO was not working at the reform school. Had this child rights NGO offered some additional funding to the school? My surprise turned to disbelief when I learned that the NGO had neither given a donation to the school nor gained approval from the school director or children to use the images in an internationally distributed report. The use of this material was misleading to its readers: the organization had done no work inside the reform school aside from distributing copies of the UNCRC to children without openly explaining what was contained inside the convention to the staff. So why were the images being used in such a misleading manner? In short, according to the photographer, because the NGO wanted to offer a variety of colorful images of children to the report's readers. The photographer also laughed and told me that access to the reform school had been so easy that the photos were pretty much there for the taking. Fine words perhaps for an independent opportunist, but shocking when the opportunist was employed by the most prominent child rights NGO working in Hanoi during that period; so much for respecting the rights of individual children the NGO came into direct contact with.

Ironically, while the agencies that support the UNCRC have a preoccupation with being seen to give children a voice, their reports do not reflect this intention. The children's words were translated and analyzed by adults. Not only did agency reports show that some agency information concerning children was inaccurate, but organizations used different definitions to categorize the same groups of children. This meant that information could not be drawn together in order to understand what was happening throughout Vietnam. Hopkins made similar observations: "Some agencies use definitions of street children, which cover only a subset of street children. A number of sources maintain that only children without homes are true street children. The youth research group in Hanoi uses Bond's definitions differently, and adds another category" (1996, 163–164).

Some NGOs referred to children in terms that betrayed their subjectivity: "One Hanoi based NGO refers to such children as children exposed to life early, which may cause offence" (ibid., 166). Agencies were also inconsistent in estimating how many children made up certain categories. Hopkins wrote, "In one report there were one thousand street children, while in another there were seven thousand" (ibid., 168). If anything, NGO reports highlight the disparity of views that exist about the circumstances of local children. The ideas of children themselves were consistently absent. Some of the NGOs did not write a yearly report because their funders had different expectations not driven by the common international agenda. They tended to be the smaller agencies that relied on private sources of income rather than bilateral and multilateral organizations.

## Conclusions

Although Vietnam has ratified the UNCRC, the UNCR has not been universally accepted either by local or expatriate people working for NGOs. My observations show that employees of NGOs that supported the UNCRC tended to have views about local people that differed from those of other NGO workers. They seemed to assume that rights for children would have uniform relevance: "They carry with them their own significant cultural categories and rapidly make sense of the alien ones in terms of their own" (Fardon 1995, 165). Moorehead has pointed to the futility of conventions that are not wholeheartedly supported and has noted, "Conventions are awkward and peculiar things, and many examples from torture to minimum age demonstrate that the new rules will hardly intimidate those states that wish to defy them" (1989, 16).

It is likely that children will be understood by the prominent NGOs working in Vietnam within a limited context, one that substantiates the NGOs' existing philosophies and those of their paymasters, generally the United Nations agencies. Conversely, NGOs that work more closely with local staff and on small-scale projects are most likely to work within the context of the Vietnamese culture. I found that those organizations had a low profile and were not commonly recognized among their larger brethren. They were alone in fitting the criteria that Cassen outlines: "When competent they have many advantages. They are non-bureaucratic, have low manpower costs and can penetrate directly into local conditions" (1994, 51). The large child-focused aid organizations that support the UNCRC pay little attention to each other or to the smaller NGOs. In those organizations, work persistently uses the general and internationally led discourse on childhood as a starting point. The small and usually religious-based agencies that do not do this are more likely to listen and respond to the individual needs of children. Different agencies remain unaware of each other's activities, so the children who are meant to be the ultimate beneficiaries of the aid programs are supported in a fragmented and often inappropriate manner that often ignores their real interests.

*Four*

# Why Children Work

Most of the Vietnamese children who appear in this book were working or had worked to earn a living at some point in their lives. This is a common feature of most countries in the South (Boyden and Holden 1991; Fyfe 1985). The recognition that many of the world's children work is a difficult and disconcerting subject to address. Those who are opposed to child work tend to think of all forms of child work as bad. While I would much rather that children did not have to work, as I show later, an all-out ban on child work could be catastrophic for individual children. Any talk of banning child work is premature, and we do children a disservice when their status as workers is overlooked or criminalized. A great deal more could be done for working children if we accepted the more realistic premise that most of them are working because they have no choice. The reality is that child work will only become a thing of the past if standards of living go up in Vietnam; to overlook this fact is to dismiss the experiences of millions of children who are working right now.

From the moment I arrived in Vietnam in 1996, working children were highly visible. On my second day in the city I woke up early to the hot sun streaming through my windows, and I remember feeling an overwhelming sense of urgency to get myself organized. Embarking on an extended period of fieldwork can be a daunting process, and before leaving for Vietnam

I had been concerned that I would never meet enough children to adequately support the type of in-depth research I would need to develop my ideas. But that day I felt irritated with myself for indulging in such self-absorbed anxieties. Compared to Xiem, the young maid who had settled me into my room the previous night, and the countless other children I would meet over the next two years, my worries were totally insignificant: like most people born in the West, I already had far more lifestyle choices than any of them would ever know.

Still chastising myself, I quickly dressed and went out onto the streets to explore the area on foot. My first objective was to find the university where I was to enroll as a language student, but in retrospect walking there was a crazy idea. Once I found out how far away the university was, I decided to use a bike to travel around the city, but on that first day I had no idea that the scale of my map was so inaccurate. I was also unaware that when Communism was at its most radical, maps had been banned for national security reasons so that the people I asked for help were completely unaccustomed to deciphering them. Most people that I showed my map to smiled at me in a way that I took to be encouragement, but in reality they were probably smiling in bafflement, because they had no clear idea of what they were looking at or perhaps why I might be showing a map to them in the first place! Not surprisingly, I was soon lost in a maze of back streets and resorted to stopping every so often to ask the way. It was while walking those streets that I began to notice that where families were running small businesses, family members of all ages worked alongside each other.

In mid-morning I stopped at a noodle stand run by a young woman and her two daughters. While the mother cooked and served up the noodles and broth, the youngest daughter, who looked about twelve years old, chopped the vegetable garnish. Her older sister took orders and carried the steaming bowls of noodle soup to each customer. Later, I walked by a photocopy shop, and the eldest daughter of the owner invited me to join the family for tea. As I sat down, her grandmother, who had been collating papers to form a book, joined us, along with a toddler who had been sitting on the floor next to her and whose job it had been to hold the papers down so they didn't flutter away in the wind. In this family, everyone talked and laughed as they worked. A seven-year-old poured us tea while her father carefully studied my map (which was sitting upside down in his hands). The eldest daughter spoke a smattering of English, and we whiled away almost an hour going over and pronouncing words. As I finally left, I turned back to wave and saw that all the children were being ushered back to the different jobs they had been doing before I arrived.

During our time together I had learned that the eldest daughter juggled work with school and that she and her siblings worked short hours in the family-owned business. Under these circumstances, work was a collective endeavor in which adults monitored the amount of work their offspring did and tasks were distributed according to age and ability. Clearly, in this family-run business, work for the children was of a very different nature to that experienced by Xiem, the young maid who worked for my landlady. Xiem had moved from the countryside at the age of fifteen and worked long hours without any breaks during the day. Unlike Xiem, neither the children nor the adults were receiving a wage, but were at least working for the family collective—the photocopy shop—in a supportive environment, juggling work and school.

## Work and Play

Like a growing number of social scientists, Samantha Punch points out that a majority of the world's children are likely to work from an early age and from a Western perspective are often assumed to be less childlike, with little, if any, time left to play. But in reality, as she found while doing fieldwork in Bolivia, children are often very successful at combining both work and play (2001). The children I met that day were doing exactly what Punch describes in Bolivia. They and their parents had been relaxed about sitting with me and talking over tea because they could catch up with their work after I had left, and the children had clearly felt free to take their ease. The boys that I later got to know who sold postcards or cleaned shoes on the streets had a similar approach to that described by Punch in Bolivia. If trade was slow, they and their friends would put their work to one side and play a game of tag or jump on a bike and cycle around until the work picked up. Work and play did not have distinctive cut-off points.

Before I moved to Vietnam, my understanding of what constituted work was informed by my immediate surroundings and experiences. Growing up in the West I understood that it was essentially adults who worked and who received payment to do so. If children worked they did so more sparingly either in the home or on a part-time basis: but even so children's work did not have the same degree of necessity as the work adults did. In the West, working to earn a living is regarded as an adult experience, and in general the subject of work is not touched upon when Western childhoods are described. For example, the sociologist Barrie Thorne, who writes about childhood in the United States, notes that the landscape of contemporary childhood includes three major sites: families, neighborhoods, and schools (1997, 29).

The expectation that children will enter the workforce only once they are adults is quite alien to many people living in the South, or majority world, today. Indeed, as the experiences of Xiem, the girl at the noodle stand, and the children working in their family photocopy shop indicate, child work is often considered essential to the whole family's survival. But what does it mean for children to be working? Many of the dominant images of child work that appear in the West are of the most dramatic kind: children are pictured in coal mines, or working hard on the factory floor next to a piece of industrial machinery. Because these types of images are so pervasive, any discussions of child work or child labor is charged with emotional content, yet the causes and effects of child work require careful and reflective discussion. It is only by spending extended periods of time with different types of working children that we begin to recognize how varied children's experience of working are, and thus what a complicated subject it is to discuss.

As childhood becomes increasingly idealized in the West as a time for play and dreaming, the reality of most children's lives is likely to be viewed critically by international child rights legislators; as a result it becomes harder to treat with the necessary objectivity. Whether in aid agency reports, media stories, or academic literature, the use of child labor is decried as being altogether bad, denying children access to a childhood in which formal education is easily accessible and is each child's integral right (Blanchet 1996). While I have sympathy with these arguments, I also recognize that there are very varied and complicated reasons for children needing to go out to work, and such arguments do not allow one to take into account the economic necessity of child work or the access to education that some children can only afford as a result of earning a living for themselves.

## Child Labor or Child Work?

In both academic and international aid circles, attempts have been made to distinguish between child labor and child work. However, like Theresa Blanchet, I argue that it is irrelevant to make such a distinction, because so little is known about how many children work throughout the world or under what conditions they are doing so. From her own fieldwork in Bangladesh, Blanchett shows that under the labor/work distinction, the work that boys do in the bidi (cigarette) factories in Kustia would qualify as child labor, since they are officially recognized as working long hours in a factory, whereas their sisters who roll the cigarette papers at home in their "spare time" for only one-third of the boys' pay would be seen as child workers, precisely because their work does not take place on a factory floor. Any measure of injustice and gender exploitation is lost when arbitrary classifications are attempted. The children I met in Vietnam referred to their monetary-based activities as work and not child labor, and so it seems most fitting for me to adopt their more commonly used term.

### Child Work Defined

If children are engaged in so many diverse forms of employment, is it possible for there to be a single definition of child work? The answer has to be a resounding no, because although working children are highly visible in some regions of the world, they are also difficult to track, since they are most often found in the informal sectors of the workplace. I have only to recall my immediate experiences in Hanoi to recognize the informal nature of many children's work: for example, my landlady, Mai, negotiated Xiem's terms of agreement with her father, so Xiem had no formally recognized employment rights, nor indeed did anyone in the city really know of her existence or how she had come to be working for Mai. The girls who worked for their parents in the photocopy shop probably did not receive a salary and worked as and when they were needed. The boys who worked on the streets cleaning shoes or selling postcards did so under their own steam and as illegal street workers. Even in the United States—the dominant superpower in the world—children work illegally (Herzog 2004). Whole families of Mexican illegal immigrants work on farms as cheap laborers, ensuring that the price of fruit and vegetables remains low for the American consumer. As Carolyn Tuttle argues, "Unlike their predecessors in Europe, they [children] no longer work in the formal sector but have moved into the informal sector, where [employment] laws do not apply or are not strictly enforced. Consequently, today's child worker toils in small manufacturing enterprises rather than factories or large industrial firms. They work as cheap, 'sweated' labor in a variety of cultures and countries but in many of the same industries" (1999, 2).

As the International Labor Office points out, children are often found working in the domain of the family on the land, which makes it very difficult to document and therefore define exactly how many children are involved, or in what forms of work. However, from the documented cases in the Southern Hemisphere alone, one can hazard a guess at the types of jobs children are doing outside the domestic setting. Children are engaged in farm labor. They dismantle car batteries to recycle their parts. They work on the streets selling post cards or cleaning shoes. Some sell themselves for sex (Montgomery 2001). They work as panhandlers in the gold and diamond mines of Angola and South Africa. They sew cloth in the garment industries of Bangladesh and Thailand. In Vietnam, Jeff Ballinger has documented poor working conditions for teenage Nike employees, unable to afford school, who instead sew sneakers and are often cheated out of their low wages when they fail to complete high daily quotas (Ballinger 1997).

So varied is child work that one child's experiences of employment will be quite different from that of another. This also means that activities that are referred to as work by one person will be understood differently by another. Jo Boyden and Margaret Holden point out "another problem is that many juvenile occupations are not defined by adults as work . . . young street workers are often thought of by adults as vagrants, beggars or thieves and not workers. But things might look very different from a child's point of view" (1991, 119). After making similar observations among working children in other parts of the world, Jo Boyden, Birgitta Ling, and Bill Myers refer to child work in very generalized terms as "those in paid employment or active in money-making tasks inside or outside the home, or involved in unpaid home maintenance for at least ten hours per week" (Boyden, Ling, and Myers 1998, 22). This, of course is only one definition of child work, but it is one that at least attempts to offer a broader understanding of what work is.

*Vietnamese Work Defined*

Formal definitions of what is and what is not work are created at the international level, and most governments now measure the amount and types of work that people do using these internationally standardized measurements, which in fact originated in the West where work is often of an entirely different nature. Therefore much of what many Vietnamese families, for example, think of as work would not appear in officially recognized documentation. Conversely a great deal of what children do within a rural setting, such as collecting water, caring for younger children, or looking after the water buffalo, may not be considered work within their immediate community. Olga Nieuwenhuys writes, "During the 1970s, anthropologists carried out extensive and painstaking time-allocation and family budget studies to show that even young children were contributing to their own sustenance by undertaking a whole range of activities in the subsistence sphere of the peasant economy" (1996, 241). So when we talk about work in the context of a country like Vietnam it is crucial to recognize that official records of what is and what is not work may not reflect real life experience.

Before concentrating on aspects of child work in Vietnam, we need to establish how people work and are rewarded in the country as a whole. Vietnam still lacks reliable contemporary ethnographic and sociologically based research, and this means there are very few comparative studies to be drawn upon when talking about indigenous attitudes toward work, and especially child work.

*Agriculture*

Vietnam still has a largely agrarian economy, which means that the majority of people still work on the land, on their own freeholds or for other people. Ninety percent of people still live in rural areas and are involved in basic industries such as agricultural production on their own or rented land. William Duiker explains that like most of its neighbors, Vietnam has been a predominantly agrarian society for more than two thousand years. And for the Vietnamese, agriculture almost by definition implies the cultivation of wet rice (1995, 129). Because of the nature of people's work, very little of the fruits of their labors is likely to be visible in the gross domestic product of the country as measured by internationally agreed accounting methods (Boyden, Ling, and Myers 1998). The family who works collectively on its land while the grandmother of the family sits at home mending fishing nets will not figure in formalized definitions of work. The child who sells postcards on the streets and who sends some of his earnings home to assist family members in the countryside, or the child who cares for younger siblings while her mother goes out to work, will also not show up in any of the official measurements recording how many people work and in what activities. And whatever work might be understood to mean today it has had different meanings in different societies and different cultures throughout history.

In the past 150 years, Vietnam has moved from being a feudal society to one in which its workers lived under French colonial rule, then to one in which the Communist movement of collective farming was introduced (Luong 1992). Hy Luong's fieldwork documents the transformation of a village in northern Vietnam during these distinct periods in Vietnam's history. He points to the common expectation that children will work. As one villager who had grown up in the 1930s recalled to him during a fieldwork interview, "Feeling bad about the family's poverty, I began working again at the age of twelve, this time as a babysitter. I was paid four piastres a year plus enough food for myself. In the colonial period children could pursue education for themselves only beyond the second or third grade if their families were wealthy. At the suggestion of a friend I soon gave up babysitting in order to apprentice as a plowman for Mayor Huu in the village of Vinh-Lai. I became an accomplished plowman at the age of fourteen or fifteen. The work schedule was heavy" (1992, 63). Other people growing up in the same village during that period recalled the pleasure that combining both school and work gave them: "I usually tended buffalo in the afternoon after my return from school—not because I had to but because I liked to get a chance to play games with other buffalo tenders" (ibid., 68).

French policy during the colonial era lent itself to educating a small elite, and for lack of funds many young Vietnamese in rural areas received virtually no education at all (Duiker 1995, 33). William Duiker writes that the "end result of the French colonial period was not a society on the verge of rapid economic development, but a classic example of a dual economy, with a small and predominantly foreign commercial sector in the cities surrounded by a mass of untrained and often poverty-stricken peasants in the villages" (ibid., 133).

### Communism

Particularly in rural areas, children have continued to work even when society was radically restructured under Communism. In 1954, villages across Vietnam were subjected to the Marxist Land Reform Act. Duiker argues that in some respects these reforms were successful: more than two million hectares of land were redistributed, and the historic domination of the landed gentry was broken. But this meant that whole communities were assigned to work in a particular manner by the state, and the physical labor of children was still necessary to ensure that expected production targets were met. By the 1960s, collectivization was substantially completed, but this did not significantly increase grain production; nor did it free all family members, including children, from having to work. Indeed, the Communist propaganda machine reinforced the value of hard labor. Propaganda posters during the height of the Communist era depict muscular men and women wearing the same unisex uniform of overalls and red scarves and working alongside each other as equals in a romanticized depiction of agricultural revolution.

During the most radical phase of Communism in the 1970s and 1980s thousands of the Vietnamese educated class were sent to study subjects as diverse as medicine, engineering, and political doctrine in the Soviet Union. Today Vietnam's privileged class is sending its offspring to study in the West, and for these people a different set of cultural attitudes toward work is being assimilated. For the majority of Vietnamese, though, work remains as it always has: a collectively driven, small-scale, family-based enterprise that can ill afford not to send children out to work.

### Statistical Evidence of Child Work

If definitions of child work are so difficult to pinpoint, is it possible to rely on international estimates about the number of children involved in child work or labor? Drawing on recent survey data, the International Labor Organization estimates that worldwide there are currently 352 million children aged five to seventeen engaged in economic activity of some kind. The organization goes on to estimate that of these, 106 million are engaged in types of work acceptable for children who have reached the minimum age for employment (usually fifteen years) or in light work such as household chores or work undertaken as part of a child's education. The remaining

246 million children are engaged in forms of work that the International Labor Organization says children should be forbidden from undertaking because of their hazardous nature. It estimates that the Asia-Pacific region harbors the largest number of child workers, and that 70 percent of all children there work in primary sectors such as agriculture, fishing, hunting, and forestry (International Labor Organization 2005, 1).

Other bodies make different estimates about how many children in the world work, and where they are most likely to do so. The Church World Service (CWS) estimated in 2002 that 250 million of the world's 2 billion children work and that a significant number are producing goods for export to consumers in the United States.

In Vietnam, information about the type of work children are doing and how many of them are in fact involved in any type of work is just as hazy and varied as elsewhere in the world. When statistics on the numbers of child workers have been accumulated, they have often been assembled from different bases and interpreted and applied differently. For example, while the Vietnamese government provides statistics on the total number of working children, UNICEF chooses to provide information about the total number of children working full-time, which is not the same thing at all. Unless one reads each body's material carefully, the different approaches can lead to confusion on the reader's part.

Vietnamese government figures claim that out of Vietnam's population of 80 million, the number of child workers between the ages of six and seventeen declined to 6.3 million in 1998. UNICEF, however, quotes from the Vietnam Living Standards Surveys (VLSS) to show that the estimated number of full-time child workers fell from 4 million to approximately 1.6 million between 1992 and 1998. In the same report, UNICEF reveals some discrepancies: it states that there has been a decline in child workers in urban areas but expresses concern that there has also been a rise in the number of children defined as being neither in school nor at work, especially for the eleven to fourteen age group in rural areas. In other words, the movements of an increasing number of children are failing to be accounted for in official surveys. Perhaps it is no coincidence then that this growing discrepancy in statistics describing the activities of some of Vietnam's children coincides with Vietnam having embraced international-standard child labor laws: laws that essentially oppose and are critical of any type of child work and can therefore result in employers trying to disguise who works for them.

### Girls Who Work

Children's gender, age, and family circumstances influence the types of jobs they end up doing, and this further disguises the extent of child work, particularly for girls. In Vietnam, while boys are more visible working independently on the streets, girls are more likely to be working in cafes, market stalls, or private homes. Girls are also more likely to do domestic work for their own families, caring for younger siblings and taking care of household chores. Some of my fieldwork took place among girls who lived in a government orphanage. While the girls did not consider that they worked, many of their responsibilities would be classed as work under different circumstances. When they returned to the orphanage from school, for example, most of their time was taken with the care of the younger children there, each girl pairing off with a particular child.

Both Nguyet and Lan, two of the girls I knew in the orphanage, told me that looking after younger children in the orphanage provided them with a surrogate family. From their perspective, this was not work. In fact, taking care of younger children added meaning to their lives. Minding, chastising, feeding, and cleaning of the younger children were of course a type of work, but like much of child work, they went unrecognized. Pamela Reynolds observed the same phenomenon in her study of children's work in subsistence agriculture in Zimbabwe, where she found that girls under ten years of age spent 56 percent of their time caring for infants and younger children—but that this did not mean that they were given less responsibility than boys for farm work; in other words, child care was not recognized as work (1991, 80–81).

## Attempts to Limit Child Work

The West has determined much of the debate about child work and labor, even though the majority of today's child workers are in the South (Seabrook 2001, 1). Some of the expatriate aid workers I interviewed in Hanoi spoke in such shocked terms about the fact that Vietnamese children work that one was virtually given the impression that child work is completely obsolete in the Western countries they came from. During a meeting

I attended on the subject of the working girl child, a Swedish aid worker who was an enthusiastic proponent of the child rights agenda even went so far as to announce to the attendees that "it is an outrage that Vietnam is letting its children work." But while child work is far more pervasive in the South, child work is still not completely a thing of the past in the West. In addition, after-school employment is commonplace, as is an expectation that children will do unpaid work in the home. In her research, Virginia Morrow found that British teenagers are often highly responsible workers in the home (1994, 130). In the 1990s Michael Lavalette did extensive research into the extent of paid employment among those under the age of sixteen living in Britain and found that far more children combine part-time work with full-time education than is commonly recognized. He concluded that the majority of children have experience of paid employment outside the home, that they work in a wide range of jobs, and that British legislation designed to ensure that working conditions are suitable remains ineffective (ibid., 199).

Of course, Western children in full-time education who do not work at least part-time at some point during their school years still make up a minority of the world population, and for most of the world's children a major site of childhood is the workplace and not school. But in the West there is now a legally based growing lack of tolerance for child work in any form, and this same intolerance has been imposed on the economically weaker countries of the South, such as Vietnam. Broadly, the West has tried two approaches to address this perceived problem: the abolition of child work, and the limitation of particular categories of work. I will discuss each in turn as it is relevant to Vietnam.

### Abolishing Child Work

The first solution to controlling child work has been simply to ban all forms of production that involve children. As I have indicated, this approach is open to failure because children are most often found working in informal sectors. But the approach also fails because in simply banning work, those who wish to abolish it are failing to address the underlying reasons for children going out to work in the first place. For example, in 1999 the United States Congress supported the Harkin Bill, which, had it been ratified, would have banned the import of all garments produced by child labor in Bangladesh. On the face of it this seemed like a good idea: if one of the largest importers of Bangladeshi-made garments in the Western world was willing to take a stand, then surely child employment would be a thing of the past? However, supporters of the Harkin Bill soon discovered that by simply closing down an avenue for employment, the bill did little more than make children who still needed to earn a living even more vulnerable to exploitation in the workplace. Monetary compensation to children and their families was too slow and children were compelled to go into alternative and often worse lines of work. Numerous Bangladeshi-based aid agencies reported that children had had little choice but to go into illegal sweatshops or into the sex industry, where they were likely to earn less and be more vulnerable to abuse than they had been in their previous jobs.

My observations in Hanoi also led me to believe that by imposing blanket opposition to any type of child work, activists leave working children even more exposed to potentially threatening working environments, because this approach can result in their work going underground. In addition, this type of blanket opposition to child work ignores the reality that support systems need to be up and running before factories are closed; otherwise the children who have just lost their jobs still need to earn a living. The NGOs in Bangladesh also reported that many of the affected children had enjoyed working in the garment factories because the jobs were of higher status than other types of employment. Thus it is inaccurate—as well as belittling the contribution of working children—to treat all forms of child work as potentially abusive.

### Limiting Certain Types of Child Work

The second approach adopted by international organizations is an attempt to define acceptable and unacceptable forms of child labor and then apply matching reform programs. The International Labor Office has defined hazardous work as that which "places too heavy a burden on the child; work that endangers his safety, health or welfare, work that takes advantage of the defenselessness of the child, work that exploits the child as a cheap substitute for adult labor, work that uses the child's effort but does nothing for his development; work that impedes the child's education or training and thus prejudices his future" (International Labor Office, Report of the Director-General 37, 69th Session, 1983).

As it stands, Article 32 of the UNCRC, which relates to child work, is open to very broad interpretation. It states that child work should not be hazardous, but it does not say what type of work is considered to fall into that category. It also states that work should not interfere with children's education, but it does not elaborate on what constitutes a good education. These expectations are based on an assumption that all governments have the resources to make all employers accountable to them, and that education is freely available to all children. In short, apart from being overly idealistic about the level of support countries in the South can afford to offer their children, the UNCRC is also supporting a very middle class set of Western values, which also give a false impression about the type of childhoods found in that part of the world. Once I began spending time among children on the streets, in the reform school, and in the orphanage I learned that they all worked or had needed to work in the past because their families relied on their incomes to provide enough food for the table, or to help cover school fees imposed by the government of Vietnam on the advice of the World Bank. None of the children felt they had any choice but to work. Yet to look at Vietnam from the distance generated by governmental and NGO reports is to assume that child work is becoming a thing of the past.

In general I found that the NGOs that focused exclusively on children were the same ones that had made a commitment to the UNCRC; these NGOs were most opposed to child work. Often a large proportion of their income (and hence assurance about their continuing existence) relied on funds granted to work on international aid agency projects. When I was in Hanoi for two years between 1996 and 1998, these NGOs were involved in a number of high-profile projects aimed at the working child. For example, PLAN International was working with the government on a project designed to reunite unaccompanied working children with their families by sending the children back to the countryside. During the process no attempt was made to compensate children and their families for the loss of income this process caused, even though an NGO-initiated report headed by Radda Barnen, another NGO, indicated that some form of family-focused poverty alleviation would be necessary to make the project a success. In contrast, a number of international NGOs working outside the remit (and funding) set by the UN agencies took what I believe was a more realistic and supportive stance. When boys entered the reform school in which one such NGO based itself, their investment in their working lives did not come to an end. Some of the boys used their time at the reform school to join training programs for skilled occupations such as mechanics or computer services, and others took up craftwork. The work they did in these classes was introduced by the NGO at the boys' direct request. Because most of the boys who attended the school would need to work when they left the school, the work training was designed to improve their employment chances. Sometimes they were also able to earn an income from the crafts that they sold.

However, in the spring of 1997 the employment training offered to boys at the reform school came under attack from visiting members of UNICEF who, after observing children working at their arts tables and mending motorbikes, accused both the director of the school and the NGO workers there of colluding in child labor. From my perspective this response to the skilled training program was shortsighted and showed a level of ignorance about the daily pressures that exist for the majority of children who live in the South. As Van Deer argues, "Paradoxically, our tendency to focus on that which divides human beings from each other, to focus on difference, is something that all humans share" (1998, 299).

According to Mr. Ha, the director of the reform school, when one of the UNICEF representatives criticized what she observed in the reform school, her wording and tone of voice gave the impression that she believed it was unusual for children to be working, and that elsewhere in the world children had more positive lifestyles. I maintain that this is not so, and Jo Boyden and Pat Holden have shown that out of necessity children work at a variety of tasks throughout the world: "In the South, the only way the urban poor can survive is by putting as many members of the household as possible to work. Where there are no State welfare payments, and where self-employment and low, unstable incomes are widespread, the labor of children is crucial" (1991, 117).

Because NGOs often rely on Western-based bilateral and unilateral funders, their areas of interest can be dictated by funders' current areas of interest, which are not necessarily their own. This means they have to rely on unreliable sources of short-term funding, which depend on the changing priorities of the international aid community, and this can make the work that they do unsustainable in the long term. Before arriving in Vietnam I was aware that the plight of street children had been very high on the international aid agenda. But I arrived in Vietnam one year after the Beijing Women's Conference, and as a result of petitions from within the women's movement the girl child was the new aid interest. The week after I arrived in Hanoi, I attended a UNICEF meeting for members of NGOs to pool their knowledge and concerns about the girl children and to discuss ways of offering support to that group. The workers who were present were particularly keen to set up a support system for girls who work.

After discussions had been under way for some time, a Vietnamese member of the audience stood up. He first pointed out that gaining access to such girls was going to be highly problematic if not impossible because of the informal nature of their work and the manner in which such girls were absorbed into the family unit of their employer's household. He then asked whether NGOs would continue to support the projects they had already set up for the working street children, who were predominantly boys. A Danish aid worker responded by saying that street children had enjoyed support for a number of years and that now the time had come to focus elsewhere. In other words, interest in one group of children was being supplanted by interest in another as the international aid focus moved arbitrarily in a new direction and the funding available to NGOs reflected that change. In aid circles, this is known as "funding-led" rather than "needs-based" project planning. Of course, NGOs cannot start or continue projects for which no funding is available, and funders often set funding priorities with little knowledge of the situation in the field. But this meant that the child rights–focused NGOs that had made themselves responsible to uphold the UNCRC were in fact not trying to improve the lot of all children, and genuinely treat them as universally the same, but were choosing to focus only on the needs of particular subgroups of children, to the potential detriment of others who did not fit some very particular and limited categories such as being a working child or a street child.

That meeting made such an impression on me that it changed the focus of my research in Vietnam. I had only attended the meeting to become familiar with the NGO community as a preamble to researching child health issues, not child rights. But the difficulties facing NGO workers, and, most importantly, the children they were seemingly having to let down as street children projects came to an end, left me incredulous. I wondered to what extent well-intentioned NGO workers were really able to make any positive change for working children. Faced with the dilemma of having to switch funding focus every few years, what were they really doing for Vietnam's working children? If they wanted to protect the working girl child, how could this be achieved using unsustainable funding when the factors contributing to a child having to work were so complex? As a result of this experience I decided to concentrate my research on working children, but by using the experiences of working children in their family and societal context as the starting point to inform what I was also learning about the work of the external aid organizations.

Following this changed perspective, let us put to one side for the moment the policies and programs promulgated by the international community, and look at the reality of children's lives as workers in Vietnam, and specifically in Hanoi, where I subsequently based myself. Their work takes many forms; for Hai, about whom I write at length in chapter 4, selling postcards on the streets provided a level of freedom that he relished. For other children, such as Binh, who cleaned shoes for a living, working provided the opportunity to have an education and to support their younger siblings in their studies. For older girls in the orphanage described in chapter 7, it took the form of domestic work and of informally providing care to younger children they considered to be their family. For Xiem it took the form of working long hours in a domestic setting with little respite. Meanwhile, boys in the reform school, who are the focus of chapter 6, were proud of the work they did because their work was part of a skilled training program that they had requested. In short, work means different things to different children, and children's experiences vary considerably.

### *The Significance of Children's Work*

At the reform school where I was to do research for almost two years, some of the children told me they had been arrested because they had taken up stealing as a means of supporting their parents, or to buy items that their families could not afford. Other boys in the reform school also spoke of the work they had done alongside their parents, on the land, in their shop, or perhaps in a café. Whatever the reason for trying to earn a living, children's earnings are unlikely to be regarded as pin money but rather as essential and necessary contributions to their own or their whole family's survival. Boyden and Holden explain that "in the South the only way the urban poor can survive is by putting as many members of the household as possible to work. Where there are no state welfare payments, and where self-employment is low, unstable incomes are widespread, the labor of children is crucial. Millions of children throughout the world work" (1991, 117). A significant number of the children I met were economic migrants to the city and had either left their families at home in the countryside or had emigrated with them to live illegally in the capital. The majority were proud that they worked and very few of them had experienced the type of exploitation experienced by large numbers of children throughout the world who work in sweatshops or in the sex industry (Montgomery 2001; Seabrook 2001).

So what happens when adults believe that children should not work and children believe that they should, or, as is the case in a country like Vietnam, they feel compelled to work for survival or to improve their life choices? One of the outcomes of this dilemma is that working children stop seeking out the support of adults who might have been able to help them. Why is there often a failure of understanding? One problem facing working children is that adults who oppose what they do really do not have enough appreciation of their circumstances or those of their families. The majority of Vietnamese I met who worked for NGOs were highly educated and from the privileged sectors of their society, and as such they were often as removed from the pressures facing the children they supported as were their expatriate coworkers. And as is often the case among more privileged members of any society, there was a tendency to externalize explanations for poverty and place responsibility outside the political context. For example, on one occasion I was sitting by the main lake in the center of Hanoi with Hang, a Vietnamese woman who worked for an NGO within the Save the Children consortium. A boy I knew whose name was Thoa came over asking to clean our shoes. After I had introduced Hang to Thoa and he had walked away, Hang said, "It is so sad that his family do not want him." Nothing that Thoa had said could have created that impression. In fact, Thoa had told me that he was working on the streets to pay for his afternoon studies and to send money home to his family.

Hang's response to her encounter with Thoa reflected similar ideas that were presented in the local newspapers and mirrored stereotyped attitudes held by the government: that working children were unwanted, or that they were victims of parental greed. On November 3, 1996, the *Vietnam News* printed the following statement about working children: "'My mother wants me to bring home money, although she is aware of how I earn my money— sleeping with men,' a sixteen-year-old girl in Cho Gao District, Tien Giang Province said. The girl said that she gave her mother all the money she was paid for each night—about forty thousand Vietnamese dong or three dollars fifty . . . it is incredible to learn that there are children forced to work on the streets by their parents." This example of press sensationalism owes nothing to objectivity.

The reality is more prosaic and less sinister. However tenuously, most of the children I knew maintained a positive contact with their families and had gone off to work for themselves without being unduly exploited, to lessen their parents' financial burden, often making their own highly appreciated contribution to the family income. By routinely demonizing working children and their families and removing working children from the streets, the government and its supporters were ignoring the loss of income that would be incurred by a child's family, thus creating greater pressure for the entire family unit. There also seems to be an implicit assumption among authorities that parents of working children care little for their children, as Hang's ill-considered remarks illustrate. In reality the majority of parents want the best for their children, and given the option would rather that their children not work. Eric Edmonds and Nina Pacenik have demonstrated that Vietnamese rice farmers whose children work alongside them stopped relying on their child's labor once rice prices went up. They report, "A 30 percent rise in the relative price of rice (as experienced in Vietnam) is associated on average with a nine percentage point decrease in child labor. Rice price increases can account for 45 percent of the decline in child labor experienced in 1993 and 1998 in Vietnam" (2003, 23). They use these findings to point out that households that are large net producers of rice appear to have taken advantage of higher income after the rice price increase to reduce child labor despite increased labor opportunities for children. So rather than criticizing the families who send their children out to work we should work toward adjusting the enormous disparities in earnings that exist across the globe, while simultaneously putting more creative funding in place to, for example, provide monetary compensation for parents who send their previously working children to school. Exactly this type of project was set up in 2003 in some parts of Brazil by the Brazilian government. In the meantime, we must recognize the realities of child work, and it is worth examining the social gains that some children reap from working.

### Working Can Improve a Child's Status

Working can improve the status of children brought up in poverty and give them satisfaction, making them equal and empowered partners within their immediate household. During my first couple of months in Hanoi I worked on a project with some Vietnamese NGO workers, one of whom was a young woman called Hoa. She had grown up in a rural village on the edge of Hue, the previous capital to the south of Hanoi but now a provincial town. When I first met Hoa I presumed that like other people working for the NGO she was opposed to child work. During my first year in Hanoi I did some research training for the agency, and Hoa and I became friendly. When she found out that I was quite skeptical about the extent to which the UNCRC would ever be effective in Vietnam, she began to tell me about her experiences of working during childhood. Rather than painting a bleak picture, Hoa described a working environment she recalled as both supportive and caring, in which her parents showed a great deal of appreciation for what she and her siblings contributed to the family. She and her siblings used to relieve their mother from her weaving after they had returned home from school, while their mother in turn kept a close watch over her children, encouraging them to complete their homework before work began and to take a rest when they showed signs of fatigue. As a result of this family cooperation Hoa had always felt very supported. Hoa's family very clearly defined and shaped her experiences of working during her childhood, so that years later she was able to recall how much she had enjoyed and gained satisfaction from her work; for example, she told me how proud she was that the money earned from weaving had enabled her and her siblings to continue to attend school. Both of her parents praised her and spoke of being in debt to her and her siblings for contributing to the family income. Hoa's family's supportive approach ensured that she had happy experiences of working and that work fitted in with her other needs and abilities.

This experience is in line with those observed by Punch among rural Bolivian children, whose parents were considerate of their children's abilities and mindful that their needs were taken into account (2001). Anne Solberg draws some similar observations about family attitude shaping Norwegian childhoods when she makes the point that "to some extent the shaping of particular childhoods is the family's task, particularly in relation to ideas of age and conceptions of independence. It is the dividing up of tasks between family members and the laying down of rules and conduct that implicitly determines what it means to be a child" (1990, 118). But what of children who work independently of their families, such as the boys I met in Hanoi who worked on the streets? As we shall see, despite having very different experiences of work from someone like Hoa, they also gained certain types of empowerment along with specific types of hardship.

### Experiences of Working Children on the Streets

Life on the streets of Hanoi could be precarious for working children. As well as being regularly persecuted by the police, who would extract bribes from them or force them to move on, they were often caught up in rivalries between gangs competing for the best sales areas in the city center. They were also vulnerable to more sinister influences such as drugs and tourists seeking sex. But with all this, I began to recognize quite quickly that individual children working on the streets of Hanoi responded quite differently to similar situations. Binh was one boy who enjoyed working on the streets of Hanoi, while other boys, like Hai, were less resilient in coping with some of the difficulties street life can bring. Hai was about fifteen years old when I first met him. He sold postcards on the streets of Hanoi and gained obvious satisfaction from his independent lifestyle. Although he had lost his mother, he did have other family and so was not strictly an orphan, but he pretended to be one for the tourists as he realized that this would increase their sympathy and hence his chances of a successful sale. During the time I knew him he was offered a number of chances to become an apprentice in different expatriate-run businesses, but he had a tendency to turn such opportunities down because he liked to be his own boss. Hai enjoyed working for himself and particularly liked the freedom to set his own hours and to come and go as he pleased.

It was very instructive for me that Hai was also keenly aware and critically vocal that all the support ostensibly available to children like him did nothing to address the real limitations on their lives: for example, that he was an illegal worker to the city and so was denied access to health care and schooling. Foreigners like me, whether tourists, researchers, part of the expatriate business community, or international aid agency workers, did take a keen interest in him and the other children who worked on the streets, but our interest was always transitory. Once we left, the boys' lives stayed the same. Indeed, for Hai life on the streets was a precarious and ultimately tragic one, as I will explain in chapter 5. In contrast, Binh, who was fourteen years old when I met him, spoke with enormous pride about the work he did and the benefits that earning money brought not only to himself but also to his whole family, who lived in the countryside. He cleaned shoes outside a prestigious hotel in the center of the city, and was proud of his achievements; he told me "my money supports the costs of the classes I go to but also pays for one of my brothers living at home to go to school."

## A Reassessment

We can see from this overview of some of the working children I met that their life experiences were very varied, often productive and positive; it is not helpful to stereotype them as all being in need of some kind of help. Of course, some individuals were vulnerable and exploited, but it is important to acknowledge that many others were not. By their very nature, external aid interventions cannot respond with sensitivity to this varied pattern of experiences, within the context of Vietnamese society. So let us return to the central question by reassessing the lives of children as individuals, and then asking whether it is right that they should work. Recently there has been a shift in the way in which children's lives are understood. Researchers have begun to recognize that most attention has focused on the detrimental effects on children's lives of experiences such as working and poverty. This has led to sweeping policies that attempt to put a stop to child work without first considering the particulars of each child's circumstances. But there is now increasing recognition that we need to understand more about situations in which children seem to thrive despite adversities that are thrust upon them. In other words, we should start acknowledging children's own capabilities and resilience. For example, Heather Montgomery, Martin Woodhead, and I have written, "One of the reasons children's temperament, level of activity and social responsiveness can be so influential on their resilience is because it affects the quality of their relationships, especially with those on whom they depend for survival, care and learning. Some children may be more effective than others in eliciting those very kinds of nurturance, emotional support and guidance which serve as protective factors" (Burr, Montgomery, and Woodhead 2003, 24).

Clearly the question of whether it is right for children to work is a loaded and very complex one. By whose standards should we assess whether it is right for a child to work? Should some forms of work be considered more acceptable than others? At what stage, if any, should children be considered capable of making independent choices about whether they enter the labor market? If we want to change the experiences of working children, then I believe this goal must be accomplished in stages—the first of which would be to research the real conditions under which children work, without immediately penalizing employers. Financial support must be offered to employers to improve the working environment. But it is also crucial that the families of working children be offered financial support to make it possible for them to remove their children from the workplace altogether. While these propositions may sound ambitious, even idealistic, it is more practical to think along these lines than it is to take the current view that dominates in the West: that child work must be prohibited immediately and entirely, without simultaneously addressing complex influences that make it impossible for children to stop working immediately. A blanket opposition to child work results in children's work being hidden from view. It doesn't stop the practice; nor does it address the fact that children work under diverse conditions and that while some would be very pleased to give up work, other children gain pleasure and social status from working.

The fact that more could be done to redress the balance between the haves and have-nots did not escape a significant number of the children I got to know. The children most negatively affected by unfair distribution of the world's resources should not be treated as passive innocents. Most importantly, rather than treating child work as a problem that is separate and removed from children's experiences in the West, we need to acknowledge that child work occurs in every part of the world. The West and its aid agencies should acknowledge that children work as a result of unequal distribution of the world's resources in favor of the more affluent members of their own country and countries in the West. I have shown here that it is still a reality that children have to work. But what then should be done about this?

Abolitionists argue for an all-out ban without acknowledging that the global world as we know it would have to change dramatically for such a ban to be enforced. Gradualists argue that over time as the world economy gets stronger money will trickle down to the poor. Neither of these approaches can hope to succeed under the present economic rules.

But it is of little use simply to rant and present such facts as so many social commentators and academics have a tendency to do without proposing solutions: to do so does not excuse one's own actions. As Paul Farmer points out, "If these individuals are privileged people like me, they understand that they have been implicated, whether directly or indirectly, in the creation or maintenance of this structural violence" (2003, 157). When I get up in the morning and throw on my sweater made somewhere in China or knock back a cup of coffee grown in Kenya, I do so in the knowledge that in all likelihood children worked to provide me with those wares. We should all make ourselves accountable at this very basic level. And rather than drawing on the bad experiences of working children, antiwork movements should shift their focus toward first introducing and reinforcing benign global influences that will protect children as they necessarily continue to work. Short of enforcing a worldwide redistribution of wealth, we should work toward all children being protected in the workplace, and this has to take a more effective form than making grandiose and unrealistic plans to ban child work altogether. In addition, if children are truly to participate in the rights movement that purports to support them, then their various views on work also need to be properly listened to before adult-led interventions are made on their behalf. Properly listening to children can make for uncomfortable and disconcerting listening.

While most social policy makers, and, indeed, society in general, fail to recognize the extent to which children work, there is real reason for concern, because this means that the reality of children's working conditions are not properly and objectively understood. And whether in Vietnam or in any wider international arena, addressing the issue of child work is very difficult when policy makers are unsure of how many children work or where they are employed. Wherever it remains normal and traditional for children to work, however, it is also certain that there will be times when they are also unfairly exploited.

*Five*

# Children on the Streets

The first children I did fieldwork among in Hanoi worked on the streets in the center of the city. In this chapter I discuss some of their experiences, in particular their responses to the different types of formal and informal support services available to them. My findings show that children who had already been on the streets for a number of years were wary of establishing contact with any type of adult-led formal services, preferring to rely on informal support from within their peer group or from among adults who did not challenge their current lifestyles.

There is a tendency to offer children associated with the street very uniform types of support, the assumption being that "street children" are essentially all the same. Most of you reading this are probably familiar with the term "street child."

My use of the term may have conjured an image in your mind of lonely, unsupported children living on the streets because they have no home, or are orphaned: begging, selling wares, or running makeshift streetside stores. All such images are legitimate, but they are also stereotypical. The children I met could not be so readily categorized.

Another problem facing the children I knew is that the wider society associates the life of a street child with deprivation. As I argue in chapter 1, we do such children a disservice when we treat them as a homogeneously disadvantaged subgroup separate from mainstream society. As I show in this chapter, most of the children I did fieldwork among did not consider themselves disadvantaged and would have probably felt it was patronizing for anyone to treat them as such. As Tim Bond, writing about children working on the streets of Ho Chi Minh City, points out so clearly, "By living on the street, a child is automatically guilty of challenging and breaking society's most basic rules, and is reminded of the fact every day by the attitudes and acts of a whole range of social workers. Most people believe or want to believe that all street children yearn, deep down, to return to a normal life. This is a comfortable and complacent belief, reflecting the unquestioned rectitude of conventional morality. To think otherwise would be to challenge things best left unchallenged" (1994, 1). Bond observes that "street children" are often stigmatized by wider society, but he also questions the generally held orthodoxy that street children would rather not be living the way that they are, that they do in fact want to return to living in a normal home, headed by adults. Rather, he argues that some children genuinely want to stay where they are and prefer to be earning their income on the streets. He notes that this life choice is beyond the comprehension of members of the wider society because it entails recognizing the benefits of life on the streets for some children and therefore raises unsettling questions about childhood in general and the limitations placed on children's lifestyles by well meaning adults.

He is suggesting, as do I, that we underestimate children, their coping strategies, and their abilities to make decisions for themselves. By joining forces with Bond's argument I am not suggesting that we do nothing to help "street children" but rather that we listen properly to each child and respond empathetically to his or her wants rather than automatically and sweepingly make decisions on each child's behalf.

Problematizing the term "street child" creates a dilemma: should I have entirely abandoned the term? Even though I originally decided to drop the term in my own work I came up against difficulties when trying to write about the children whose experiences are discussed here without referring to the street. This is because when engaging with existing literature and social policy on this issue it becomes virtually impossible to do so without using the dominant terms of reference already adopted by practitioners and academics alike. On reflection, then, the term "street child" has some use but only as a very loose generic, so while I use this term, I do so with reservation. I am not alone in reaching this compromise. Even though the anthropologist Tobias Hecht uses the term "street child" in his ethnographic study of children living on the streets in South America, he nevertheless points out that overfocusing on street children detracts attention from the issue of widespread poverty and abuse that affects children living in other circumstances (1998).

Bruno Glauser, an academic and social worker working in South America, also uses the term but with reservation. He notes that the term implies that such children predominantly and permanently live and sleep on the streets and that they have a lack of customary contacts or links with adults in the family and in wider society (1990).

## *The Problem with Defining Types of Street Children*

The term "street child" is also problematic because it is an umbrella term that is subdivided in different ways by different authorities and commentators in attempts to distinguish between different types of children of the streets. But it has been estimated that homeless street children sleeping outdoors in such places as alleys, street pavements, and storefronts comprise only about 20 percent of the world's street children (Glauser 1990). Research carried out in Kenya by Kilbride, Suda, and Njeru shows that about 80 percent of street children in Kenya return to their homes frequently to sleep even though they are seen being "on" the streets where they eke out a daily living (2000, 2). Judith Ennew has pointed to an early definition used in 1983 by the Inter-NGO Programme for Street Children and Street Youth: it refers very generally to street children as children for whom the street has replaced the family as their real home, a situation in which there is no protection, supervision, or direction from responsible adults (1994). But over the years the term has been qualified and redefined in attempts to make it more specific. For example, UNICEF makes a distinction between children on the street who return to their family home at night and those who either live there permanently or have a limited and risky access to housing and hence spend most of their time on the streets. This categorization is also problematic because it makes too fine a distinction between children who return home and those who do not. In 1992 the NGO Childhope Asia defined three categories of street children: abandoned and homeless children; children who go home to their families; and children of street families. Adams, Gullotta, and Clancy (1985) have also distinguished three groups of street children, but have instead done so on a psychosocial basis. They have categorized them as children who flee the home because of family conflict, bad social relationships, and alienation; children who are rejected by their parents or are forced to leave home; and children who are the products of rejection by society. But what does any of this mean in reality? Is it really possible to make the distinction that Adams, Gullotta, and Clancy do between children who have experienced family conflict and those who are rejected by their parents? Such distinctions come across as unnecessarily pedantic.

One could ask what relevance these categories might have to the very children who inform such studies. A number of children I met during fieldwork debunked these rigid categories. For example, Hai, who told me he was fifteen years old and that he had worked on the streets of Hanoi for the past five years, maintained regular contact with members of his extended family and would go home either to his grandmother or his uncle for set parts of the year. In the past he had helped his uncle with his business for up to three months at a time, and his grandmother was eager for him to live permanently with her. But during the time when he worked on the streets he gave the false impression that his life on the streets was a permanent state and that his family had no interest in him. While it is essential that we find out why children are leaving their homes, there are now scores of studies in the public domain that continue to be produced within academia and the NGO community that duplicate each other: first by analyzing what a street child is and then by adding a new angle on current discourse.

### Confusion Caused by Categorizing Street Children

According to the Vietnamese government's Committee for the Protection and Care of Children (CPCC), there are currently twenty-one thousand street children in Vietnam (Reuters, report in *Vietnam News*, March 3, 2004). As I explained in chapter 4, the majority of Vietnamese children still work on the land. Those who work on the streets in urban areas have come to be called "street children." But the term is still relatively new, and although the international community has embraced it, other terms for such children exist at the local level. In Vietnam the thousands of adolescents who live on the streets, particularly in Ho Chi Minh City (Saigon), are locally known as *bui doi* or "children of the dust."

In Vietnam during 1996 two different consultants were doing research among children associated with the streets. Tim Bond was based in the south of Vietnam and working extensively among children working the streets of Ho Chi Minh City. When Bond's report came out he was very critical of the term "street child" and pointed out to its negative connotations (1996). Nevertheless, he offered the reader three categories: children who lived and worked on the streets by themselves; those who lived and worked on the streets alongside their parents; and those who were intermittently on the streets and returned home. After Bond's report was published, Jonathan Caseley, another expatriate who worked as a consultant to aid agencies, was commissioned by a consortium of child-focused aid agencies to write a report on street children living in Hanoi, initially embracing Bond's categories. Caseley, however, went on to add a fourth category that covered children who worked as part of a group. Bond had intended for his categories to be adopted throughout Vietnam so that an overall picture of what was happening among some "street children" could be developed (Caseley and Buom 1996).

Caseley told me that when he went out onto the streets, he and his research team did so with a prewritten open-ended questionnaire. Predesigned questionnaires presume a certain amount of accurate knowledge on behalf of the researcher prior to interviews taking place. Caseley's questionnaire did include questions about children's families and so did not make the assumption that street children are abandoned, but because his questionnaire did not include questions about informal forms of support available to the children, he and his research team never came to realize the significance of that type of support for some children and so were not struck by its level of importance. But while Caseley's interpretations were based on a formal questionnaire survey with its built-in inflexibility, Bond had based his categories on intimate ethnographic accounts among children with whom he had a long-standing relationship. Of the two "experts" it was Tim Bond who was more grounded in his thinking and more knowledgeable about the daily life experiences of street children. Because Caseley partially responded to Bond's category guidelines but then added a further (and in my view confusing) subcategory, it is now difficult to merge findings from different parts of the country or to attempt to achieve an absolute overview of what happens in children's lives in Vietnam.

The fact that these conflicting categories of street children were failing to dovetail did not escape other observers. During the same period that Bond and Caseley were doing their research, Susan Hopkins was preparing an independent report on child-focused interventions among Hanoi-based NGOs. She wrote, "Some agencies use definitions of street children which cover only a subset of street children. A number of sources maintain that only children without homes are true street children. The youth research group in Hanoi [headed by Jonathon Caseley] uses Bond's definitions differently, and adds another category" (1996, 163–164).

### "Street Children" Do Not Relate to the Term

One day in April 1997, I asked Hai and Tan, who sold postcards outside the post office, whether they had heard of the term "street child" and whether they thought the term applied to them. Neither of the boys had heard of or ever used the term. They knew of the Vietnamese term "children of the dust" or "the dust of life" because it was used in everyday discourse, and they had read the term in the local newspapers, but nevertheless they did not think that any of these categories applied to them. In fact, most of the children I knew could not relate to these stereotypical ideas about their lives. Instead they took pride in their independence and worked hard to maintain a certain level of professionalism in their working lives. For example, Hiep told me that he always wore a clean T-shirt because he needed to look smart to attract customers; as leader of his group, he encouraged his friends to do likewise. Hai spoke of wanting to look his best, and of always wearing clean clothes, but he also pointed out that he would never wear his best clothes while working because he needed to look a little rundown to attract the sympathy of tourists. The boys I met who worked on the streets gave many reasons for being there, such as becoming economic migrants to help support their families, or leaving home because a parent had died, or earning money to support their education, or in one instance earning money to contribute to the costs of the orphanage where he lived. It was both their family's poverty and a lack of comprehensive formalized support at state level that made stopping work so hard. This is because Vietnam has limited resources and burgeoning international debts; the country does not have the resources to sink into a comprehensive social support system, and at best the support available to such children is patchy. Most of the literature on street children, whether it be in academic literature or NGO reports, glosses over this crucial point and also fails to examine how comprehensive the current support is. The same body of literature also focuses on the difficulties that children face and tends to ignore the occasions where children make a success of their experiences.

### The Fieldwork Environment

Within hours of arriving in Hanoi I had made my way down to the shore of Hoan Kiem Lake (the Lake of the Restored Sword in the center of the city) for the first time. I strolled for a while along the grass-lined pathways, passing old men huddled over chessboards, women cradling their tea stands while chatting with their customers, and young girls wandering in the sun as they tried halfheartedly to tempt passersby to sample their sweaty cakes or dried-out buns.

As soon as I sat myself on a nearby bench, children seemed to come out of nowhere to swarm around me. Postcards, cakes, and shoe polish were thrust in my face. It seemed that for at least five minutes there was no respite from the sales pitches that confronted me. I was a sitting duck. Clumsily and with a nervous croak I spoke my first real words of Vietnamese, the first attempt being a profound "Hello, no thank you," which, although rudimentary, immediately stopped some of the children in their tracks. A young boy who looked about ten years old said, "oh you speak Vietnamese; I would like to practice my English." He quickly introduced himself as Hiep and shooed the other children away, leaving only himself and a few friends, all of whom gathered around to try out their phrases on me. We spent the next couple of hours alternately translating sentences into English or Vietnamese. I was impressed by how patient Hiep and his friends were. As I mechanically banged out my words, he would patiently repeat words back to me over and over, until parrot-fashion I began to mimic his rhythm and pitch.

That afternoon I learned that Hiep and his friends made a living cleaning the shoes of customers who came to Hoan Kiem Lake. The five boys, aged between twelve and fourteen, supported each other by pooling the money they earned to pay for food and the rent on a room that they shared, which was located in a riverside neighborhood to the east of the lake. Hiep told me that they had come to the city separately from different areas of the countryside in order to support themselves and not be a financial burden to their extended families. I wondered why it was that they were so willing to spend time with me instead of trying to do more shoe shining, and at the end of our meeting offered them some money as a thank-you. It was the wrong thing to do: Hiep was affronted by my gesture, and instead we came to an agreement that I would be there again the next day to carry on with our meetings. I had made a glaring mistake because I had unintentionally treated Hiep as one of life's victims, and, worse still, had seemingly tried to pay him off for merely talking to me. I immediately apologized for my blunder and was lucky that he had the generosity to forgive me. Thus began my first period of doing participatory observation among children in Hanoi.

By adopting participatory observation as a method for doing research among these boys, I tended to watch and slowly learn from them rather than force questions their way and perhaps come to erroneous conclusions. Watching children day after day alongside the lakeshore, I learned a great deal about their groupings and the level of permanence or impermanence that particular children attached to the work they did. It was impossible to become familiar with all the children, so I chose to focus on what I observed to be four quite distinct groups: Hiep and his friends, who cleaned shoes for a living at the south end of Hoam Kiem Lake; Hai and his friends who sold postcards and who were also located at the south end of Hoam Kiem; Thoa and Binh, who worked as a pair cleaning shoes outside a café nearby; and Lac and his friends, who worked cleaning shoes farther out from the center of the city at the end of a street near where I lived. In addition, there were the children who at various times worked on the streets, but who I first met while they were in a reform school or through my visits to a government orphanage (we will visit these institutions in later chapters).

One of the features that all the children had in common was that they worked together in single-sex groupings and within a similar age range. In general, boys tended either to sell postcards or clean shoes for a living, while girls generally sold food products of some kind. However, girls were very much a minority on the street and were far more likely to work in people's houses as maids or as assistants in the markets and cafés. A Vietnam-based statistic suggests that boys outnumber girls on the street by an estimated twelve to one (Cuc and Flamm 1996, 2). On the one occasion when I did meet girls who were selling postcards, they were being mercilessly harassed by Hai and his friends, who told anyone they met that the girls were really prostitutes, and that, worse still, they lived with their families in Hanoi and were only pretending that they needed street work.

The majority of these children had migrated to the city from the countryside. However, being on the street was not necessarily linked to urban migration. Hang, Phuong, and Sern were three boys I met at the reform school where I was also doing fieldwork. After they had served their time there they worked and then slept in the markets rather than return to their families at night. All three boys spoke of the streets as a place of adventure and independence, but Phuong in particular also confided that he did not want to go home because his stepmother never made him welcome. He told me that on the rare occasions when he did go home, she made him sleep in the pigsty.

### Working on the Streets to Pay for Education

In the two preceding chapters I talked extensively about the reasons for children working in the South and made particular reference to internationally led child-focused directives. In Hanoi, I learned that children who had migrated from rural areas to work on the streets sometimes had particular motivations for doing so that belie any expectation that they were part of a subsection of society that did not retain mainstream values. Khoa and Binh, two of the boys I knew well, told me that they moved to Hanoi to clean shoes for a living so that they could afford to pay fees and so attend school.

Khoa and Binh worked cleaning shoes outside an expensive café that attracted many expatriates. By holding on to this location, the boys had been able to befriend particular people who gave them more generous amounts of money that enabled them to split their day into shifts between them. When one was working the other was in school and vice versa. Khoa also spoke proudly of being able to earn enough to pay for his brother in the countryside to go to school. However, it is important to note that the boys attended "compassion classes," set up for the purpose of providing children who are unable to keep the regular hours of mainstream schooling with some education. This placed the boys at a disadvantage because they would be competing with the privileged minority with Communist Party connections.

### Negotiating and Defending Work Territories

Each group of children I met had marked out a small area in which they expected to be the dominant workers, and as a consequence they were constantly marking and redefining their territories and treating those outside their set as a potential threat. Children who worked by the lakeside not only competed with each other for space but also worked to keep other children from establishing themselves in their areas. I first realized the importance of territorial areas when I was sitting at the south end of the lake near an outdoor café that, because of its location, was particularly attractive to expatriates and tourists. On one occasion I watched as a young boy I had never seen before ran up to Hiep and pinched him hard on the arm. Hiep shouted back but was quickly surrounded by two of the boy's friends, who shouted at him and told him to move on. When I first met Hiep he told me that he had been working in that area for over a year, but it now seemed that the territory of Hiep and his group was under threat.

Over the next few weeks the groups of Hiep and the new boy began to compete more openly for business from the café's customers. Three different expatriates on separate occasions told me they had begun to feel so harassed by the continual attention that they had decided to avoid the café and go elsewhere. In one case an expatriate aid worker opted to wear plastic sandals to avoid the attention of children continually asking if they could polish his shoes.

Soon afterward, as they noticed trade dropping off, the owners of the cafe came up with a solution: they would choose particular boys to establish their work around the area of the café and would offer them legitimacy by giving them café T-shirts to wear. This was obviously an opportunity to be coveted because of the lucrative nature of the work and the level of permanence created. On the day that Hiep rushed up to me wearing his café T-shirt, he was brimming with pride. It promised him and his friends a more stable income than he had ever known since moving to Hanoi, and it showed: he looked more relaxed, and over the next few months put on a little weight and started talking more often of going to evening school. Yet one month later, Tao, the boy who led the other group who worked around the café, was bullying Hiep again and asking him for a cut of his income to stay in the area. It all became too much for Hiep, and after a long drawn out battle in which Hiep became more and more despondent, he and his friends retreated to the far less lucrative northern side of the lake.

I was never able to find out whether the café owners had played a part in Hiep's departure from the area, but it was quite clear that Tao had the edge as a salesman. His grasp of English was better than Hiep's, and he was also only twelve years old. The boys in Hiep's group were all about fourteen to fifteen years old, while Tao and his friends were a couple of years younger, a fact they used to their advantage by emphasizing their age (and by implication their vulnerability) when trying to get work from the café customers.

About a week before Hiep and his group were forced out of the area I noticed that an old lady was always crouched behind a tree in the vicinity of the café whenever Tao and his friends were working. She would observe the café crowd and occasionally call out to Tao, who would drop whatever he was doing to run to her side. She would surreptitiously whisper in his ear and he would run off, apparently to follow her advice. I sat for an hour watching this go on and realized that the old lady was helping Tao guide his group so that they could continually attract potential customers away from Hiep and his friends. If Tao and his group were being guided by the old lady, then the likelihood was that they were also working for her. Later Tao told me that the old lady was his grandmother, who was his sole carer. In contrast, Hiep relied on the peers in his group for support and lacked some of Tao's confidence; it was this lack of confidence that had perhaps given Tao an edge over him This leads me on to discuss a most important component of the working life of these children: they are often not left on their own, and adults are frequently available and sympathetic to their needs.

### Supportive Adults

One of the most striking aspects of doing fieldwork among the children on the streets was that their lives did not reflect dominant images being used in the international aid world. Aid agency campaigns regularly use images of children alone and unsupported on streets. Such representations imply that a child is without family and friends and is perhaps abandoned and destitute. This assumes that they have a great deal in common, and worse still it assumes that their own communities are failing such children.

As the anthropologists Arthur Kleinman and Joan Kleinman point out, this approach projects erroneous images of the stranded and destitute child, often to heighten the response to fundraising campaigns used by some of the most prominent NGOs. More significantly, these widely projected images create stereotypes that do not reflect the lives of all children (Kleinman and Kleinman 1996) but nonetheless become the understood norm. As my fieldwork observations confirmed, not only did some children garner support from their peers, but they also were able to rely on support networks among sympathetic adults within the wider community. We ignore the vitality of the informal support network for street children at a cost, because in doing so the image of the marginalized child is allowed to prevail; as a result inappropriate types of interventions are sometimes developed.

Thus, when I chatted with Tao he told me that he and his grandmother had moved together to Hanoi to find work because she was too old and frail to work on the land. They and Tao's three friends all lived near the railway station in a dilapidated room, but according to Tao it was still a struggle to get by and he felt responsible for his grandmother's welfare because of the support she gave him at a time in her life when she needed rest. Similarly, I observed that Vietnamese adults who ran their own businesses also informally adopted other children. When a café was developed outside one of the premium hotels in Hanoi, Khoa and Binh (who unlike Hiep and his group had managed to maintain their position at the original lake café) moved with the café owners to the new location and continued to clean shoes; they were closely looked after and protected by the waiting staff.

In a completely different area of the city, the people who ran the café on the end of my street had welcomed boys to approach their customers to offer their shoe-cleaning service. In another café five minutes walk from my house, a boy who had started off homeless and had worked on the streets for five years had been invited to live permanently with the family who owned the cafe and had built up enough work by cleaning shoes and helping in the café that he was encouraged by the family to go to school every afternoon.

So why isn't this type of informal support, which is so vital to the welfare of children who make their living on the streets and independently of their families, acknowledged in the dominant aid agency literature on street children? There are at least two reasons. The first reason is that street child literature is adult centered and grounded in a dominant Western discourse of what constitutes an acceptable childhood (Glauser 1990; Panter-Brick 2001). Perhaps we want to think of street children as abandoned because to do otherwise potentially casts the blame for their difficulties outside their immediate world. If parents actually love and care for these children, why are they having to work? A second reason might be that aid agencies tend to have limited resources, so they are unable to afford or even begin to appreciate the value of doing longitudinal studies among children and so have to fall back on gross generalizations.

### *Portrait of a Postcard Seller: Hai*

The postcard sellers were another quite distinct group of children who worked around the lakeside. One such person was Hai, who I met within a couple of weeks of meeting Hiep. Hai sometimes told me he was fourteen, and sometimes sixteen. Whatever his actual age, there were parallels between his experiences and those of Hiep, but also clear difference in their coping strategies once working on the streets. Like Hiep, Hai had moved to the city from the countryside about five years before, and also like Hiep he spoke of having lost his parents. As with Hiep, we originally got to know each other because he wanted to practice his English and I my Vietnamese. But, unlike Hiep, he had a more restless and resentful air about him. One of his opening gambits was to tell potential customers that he was an orphan, and also that he had an illness that would leave him unable to work by the time he was an adult. When I first had a conversation with Hai, he also gave me the line that I later observed him giving over the two-year period to countless tourists and expatriates who like myself lived in the city and took a supportive interest in children working on the streets. His approach was to sidle up to one, wave a few books of postcards under a nose, ask for a U.S. dollar for each book, and in one long breath say, "I have no family my mother is dead my father is dead I am all alone please give me money so I can feed myself and go to school." Then his friends would crowd around and give you a plaintive look or giggle and nudge each other. The approach often worked: who would not give money to a hardworking and ambitious orphan?

It was not until six months after we first met that he started to relax enough in my presence to tell me his real life story. The change in Hai's attitude came about when I found him crying because an older boy had been making fun of his spotty teenage face. I had never seen Hai so upset before and invited him to join me for ice cream in an attempt to cheer him up. Once our ice creams came to the table he looked across at me and said, "I am not really an orphan you know." I grinned back and said, "Well, I thought you might not be," and Hai then asked me why I had not challenged his story. I explained that I did not think it was my place to do so. He then told me that it had been his decision to leave his family behind in the countryside and migrate to the city to work independently. But as he pointed out, "Foreigners do not want to hear that I have family: they are less likely to give me money because they will think that I don't need their help so much." Hai also explained that he and his friends routinely took a couple of years off their real age because younger children were likely to attract more sympathy and therefore earn more money than their older counterparts. This was also part of the reason that he and his friends worked together in groups that included children of different ages. While they all earned money, they also pooled their earnings and drew on each others' strengths, with the older children, in their mid-teens like Hai, protecting and supporting the younger ones, who were sometimes as young as seven years old. Younger children were often the ones to initiate contact with tourists that might then lead to a sale. There was clearly a lot more to the working strategies of the children than appeared at first observation. During this conversation Hai was quite upbeat about what he did and the life choices he had made.

After his mother died, he and his younger brother had gone to live with their grandmother, who was very supportive and good to both of them. She sent the boys to school and had high expectations for both of them. However, Hai did not settle in school. He found it hard work and often played truant. He also became increasingly aware that his grandmother was struggling financially to keep both him and his brother in school. He had heard that children earned good money in the capital, and so decided at the age of twelve to move there and live independently of adult care. Hai enjoyed working for himself and particularly liked the freedoms this allowed him to set his own hours and to come and go as he pleased.

In contrast to Hiep, who told me that he wanted only to get by and have enough to eat, Hai sometimes stated that he wanted to earn enough to go to school. But as we got to know each other better he confided that he only told people he wanted to go to school because they would assume that he would use their postcard money for that purpose. And when I asked Khoa and Binh whether they knew Hai, they were both critical of the way he worked as little as possible in order to have time to enjoy himself playing pool and gambling. Hiep also told me that Hai was no good and that he sometimes wasted his money on drugs.

At other times Hai spoke of wanting to train to work in a restaurant. On the face of it the possibility that he might be able to go from working on the street into a restaurant seemed unlikely, but such opportunities were possible. A year into my stay, an Australian expatriate offered to train him to work as an apprentice in his restaurant. Although Hai and I then spent the following two weeks meeting in cafés and going through menus so that he could improve his restaurant-related vocabulary, he eventually turned the offer down, much to the bafflement of the expatriate. A couple of weeks later, quite by chance, I met the café owner, who was quite disappointed in Hai. This expatriate was not alone in thinking this way about Hai. During an interview I conducted with the director of a Dutch NGO, he told me to keep away from Hai because he would do anything to get attention and because of this gave the impression that he was interested in receiving assistance when he later revealed, by letting people down, that he was not.

I wondered if this was because in the eyes of these adults, and particularly the Dutch NGO director who spoke of Hai with such contempt, Hai apparently defied the grateful response they expected and by letting people down had shown himself to be ungrateful; I did not agree with this view. Hai had grown to enjoy his independence but was perceptive enough to refer to mainstream aspirations in order to get what he needed: a regular income, attention, and opportunities to consider a future that did not involve working on the streets. The streets were the most permanent feature in Hai's life and it would take a great deal for him to walk away from the security of a familiar environment and replace it with an unknown one. Working children like Hai who recognize that underlying power differentials directly affect how their lives are shaped are less likely to show the type of appreciation benevolent adults and charity groups expect, because to challenge their expectations is also to challenge the very nature of top-down power relationships.

Hai's ability to garner informal support was not confined to members of the expatriate community. Hai and his friends worked next to the main post office and alongside women who came into the city to sell fruit. All day they would talk among themselves and help each other. While Hai might get the women their lunch, they might lend him and his friends money or, as I observed on at least two occasions, chide Hai to go to the doctor when he seemed unwell. These women knew Hai's daily routine and looked out for him.

Toward the end of my time in Hanoi, Hai began to sleep late and work more sporadically. His friends, particularly Tan, who had sold postcards alongside him for the previous two years, were concerned about the change in Hai's behavior and confided in me that Hai was smoking more and more opium. The day before I was due to leave Hanoi and return to England, Hai and I had arranged to meet to say good-bye and swap addresses, but Hai never showed up. Two years later, after I gave a paper at an anthropology conference in Chicago, a woman in the audience approached me and asked whether I had known all the boys in the center of Hanoi, because she had recently been to Hanoi and had got to know a boy called Hai. When I told her that I had known him well, she said that Hai was now HIV positive, and although he had been in and out of drug addiction clinics he was still using drugs. I was devastated to hear this news. In sharp contrast, his friend Tan told me as I left that he was already making plans to return to live with his parents. Working on the street was a temporary phase of Tan's life, and with his older brother getting married there were new responsibilities for him at home. But Hai had irretrievably lost his way.

The reason I refer to Hai's experiences is to highlight the fact that adults place very particular expectations on children. Children do respond quite differently to street life, and external factors also influence their lifestyle choices. Hai was unusual in his willingness to speak about the lack of opportunities his family had in comparison with other people. His motivation for moving to the street had been to support himself and to enable his grandmother to afford for his younger brother to attend school. This was hardly the behavior of a thoughtless and corrupt individual, more like the behavior of a kid who is starkly aware of the poverty and lack of opportunities that surrounded him in his rural province of birth.

## Coping within the System

Without exception, the children who worked on the streets of Hanoi received mixed and confusing messages from assorted authority figures about their status as working children and adults. Officially, it was illegal to work in the informal economy and the police were there to enforce this. It was not unusual to see police sweep into a market area or alongside busy roads and round up people who had set up trade selling fruit and vegetables. This was always very distressing to watch, as people frantically gathered up their wares and ran in all directions trying to avoid being grabbed. Once people were caught, their goods would be confiscated. The majority of these people had traveled great distances on foot or bicycle from rural areas to sell whatever they had that was in season, and such a loss would severely dent a family income. Over my two-year stay in Hanoi I lost count of the number of times I witnessed these police raids. But on at least two occasions I watched people try to resist the police and then slump down in tears after they had gone on their way.

Similar raids were made among the children and adults who worked around the lakeside. But it was possible to establish a permanent life earning money on the streets if one were prepared to pay bribes to legitimize one's status. Hai told me that if any of the children wanted to keep working in the area they needed to give the police the equivalent of ten U.S. dollars a month. Other children, including Thoa and Binh, confirmed this. On two occasions Hai was unable to pay the bribe and ended up being placed in a reform school like the one that I visited. He told me that he had organized his friend Ly, who also sold postcards in the same area, to bring twenty dollars to the reform school to bribe a school guard to give him his freedom.

Like teachers, police officers would have a difficult time surviving financially without extra income, in this case from collecting these informal fines, not only from children working on the street but also for traffic infractions. Most studies of corruption show that such practices result from the state's failure to pay a living wage to its employees; workers in Vietnam's state-owned electric and phone companies, for example, were also known to collect bribes from customers in order to ensure service continuity. Thus while police preyed on children working on the streets and illegal venders as easy targets, those living within the law were also subject to their financial demands.

Because some police were willing to accept bribes from children who worked on the streets, they were complicit in undermining the official government policy of clearing the streets of informal workers. Vietnamese officials and the media demonized the children' presence, but I would argue that far from being marginal workers, most of the children and adults who illegally worked on the streets were an integral part of the local economy. With their earnings they supported not only themselves but also local and roaming retail businesses. Given the children's precarious position in the city, the constant threat of arrest, and their lack of opportunity to take part in mainstream schooling, it was ironic that their earnings also sometimes subsidized government-employed police and teacher's incomes. In addition, children like Khoa also sent money back to the countryside to support other family members. The contribution of these particular children make to the local economy and their wider community went unrecognized by members of the international aid community.

### Remand

When he was arrested, Hai would not have been sent to the school that I visited, because it was predominantly for children whose parents lived in the vicinity of Hanoi. It was also a reform school that expected most children to stay for two-year periods rather than short-term stints. On one occasion, however, I did discover a boy called Luong, who I had sometimes seen selling postcards in the same area as Hai, in the school's isolation room. We were shocked to see each other. On the day I visited, Luong had already been at the school for two days and had been subject to the indoctrinatory head shave. After telling me that he had been arrested for selling drugs, he burst in to tears, because this meant being sent to a remote country province, to a reform school that we both knew practiced hard labor as a form of reform. It was in fact a re-education center for children where emphasis was placed on physical labor as a form of punishment and rehabilitation, combined with doctrinaire teaching to reeducate them to conform to the Communist society's accepted traditions. Although Luong had stood out for being a loner on the streets and had not worked with Hai, he asked me to tell Hai and his group where he was and what had happened to him. It was an upsetting farewell. Although I had not known Luong very well he had always been friendly and eager to chat whenever we met. Foreigners were not allowed to visit the reform school that he was being sent to, but I guessed that he was going to have a hard time and that it was unlikely that I would meet him again. However, when I duly gave Luong's good-bye message to Hai, he was very dismissive of his fate and told me they were all glad that Luong was no longer around, because his drug dealing had made them all more vulnerable to police arrest.

For a while Hiep and his friends managed to get by at the north end of the lake, but their demise as a group came when they were arrested by the police at a time when they lacked their normal level of savings, and were unable to pay a bribe for their freedom to return to the streets. Of all the boys I knew, Hiep's group experienced the most dramatic decline in circumstances. When I met him a day after his release he had no box in which to store his equipment because it had been confiscated, and he was down to a tin of shoe polish and a toothbrush. He had obviously lost weight and was wearing an old T-shirt. But all the boys who worked in the neighborhood were very concerned about him, and he was sleeping on a friend's floor to save money while he got his work back in order. There was no question that Hiep would choose to return to the countryside. He knew that once he had enough spare cash then he would be able to bribe the police, so avoiding the type of arrest that he had just experienced.

### Formal Support

In their work on street child experiences in Kenya, Kilbride, Suda, and Njeru write that "early attempts to assist street children were frequently motivated by good will, charitable, and other humanitarian motives. Street children were seen almost entirely as victims with no agency of their own, such as a capacity to figure out appropriate strategies to maximize benefits to be gained by manipulating those seeking to help them. In short, there was little vertical linkage between donors' motives and those of the children perceived by them exclusively as 'victims'" (2000, 130).

On the face of it, the child rights movement, because of its emphasis on child participation, offers a new and more inclusive approach for working with children who work on the streets: one that takes us away from a past described by Kilbride, Suda, and Njeru in which children living in such circumstances were treated as victims. The UNCRC has also ostensibly been embraced by Vietnamese support services. But even so, support is patchy, primarily because funding is sporadic and projects are often duplicated. As I discussed in chapter 4, particular categories of children also become the focal point for international funders and thus the NGOs that rely on them. When I first met members of the dominant child rights NGOs working in Hanoi, they were faced with a sea change because the biggest funders were redirecting their interest away from the street child and toward the girl child. Hai who sold postcards outside the central lake in town, was particularly vocal on this issue. When he and I met we would have a friendly chat and perhaps go for a soda or ice cream, but on one very memorable occasion he scowled when I pulled up on my bicycle to say hello and immediately started telling me to go away. I was worried because this was out of character, so instead of moving off I stayed and asked what was wrong. "What do you think is wrong: all I do is sell, sell, sell, and I trust you, then you leave, go back to your rich country, to your comfortable lives, you don't really care, I am a little person, and I hate you all, you stupid foreigners with your rich lives."

I was momentarily taken aback by the astuteness and directness of his comments: although I had never said so to him, I felt similarly uncomfortable about my presence. I told Hai that I knew that things were far tougher for him than they would ever be for the majority of foreigners he met.

### Removal to Birthplace

During 1996 MOLISA decided to focus its attention on funding CPCC to get children off the streets and back home to the countryside. This was officially referred to as a repatriation program. During the period I lived in Vietnam, the government backed this plan, with the support of the international child-focused aid agencies Radda Barnen and PLAN International. PLAN International, which is a child rights advocacy NGO, trained local staff from CPCC to do outreach work with the children with a view to sending them back to their rural homes. This repatriation program was a disaster as far as many of the children were concerned. The boys who were most obviously affected by the policy of "persuasive" return to the countryside were among those who worked around the lakeside in the center of the city.

Like many other children, Hiep and his close friend, Cuc, were sent back to their home province and reunited with their families, but no provision was made to help their families cope with the extra costs of supporting a nonearning person. Not surprisingly, a significant percentage of the children quickly returned to the city. Within two weeks both Hiep and Cuc were working cleaning shoes again at the north end of the lake. They both told me that their quick return to Hanoi caused them some problems with the police. Six months later Hiep was again forcibly returned to the countryside and again he immediately returned to the city because, as he said, "life in the countryside is slow and I miss the city, and I can earn more money here than I can working in the fields at home. Here I earn enough to support myself and I've lived independently for so long and like it that way." Luckily, in the case of the work he did it was relatively easy to reestablish himself.

The majority of boys I knew told me that their standard of living was better than that of their peers in the countryside, and some of them, for example Khoa and Binh, worked hard to earn a living so that they could fulfill quite mainstream ambitions such as attending school and contributing to the family income. When I first talked to them, Binh stood tall, grinning from ear to ear, with his chest puffed out as he told his story. Binh missed his family but maintained that it had been his idea to move to the capital; as he said, "If I didn't earn money then none of us could afford to go to school." Like all the other children I knew he very much looked forward to Tet, the Vietnamese new year, because during this period he traveled home to be with his parents, who, as was obvious by the excitement he showed, were very proud of him. These boys did not fit the dominant image of the rootless, downtrodden, disheveled, and abandoned child in the dominant street child literature developed by international aid agencies that the media and members of the general public are likely to embrace.

While PLAN International was absorbed in helping MOLISA and CPCC train outreach workers to assist children on the street and to return them to the countryside, the organization was faced with the classic dilemma of wishing both to create childhoods where children lived more acceptably alongside their parents while at the same time completely ignoring the children's right to self-empowerment. PLAN's approach clearly put adult wishes above those of the child: something that in theory the UNCRC aims to redress. The problem was that PLAN International ostensibly supported the UNCRC. This was a type of dilemma faced by numerous NGOs working in Vietnam, where government child focused policy is often in direct conflict with the UNCRC.

In response to this project, NGO workers at Radda Barnen addressed follow-up research to the question of why the repatriation program was failing. It advised that families of returnees from the street needed financial and in some cases psychosocial support if they were to make a success of the change in their circumstances. A couple of months after I arrived in Vietnam I was hired to support the Vietnamese team of researchers in compiling the final draft of the report. As far as I know the report was never very widely distributed, and if it was it certainly did not have any impact on the repatriation policy, which continued unabated.

### Supportive Forms of Formal Support

So far I have been quite critical of the forms of support available to children who worked on the streets. The work of the police, MOLISA, and some of the supporting aid agencies, such as PLAN International, did not strike me as being relevant to the needs of the children I knew. Conversely, I found that the work of the smaller aid agencies that adopted local, rather than international, agendas in their projects was more relevant to children's lives.

One example was a small-scale Hanoi-based NGO named after a Vietnamese flower that blooms in the spring and is called Hoa Sua. Hoa Sua was set up and overseen by a French woman with a baking and catering background who successfully set up a catering school attached to the Hoa Sua Restaurant and Bakery. The majority of the staff were teenagers who had previously worked on the streets or in people's houses. After their training, permanent placements were found for them in hotels and restaurants. Although the organization preferred to take children born in Hanoi, who therefore had the right to live and work in the city, it did sometimes consider applications from children who had emigrated from rural areas.

Twice Hai had been considered to work there, yet both times he turned the program down at the last minute because, as he told me, he liked his independence. However, Twan and Ly, two boys from the reform school, were offered places, with the support of the reform school director and Jack, the director of the partner NGO that worked at the reform school. Unfortunately, within a couple of weeks of joining the program they had set up a protection racket outside the school and were threatening and taking money from a couple of neighboring shopkeepers. Not only were they banned from

attending Hoa Sua, but Jack was told that no other graduates from the reform school would now be welcome. This turn of events came as a great
shock to Jack, who had not known the boys outside the context of the strictly
run reform school.

If anything, the outcome for Twan and Ly reinforced my argument that
we do a disservice to children when we categorize them too readily into
one homogenous grouping. Twan and Ly had qualified to enter the Hoa
Sua program because of their past experiences of living on the streets. It
was likely that many influences other than working on the streets and going to the reform school had also shaped the choices they made. Other children from the reform school had already successfully taken catering courses
elsewhere, and in light of this, it seems unfair that all children from the reform school were now banned. However, places at Hoa Sua were in high
demand so perhaps that is why its administrators felt justified in making
their decision.

### A Successful Program

Other programs that recognized how the local environment shaped
children's lives were run on small-scale lines similar to Jack's NGO and also
developed new project ideas in response to children's experiences. Some
of these programs were Vietnamese NGOs. One such project offered children a skilled training program in motorbike mechanics, while realistically
allowing them to carry on working. The man who ran the program accepted
that some of the children used drugs and thus, for example, was willing to
invite Hai to join the program even when he was smoking heroin. The old
Vietnamese man who ran the center was highly successful at getting
through to Hai, so much so that Hai stayed off drugs for six months after
he had left the program.

Over time I became very impressed with the work that Jack's small
United States–based NGO did. The expatriate directors were in Vietnam
solely to do humanitarian work and to offer support that answered needs
expressed by and with the full cooperation of local people. When they realized that some children were leaving the reform school only to return directly to working on the streets, and that some children were not able to
return to their families, they set up a halfway house for any boy who needed
its services. This support service truly worked with the boys and answered

to their needs. For example, when Phuong moved in he asked to take classes in English and in air conditioner repair work, because these skills would give him a level of economic independence that would take him away from working on the streets and into a more lucrative line of business. Phuong's objective was to live independently of his stepmother, so by really listening to and supporting Phuong's ambitions, the NGO and the reform school were supporting his wish to live independently of his family. This form of support contrasted greatly with MOLISA's official policy of permanently reuniting street children with their families. More importantly, this work was also of more practical use to children on the streets than the work being done by the two prominent international aid agencies that upheld the UNCRC and ostensibly supported child rights.

## Conclusions

It never occurred to the children I met that they should not be working. Most of them had immediate concerns for their day-to-day survival and when asked if they thought having to work was wrong they would often look confused, as if such a question had never occurred to them. But this does not make it right that they have to work, and in making the arguments in this book I do not want to normalize these children's experiences to the point that the reader might think that life on the street is full of opportunity, or that we should just accept that children work on the streets in some parts of the world. There is no doubt that the life of a street child is hard and risky. Someone like Hai was given many opportunities to leave the streets, but these opportunities did not address the false comfort he gained from the familiarity of street life. His life was full of uncertainty and transient people (like myself), but because the street was the place he knew best he simply could not leave it behind. When I left Vietnam I knew that I would probably not see Hai again: he had a high-risk lifestyle and because of this it was likely that he would experience an early death, perhaps drug or HIV related.

Many children who live and work on the streets do contribute to the local economy, and some also improve their standard of living and ability to achieve mainstream goals in contrast to the peers they left behind in the countryside (Boyden and Holden 1991; Ennew 1994). This possibility challenges dominant Western-grounded childhood discourses and mainstream

Vietnamese treatment of street children. It asks us to take into serious account the local experiences of children and consider the complex dilemmas of those children like Hai when he pointed out to me that he was born into poverty and that the current cost of living in Vietnam (shaped by both international and domestic policy) made it very difficult for him to take advantage of opportunities that other people assume to be his right.

The more positive experiences of Khoa, Binh, and Tien also demonstrate that working on the street can be beneficial. This is all the more reason for official bodies to stop treating children who work on the streets as a homogenous group destined to lead deviant and unfulfilled lives. Instead they should start to acknowledge children's strengths and recognize that different influences shape their various lives. It should not be assumed that all children who work on the streets are having difficult experiences; for some, street work is a positive and transitory period: "Researchers in South America have also noted that street children have better physical health overall, and are better nourished than their siblings at home" (Ennew 1994, 20).

So what should be done? I think it is very important that we try to improve working children's lives, but my experiences in Vietnam led me to the conclusion that the intentions of the aid agencies working through the UNCRC were too ambitious and too far removed from local ideals and expectations. The term "street child" should be recognized for its limitations, and perhaps then the needs of the individuals currently overshadowed by such a loaded term might be properly seen and thus they might be respected for all that they have achieved instead of simply being criminalized or infantilized for leading lifestyles that challenge idealized notions of childhood. A small group of NGO workers and local people were already doing a great deal to assist these children, but their contribution went largely unrecognized by the most visible NGOs. The fruit sellers who looked out for Hai and his friends and the café owner who took a working boy in and gave him shelter are the people who gave me hope; they understood the immediate world of the boys and recognized that the need to work was not going to go away any time soon and that the children they looked out for had quite limited options.

*Six*

# Life in a Reform School

At the start of my time in Hanoi I did not expect to find children being routinely sent to reform centers, and I could not have predicted that this discovery would result in my doing fieldwork in a reform center. While I was doing fieldwork in the city, however, I was repeatedly a firsthand witness to routine arrests of child street workers. For example, I had been meeting with Hiep for little over a month when we got caught up in a police raid. I was sitting by the side of Hoan Kiem Lake with him when without warning police rode up on motorbikes and all the working children in our vicinity began to shout warnings to each other and run off in different directions. Hiep, whose shoe-cleaning box was by his feet, panicked and froze as he saw all the children either disappearing down alleys or being arrested. By this point the police were everywhere, chasing children in all directions, and if he had set off Hiep would have drawn unwanted attention to himself. So I grabbed his box from under his arm, threw it in my bicycle basket, covered it with my sweater, and pulled him down onto the bench, whispering that we should continue as if we were still deep in study.

Once the police had disappeared Hiep put down the book and we grinned accomplice's smiles at each other. It was then that he started telling me about his experiences of being arrested. Judging by the number of arrests I bore witness to, I might just as easily have met Hiep for the first time in a reform center; equally, if some of the boys I later met in the reform school had not had the misfortune to be picked up by the police, we might have first come across each other on the streets, because by working on the streets or begging on the streets they were breaking the law.

Understanding this aspect of their lives is important to gaining a complete view of their circumstances, so in this chapter I follow the progress of children who had been arrested for some form of petty crime or for working on the streets and then placed in a reform center. In particular, I look at the manner in which the experiences of children in the reform school were shaped by a merging and shifting of two quite disparate influences: that of the dogma-led Communist approach to re-education and that of the more flexible approach adopted by the progressive Vietnamese director of the reform school, supported by an enlightened NGO. During my time at the school, I was also able to observe how between them the school's director and the NGO workers gradually moved away from merely imparting political doctrine to the children in their care toward recognizing the complex needs of each child and markedly improving the children's chances of achieving a better life.

### Gaining Access

Vietnam has a poor human rights record, with many arrests and imprisonments occurring without trial. By the very nature of Vietnamese society and the secretiveness of its government, the reform centers to which the children are sent are difficult to gain access to, since their existence is an acknowledgment that not all is well within the politically controlled environment. For example, such is the secrecy that surrounds hard labor centers that foreigners are very rarely allowed access, and so I was never able to follow up what happened to Luong, the boy arrested for selling drugs whose experiences I describe in chapter 5.

While living in Hanoi and researching the work of the numerous NGOs I was lucky to make contact with some expatriate staff of an international NGO that had been asked by the director of a reform school to help with his teaching program. The staff were willing to let me accompany them on the understanding that Mr. Son, the school's director, and Jack, the NGO's site leader, were happy to give me permission. I ended up spending nearly two years visiting the school, initially on a weekly basis and for the final year on a twice-weekly basis, following not only the children's progress but also observing the improvements the school's managers introduced to help them. I was fortunate that my fieldwork took place in a reform school where, because of its experimental nature, I was able to observe some of the very positive changes that were to take place.

As a relatively neutral observer at the school I was placed in a unique position, able to observe, on the one hand, the children's experiences and those of the Vietnamese staff and resident NGO workers, and, on the other, what I quickly began to see as the counterproductive actions of child rights activists of other international NGOs, who visited the reform school from time to time. These visitors had only a superficial understanding of the school's work and were undermining its activities by their dogmatic and ill-informed promotion of the UNCRC. Their organizations not only wrongly challenged the work of the school's staff but, more worryingly, overlooked the needs of the very children they purported to care about.

Before we look at the school itself, it is first necessary to examine briefly how the Communist regime imposes its will both over these children and over the domestic and international organizations such as NGOs who get involved. At this point we need to remind ourselves briefly of the role of the Communist state in the context of the control it attempts to exert over its citizenry (in this case, what it saw as aberrant children) and over the various organizations who become involved.

## Re-education

Since the beginning of the Communist era, Vietnam, like China and Russia before it, has created numerous prisons that emphasize the political re-education of inmates. Such establishments often use Communist termi-nology—and in Vietnam the writings of Ho Chi Minh—to teach inmates how to become good citizens. However, Ramesh Thakur observes that it was the south of Vietnam that housed the first of the country's re-education cen-ters, and as such it was not the Communists who first supported the idea of "re-education" in the Vietnam context. Thakur reported that "Phu Loi was a South Vietnamese 'civic re-education center.'" In his work he noted that "there was a scandal of sorts concerning rumors of poisonings in the cen-ter in December 1958" (1984, 127).

North Vietnam's Communist government introduced legislation in 1961 providing for detention without trial for the purpose of political re-education. The North Vietnamese originally looked toward the Chinese model of Communism, so it is likely that at that time the Communist model of re-education mirrored the Chinese model. In 1961 Robert Lifton reported that in China "penal institutions are referred to as re-education centers, meditation houses, or even hospitals for ideological reform. Four types of institutions are described in Chinese communist prison codes: the Detention House, the Prison, the Labor Service for Reform Corps, and the Juvenile Delinquents Institute" (1961, 14). His description of the reform process mirrors what I initially observed taking place in the reform school: "In dealing with the criminals, there shall be regularly adopted measures of corrective study classes, individual interviews, study of assigned documents, and organized discussions, to educate them in the admission of guilt and obedience to the law, political and current events, labor production, and culture, so as to expose the nature of the crime committed, thoroughly wipe out criminal thoughts, and establish a new moral code" (ibid., 17).

After the fall of Saigon and the reunification of Vietnam, re-education centers were set up across the southern part of the country for military officers and civil servants of the former Republic of Vietnam, people who were considered to have led privileged lives during the colonial period and under the South Vietnam regime. Many people were locked up without trial for years. Information gathered by Amnesty International from past prisoners indicates that a number of camps (for example Z30A and Z30D in Dong Nai and Thuan Hai provinces) were still holding several thousand inmates—many of them classified as "political" prisoners—some sixteen years after the war's end. (Amnesty International 1991, 208; Worden 2005). Even today, in a climate of increasing international cooperation and economic inclusion, Vietnam's human rights record is still quite dismal and all evidence shows that the situation is not getting any better. It thus appears that rather than bow to international pressure to improve the manner in which it treats its dissidents, Vietnam will continue to go its own way.

### Incarceration of Children: An International Phenomenon

Some international aid and NGO workers who visited the reform school reacted as if the children's circumstances were exceptional and unacceptable and gave the incorrect impression that such practices did not occur and had never occurred in their countries of origin. Yet the very notion of a reform school for children finds its origins in the West: David Rothman writes, "Although the New York House of Refuge (which opened in January 1825) is generally acknowledged to be the first of the early reform schools, several institutions of somewhat similar character already existed in England and Europe" (1995, 364). He notes, "Deference to authority was the organizing principle of most reform schools. Corporal punishment was the norm; inmates were whipped or placed in solitary confinement for failing to conform to the daily regimen" (ibid., 368).

So while it is standard practice for Vietnam to lock up its aberrant children, it should not be assumed that by doing this the country sets an unusual precedent. It is standard practice for children to be locked up in many parts of the world, often without trial, including the United States of America. Amnesty International's 2003 Human Rights report states, "The United States has carried out the only four executions of child offenders known in the world since the Special Session. Some eighty child offenders await execution in the USA for crimes committed when they were sixteen or seventeen years old. The USA is responsible for 65 percent of the executions of child offenders known to have been carried out worldwide since February 1995. Many other child offenders, as young as twelve years old at the time of the crime, are serving sentences of life imprisonment without the possibility of parole" (Amnesty International 2003). Angela Neustatter also points out that a substantial number of children are being imprisoned in Europe and that of all the European states, parts of the United Kingdom currently have the largest number of children behind bars. Referring to the Council of Europe Annual Penal Statistics, Neustatter reports that in September 2000 the Netherlands had 6.4 percent of the prison population under the age of twenty-one in prison, while for England and Wales the percentage was 16.3 percent (2002, 12). So Vietnam is, unfortunately, not exceptional in its sometimes harsh treatment of children and young adults who come into contact with the law.

## Limitations

As I noted in chapter 3, working in the reform school provided the Butterfly Trust with a rare opportunity because in Vietnam NGOs are closely accountable to the Ministry of Labor, Industry, and Social Affairs (MOLISA). Indeed, all NGOs have to hire their staff through MOLISA; if a potential staff member was not approved by the state, he or she could not work for the organization. It was privately suggested to me by some expatriates that via this process only Party loyalists would have such regular contact with foreigners, and by this means the state kept watch over the activities of foreign NGOs. This had obvious repercussions for NGOs, because it meant that the work they did was shaped by government directives and in some cases not by the internationally upheld human rights objectives they supported. Not surprisingly, few members of the international NGO community would speak openly about the subsequent limitations this created for them and their colleagues. One NGO director I met resigned and left the country in protest on being "unofficially" told that the state would not allow his organization to pursue its interest in working with street children in a small town in the central region on the country.

Given Vietnam's general human rights record, we should not be surprised that some of Vietnam's children continue to be locked up, or that child rights supporters are met with such baffled resistance by local officials and Vietnamese NGO workers. Again, insensitivity to local cultural norms by international agencies and NGOs, whether toward traditional values or those imposed by a Communist regime, is one of the root causes for misunderstanding. In the light of limitations imposed by the state, any improvements to people's lives are bound to appear piecemeal, but should they be treated as such? I argue that the small step-by-step successes in humanitarian liberalization that were achieved (such as those that I witnessed in the reform school) provide room for optimism, even though such improvements were overlooked by NGOs whose objectives were to achieve major, often rapid, changes through implementing large-scale international objectives like the application of the UNCRC.

## An Introduction to the Reform School and Its Staff

The school was quite far from the center of Hanoi, and it was cold, windy, and raining when I visited it for the first time with the members of the NGO. On that first day, in November 1996, I was nervous: I had no idea of what to expect, whether or not the boys would take to me, or if I would even be able to make myself understood using my still-rudimentary

Vietnamese. As the car swung into the drive, I was immediately struck by the mud and dirt surrounding the school's run-down buildings. While the school's dilapidated state might have unsettled me when I first arrived in Vietnam, I had since recognized that there was nothing particularly striking about this scene. Many of Vietnam's schools do not have the resources to pave play areas or keep buildings in pristine condition. But the real difference lay with the children who came out of the huts to greet us. I was disturbed to see how inadequately they were dressed for the poor weather: many wore open-toed plastic slip-on shoes, and in some cases they had on only thin cotton shirts. They were splashed with mud from the yard, and I noticed that some of the boys had facial rashes, which they constantly scratched with muddy hands. Although some of the children were obviously very pleased to see Jack, the NGO director, they looked generally unhappy.

### The Physical Environment

The reform school had been built to hold eighty children and was overcrowded. On my first visit it held 123 boys between the ages of ten and fifteen. They lived in cabins each sleeping up to twenty children on wooden platforms or bunk beds. During the day these buildings were open and the boys wandered in and out, but by 9:30 p.m. (and sometimes earlier) they were locked into their cabins for the night. These cabins were sparsely furnished; they had concrete floors and yellow walls that were often crumbling and damp. A small, barred window next to the door had no glass, but a shutter closed against the elements. By Western standards it was rough and rudimentary; by Vietnamese standards it was not luxurious, but it was adequate. The boys slept directly on the wooden board, which is normal in that society, but they never had enough blankets, and during the winter they spoke about how cold they were.

### The School Timetable

The guards enforced a strict timetable with the boys. They were expected to get up at 7 a.m., do a half-hour's group exercise, eat a small breakfast, which was often a lump of cold sticky rice, and attend morning class. Before class started, a roll call checked that everyone was present. The children were usually in their communal huts by 9 p.m., with the doors locked by 9:30 p.m., and at that time the entrance was locked until 6 the following morning. In a discussion that I had with Chinh (a Vietnamese NGO worker with the Butterfly Trust) and his class in April 1997, they complained that during the preceding week they had been locked in their cabins at 7 every night. According to the Vietnamese teachers who came to the school to teach every morning, this rigid timetable was designed to introduce a level of discipline that the boys lacked.

However, in conversations I had with some of the boys, I thought they showed an impressive level of self-instilled responsibility and discipline. For example, Phan Anh was released a couple of months after I started visiting the school, but rather than going back to his formal schooling he asked Jack if after his release he could support his ambition to train as a mechanic so that he could set up a motorbike garage to support his aging grandmother who was his sole caretaker.

### The Butterfly Trust

My first impression was that life for the boys in this reform school was extremely bleak. However, over the coming months my negative first impression of the school shifted somewhat. As a result of the NGO's influence, conditions slowly began to improve. The guards who ran the school began to build more collaborative ties with the NGO and adopted some of the Butterfly Trust's more positive methods. I also began to have an increasing appreciation for the children's ability to adapt to the conditions and develop informal support networks inside the school.

Because the Ministry of Interior was proud of the school and eager to develop its program further, it took the step of inviting this particular NGO to work alongside the guards. Other NGOs also wanted to work in the reform school, but the school's Vietnamese director wanted to work almost exclusively with the Butterfly Trust. Jack, the Trust's expatriate director, never knew for certain how it was that his NGO came to be given this opportunity, but he was told by Mr. Son, the director of the school, that it had been because the NGO had a good reputation among the Vietnamese for working in a supportive manner and for understanding their local circumstances.

The Butterfly Trust has its headquarters in the West but has local offices in many countries throughout the world. It is a Christian charity but was in Vietnam strictly to do humanitarian work, as evangelizing is strictly prohibited. Jack, the head of the project associated with the school, was an American who worked very closely with two of his Vietnamese aid workers, Chinh and Tung. The NGO had a local focus and involved its Vietnamese partners heavily in all aspects of its work. Although it was initially invited into the reform school on a short-term basis, the school director was so impressed with the way the aid workers worked alongside his staff that he invited its members to stay on and develop more long-term projects. Jack was particularly committed to the work at the reform school and was grateful that his organization had been invited to work there. While relationships between the NGO and the guards are not the central focus of this chapter, their shifting relationship is of significance because it set the tone for the boys' response to the school environment and is key to understanding more about how the boys came to be treated with increasing respect—both inside the school and once their time at the school had come to an end.

### The Philosophy of the Reform School Staff

According to the Ministry of the Interior, the aim of the school was to reeducate children and teach them the error of their ways. A large billboard over the school entrance displayed a quote by Ho Chi Minh: "A child is like a young tree, when you tend to it, give it love and nurture, it will flourish." Ho Chi Minh's quote may have been written to inspire individual interest in children, but what "nurturing a child" meant during my early months at the school was still prescriptive. The boys were given little chance to act outside the dictated rules, and their different experiences before entering the school did not seem to inform the direction their re-education took. Instead, they were initially stripped of their clothes and personal objects and given a short haircut, as if their pasts—and more significantly their individual identities—were being symbolically stripped away. The sociologist Irving Goffman points out in his work on asylums that institutions very often set out to suppress and ignore the inmates' individual identities and that a new culture is created, "symbolized by the barrier to social intercourse with the outside and to departure that is often built right into the physical plant" (1966, 4). This was certainly the case at the reform school, where some practices were grounded in the Communist past and the informer mentality that prevails in many prison-type settings (Bortner 1988).

*Arriving at the School*

Over the two years that I visited I would see many children arrive at the reform school, although the Ministry of the Interior was very cautious about allowing people to observe procedures for preparing children to enter it. As a result I had to rely on what boys in the reform school told me about the entrance process. Experiences varied: some children told me that they had been held in a local prison cell and then transferred directly to the reform school. Whether they received legal advice remains questionable. Tim Bond wrote that street children he worked with in Ho Chi Minh City rarely had the benefit of legal advice and did not receive fair treatment from the guards (1996, 2). One boy told me that during sentencing he was "told by a guard what to say," but he was reluctant to tell me any more, so this might have meant either that the boy was not given a chance to speak openly or that the guard had been trying supportively to guide him through the sentencing process. Most boys received sentences of between six months and two years, and the majority of them were in the school for the maximum sentence. Because they usually came from the Hanoi area, their families could visit during the official visiting hours, which changed from month to month.

When a child came to the school, he arrived in a small Ministry of the Interior van with a tiny barred window. The lights on the roof would be flashing, and a siren usually went off as it entered the yard. All the boys would run to gather around, peering inside and trying to discover whether they knew the new arrival. Whatever a boy's experiences were just prior to coming to the school, once he was let out of the van he was taken to a side room by a guard who laid out the school's rules and expectations. The boys had their personal clothing taken away; then they were dressed in a school uniform, had their heads shaved, and were placed in the school lockup. This was a brick building with bars across the front; it was located at the far end of the schoolyard. Every week, boys I knew would direct me to the lockup if there were new boys inside, or if one of them had been put there as a result of getting in trouble. A bolder boy such as Phan Anh or Thang would always come forward and act as spokesperson for the others.

Jack and I realized after some time that a boy called Tuyet was always inside an adjacent lockup when new boys arrived. We guessed he had been placed there to listen to their conversations and report back anything that might concern the guards. Tuyet appeared to be regarded with guarded respect among the other boys but was also feared by some of the younger ones. Because he always sat in the adjacent cell, his role was commonly recognized but kept secret from the new entrants. Gresham Sykes, who completed a groundbreaking study of prison life in the United States, argues that being an informer makes inmates very unpopular among his or her peers (1958, 87). So while Tuyet appeared to enjoy superficial respect from the other children, this was probably based on fear of his role, and he was often excluded from their more private gatherings. I noticed that when Phan Anh and Thang managed to get hold of candy from outside the school, Tuyet was one of the last to be given any.

### Disciplinary Methods

The form of discipline introduced in the school was of a very particular kind, designed to enforce conformity. Tim Bond, who works with children who have been sent to a reform school in Ho Chi Minh City, told me that the strict routine in the school where he worked was designed to "break the spirit of the boys, to make them conform to the expectation that they would become law abiding citizens," and this tallies with my own observations. Bond was always quietly pleased when a child rebelled or tried to run away, but I observed that children's lives were made much easier if they conformed, at least outwardly. They were less likely to be put in the lockups and drew less attention from the guards, which meant that they were trusted more and had greater opportunity to participate in the informal networks.

What I saw was far removed from the type of living conditions that I had seen in a reform school I once visited as a social worker in England, and some practices seemed deliberately designed to create discomfort. For example, I found it disturbing that boys were locked up in dark and dirty cell blocks as part of their settling-in period during their first week at the school, or when they misbehaved.

It was always difficult to predict how guards might react to our spending time with the new boys. We would either be told to move away from the lockups, or guards would join us and listen to our conversations. When I discovered that Luong had been brought off the streets of Hanoi and into the school, it was a guard called Bich and a boy from Jack's class named Vu who were with me and who told me that Luong was destined to be sent to a hard labor camp in a remote rural area because, unlike children in the reform school, he did not have family living in the city, and he had been arrested more often in the past.

On my second visit to the school the guards' behavior was more severe than it had been during the previous week. For example, I noticed that they continually circled the buildings and peered into the classrooms where children were having lessons. Whenever a guard was in close proximity, the boys' shoulders stiffened, and they frowned intently over their books. My initial impression of the guards recalls the words of Franklin, who observed the condition of American prisons and argued that guards were often overwary and corrupt (1998, xiii). Once the guards began to relax with the boys I realized that some of their behavior must have been as a result of a senior directive. Clearly, like the children, the guards existed within an established hierarchy. This to be expected: Bartoller argues that "total institutions have a staff subculture as well as an inmate subculture" (1976, 100).

*One Guard's Approach.*  Nang was a guard all the boys were scared of and tried to avoid. He did not seem to be very popular with his colleagues either and often sat alone in the office drinking beer. When the mood took him, he would enter the yard and, seemingly at random, grab a boy by the hair, pull him down to the ground, and hold him as he either begged to be released or, more often, remained silent. On at least five occasions Jack and I watched as he dragged a child into a corner and repeatedly kicked and hit him. During such incidents other children would make themselves scarce, and no other guards intervened.

In the third week of April 1997, Nang staggered drunkenly into the room in which Chinh was teaching and I was sitting at the back observing the class. As he went down the aisle, he randomly hit boys on the backs of their heads. The atmosphere was one of absolute fear. Chinh tried to carry on teaching. I sat for a while, telling myself that as an impartial observer it was not my place to intervene. But his swipes were getting more aggressive, so I decided to try and stop him. Realizing that it would be difficult to challenge this behavior—particularly because I suspected that this might result in an even harder beating for a child once either I or the NGO workers were no longer present—I asked him to leave because he was smoking a cigarette. To my surprise he looked up for a moment, smiled, and staggered backward out of the room.

Obviously, such behavior raised ethical issues. In a subsequent discussion in April 1997, Jack and I debated whether our presence could be construed as tacitly approving the current regime, which seemed to accept Nang's physical abuse. From what the boys said, we knew that Nang was beating a number of children. While this was exceptional behavior, other guards were still failing to protect the children, but I think that eventually someone must have said something to the director: in May of the same year some of the boys told us that Nang was no longer beating anyone. Nang's duties also seemed to have changed, and he was not left alone with children as he had been in the past. I wondered what Nang's motivation was, or if he was even aware of any. He certainly seemed to despise the boys. In that setting, what was most striking was that the guards had absolute power. They could choose who was allowed access to the children. If their position was under threat or they felt that they were being criticized, it was easy for them to take a stand. Meanwhile, because of their precarious position in the school, the NGO workers did not initially feel able to intervene openly. Their presence ultimately had a very positive effect on the guards, as by example they showed that it is possible to win trust and thus make changes to children's lives without using physical oppression.

### Indoctrination

Bortner makes a point about rehabilitation that confirms my observations of life in the school during 1996: "Despite rhetoric, few institutions are dedicated to or structured in a manner that will provide the resources for confronting and solving problems . . . juveniles learn that the majority of their time in the institution will be spent learning the organizational rules" (1988, 349). When the school was first set up, a strong emphasis was placed on re-education of children through the political writing of Ho Chi Minh. Every morning the children gathered for their morning register call, and on one occasion in December 1996 I watched as some of Ho Chi Minh's writings were shared with them. The lecture on Ho Chi Minh was delivered by a guard and seemed to focus on the role of a good Communist, which was to conform to society's rules. Half an hour later, when the lecture had come to an end, Phan Anh marched up to Jack and told him, tongue-in-cheek, that he thought he was now a good Communist—particularly, he said, because he was wearing open-toed rubber sandals similar to those worn by Ho Chi Minh. As boys gathered around Phan Anh to share the joke, he repeated over again, "I am like our Uncle Ho [Chi Minh], my sandals demonstrate this. Now that I understand our leader I can have my freedom." "Uncle Ho" is the commonly used affectionate yet respectful designation, so Phan Anh's ironic take was even more sophisticated for at once showing respect yet also gently mocking. Phan Anh's ability to poke fun at the treatment they all received made him very popular among the other children and also among the NGO staff. More significantly, he recognized that the NGO workers, and particularly Jack, were at least his tacit allies in this game.

The boys in Jack's class thought up an ironic word game in which they asked Jack and other people, like me, for their freedom in English, which most of the guards did not understand. On that day in December, during the break in morning lessons, Jack's students stayed in the classroom and continued jokingly to ask for their freedom. They also referred to their Uncle Ho as someone they could identify with, not because of his writing but because he had had his freedom curtailed when he was in prison in China. Thus they had turned the doctrine on its head and were referring to Ho Chi Minh not as a Communist leader but rather as someone who had been victimized in what they felt to be a similar fashion to themselves. This is significant, because while the guards thought that the boys' references to Ho Chi Minh were a confirmation of an acceptance of the dogma (and hence also their own position as authority figures emphasizing responsibilities as Vietnamese citizens), the children were actually identifying with Ho Chi Minh as a political prisoner who like them had spent part of his life having his freedoms curtailed.

### Room for Optimism

It was the Ministry of the Interior that had set up the reform school, and it tightly controlled who came into and out of the institution. While the Ministry still emphasized reforming children through lectures on political doctrine, the Butterfly Trust became increasingly influential in shifting the focus toward providing a more general formal education, something that was not readily available in the boys' everyday lives. This was both because of lack of funds and because some of the children were illegal residents of Hanoi, making them ineligible for schooling there. The Butterfly Trust made extra funding available in 1995 for the director to hire a few teachers to provide basic classes in mathematics, writing skills, and English. During the same period, at the request of the children, the NGO also gave them the opportunity to pursue vocational training in woodwork, basic motorbike mechanics, or as air conditioner engineers. Despite, or perhaps because of this, some members of the wider international aid community still considered the school to be essentially a prison. Some visitors from the United Nations also categorically (but erroneously) told Mr. Son, the director of the school, that such places did not exist in their home countries.

Certainly, there should always be concern about the philosophy that underlies the imprisonment of children. I argue, however, that being overtly critical of Vietnam's practices, as some aid and NGO workers were when they visited the reform school, did nothing to help improve the children's experiences. If anything, these visitors further alienated school staff, making it less likely that they would try to understand and apply any of the child rights practices advocated and supported by some NGOs and ostensibly by the Vietnamese government.

### The UNCRC Philosophy: Consequences

As I have explained, the Butterfly Trust's employees were reticent about taking a stand to improve the disciplinary regime inside the school, preferring instead to make gradual changes by demonstrating through their own behavior that relations with the children could be better and more productive. As an observer, it was clear to me that this gradual approach was essential because the naturally conservative authorities would only become receptive over a period of time: any proposals for sudden changes would undoubtedly have produced a strong negative reaction.

However, visiting workers from other NGOs, unaware of this deliberate and necessarily subtle approach, made direct criticisms during their visits by referring to the UNCRC to support their concerns about how the boys were being treated. Six months after I first visited at the school, one of the dominant NGOs that supported the UNCRC unexpectedly turned up at the school with Vietnamese translations of the UNCRC, which they handed out to the students before guards were aware of the contents. The next day, when Jack and I arrived, we discovered boys in his classroom tearing pages from the UNCRC pamphlets and rolling cigarettes from them. We were surprised, and as we tried to work out how they had gotten hold of the UNCRC, boys crowded around Jack and chanted laughingly, "Freedom, we want our freedom now!" followed by "We have the right to freedom." The more astute children in the class, such as Thang and Diep, asked, "OK, Mr. Jack you give us some money and then we will have our freedom." In other words, they knew, as did we, that the only way they could be released early was if they bribed their way out of the school.

No amount of pressure from child rights activists was going to have any influence over the treatment of children during that time, for several reasons. First, although it was ratified and supported by the Vietnamese government, at least in principle, the UNCRC was still relatively unknown to most Vietnamese. Second, the infrastructure was not in place for it to be adhered to. Jack and I believed that by turning up in a reform school with copies of the UNCRC, the NGO involved had done more damage than good. Human rights laws will only be adhered to with the proper support systems in place and if the government in question is positively inclined to implement it. Even if the children had been given the necessary financial resources, they would not have been able to find local lawyers who could have or even would have been willing to make a successful claim that children were being inappropriately locked up. Further, the guards followed directives from the Ministry of the Interior, which was the same organization that managed the regular rounding up of working children on the streets of the city, an activity that no regime that endorsed the UNCRC could possibly support.

Such visits resulted in the director of the school banning those NGOs that, as he stated, showed no respect for or understanding of what he was trying to do. The school was one of the first of its kind and as such was considered experimental and quite radical by the authorities that had initiated the project. Previously, as in other parts of the world, children who got in trouble were locked up in adult prisons and in hard labor camps. Any criticism of the school from outsiders, however ignorant, would jeopardize Mr. Son's reform program and possibly lead to the boys being put back into inappropriate prisons.

From the director's perspective the school was revolutionary in that it offered children a chance to reform their behavior and start again. Being privy to such information further convinced me that the direct approach adopted by some NGOs toward the school was highly inappropriate, culturally insensitive, and even arrogant. Certainly it never did anything to improve the boys' circumstances. In reality, it led to such NGOs being refused future access and thus being of no help to the children they wanted to assist. As Lifton wrote of China, "In all of this it is most important to realize that what we see as a set of coercive maneuvers, the Chinese communists view as a morally uplifting, harmonizing, and scientifically therapeutic experience" (1961, 15).

## The Boys' Coping Strategies

I turn now to an examination of the internal dynamics of the school, particularly the informal networks established by the boys and the various coping strategies they adopted. Both the boys and the guards were affected by the formal and informal organizations, and recognizing the significance of each is fundamental to understanding the influences that shaped the boys' lives. My observations were partly informed by actor network theory (Castell 1996; Pile and Thrift 1995), and using this approach I identified networks among the children, child-focused organizations, and individual people working for those organizations. I have observed throughout this book that where authorities or supporting organizations claimed to have particular understanding of children, such as "street children," they were often unaware of some of the influences on the children's lives, and this often resulted in inappropriate remedial programs. But my findings also suggest that neither children nor organizations had a complete understanding of their own or each other's circumstances, although the police, for example, worked within both formal and informal structures that impacted upon their level of involvement with children in the school. Meanwhile, the children were organized both formally by the police and informally among their peers. In general, however, the formal organizations did not recognize the importance of informal structures, and this was to the detriment of the children they were trying to assist.

### Status and Hierarchy

Each residence hut had a group leader assigned by the guards. Group leaders were usually replaced regularly, because to keep the position meant behaving appropriately, for example, not fighting or abusing their powers. Responsibilities included holding a key to the hut and to a security box used for storing the boys' valuables. The leader was also responsible for reporting to the guards during roll call. Control was thus maintained using the well-known approach of positioning inmates within a hierarchy (Douglas 1986; Goffman 1961).

Another much-coveted role was to be the boy, identified by a red and gold bandanna pinned on the upper part of his sleeve, who hit the gong that heralded the start and finish of time periods. Again, the position was reassigned if a holder misbehaved. It had the additional attraction of being open to children regardless of their size. The children most enjoyed the power of being in command of the gong when it was used to end lessons. On one occasion when I was sitting in on Chinh's English class a young boy called Thiep was in charge of the gong. Thiep was then fifteen and had been in the school for three months when I arrived; he usually sat at the back of the class and often appeared to be depressed. Sometimes I would sit next to him and we would talk about his mother and how much he was missing her. When he was in charge of signaling when classes were coming to an end he was unusually buoyant, in part because he enjoyed the responsibility but also because he got so much attention from the other boys, who often begged him to ring the gong well before class was due to end. Thiep was successful in holding on to this coveted position for three weeks. When the role was given to someone else he slipped back into a dark depression, and when I sat next to him during his lessons and asked what had happened, the only explanation that he gave was that he had gotten bored. But there was more to it than that. His role as gong striker had briefly improved his position in the school hierarchy on both a formal level, as the guards had demonstrated that they trusted him with formal duties, and within the informal support structure, because his peers were dependent on his signal if they wanted to be released from their classes. The guards allowed for a certain amount of leniency in the time at which the gong was struck, so Thiep had been able to improve his status by occasionally letting the boys out of class a few minutes early or sending them back a few minutes late.

Boys also learned how to position themselves and gain a particular rank in the informal network. This process started as soon as children were placed in the lockup as part of their orientation, and it continued when new boys were released from lockup and assigned to residence huts. When a new boy turned up, the more powerful boys in the hut would have him perform menial duties such as sweeping the hut floor and washing clothes, but it was usually possible for a child to challenge this role if he exerted his will. How the boys positioned themselves and formed groups within their informal networks inside the school was of importance in confirming their sense of identity and defending their self-worth against the institutionalization process. The guards also recognized this at some level. While the groupings that existed did not take the form of formalized gangs, they were distinctive enough to be noticeable. Not all children identified with particular groups, but there were three groups, all of which could be identified by their tattoos (see chapter 8). The formal and informal organizational structures were not entirely separate from each other; instead they informed and influenced each other to various degrees. Jack's influence on his class was a graphic example of this.

### Jack's Influence

I am not sure whether Jack was ever aware of the level of influence that I at least felt he had over the children's informal power structure. As well as being assigned to huts, boys were also given a test for educational achievement and placed in different classes. There were five separate classrooms, and classes were run on a rota system so that the majority were taught either in the morning or in the evening. Jack and Chinh were allocated smaller English classes than the Vietnamese teachers. Boys in Jack's class had scored the best marks in English. The class was half the size of the others, and he could therefore adopt a different teaching style. The boys got far more individual attention and personal direction, and they recognized their privileged position. An added attraction was that they had a foreigner giving them attention; this was an enviable position and gave them higher status, thus making it easier for them to exert more influence in the informal network. Initially this surprised me, because one might think that the toughest and most rebellious children would be in charge of the informal network, but this was clearly not the case. Later, when Vu's group did challenge the status quo, I realized that the guards also had some influence over which boys were in charge of the informal network.

### Group Hierarchies

The dominant group inside the school was that run by Phan Anh, one of the boys in Jack's class. The guards were aware that Phan Anh had a great deal of influence over the behavior of other children, and because he was charming and subtle in his challenge to the system he was both supported and treated respectfully by the guards. His position as informal leader of a particular group of boys in Jack's class meant that he enjoyed the other children's respect and had a guaranteed audience whenever he made a joke. Thus, when he jokingly mentioned that he wore the same footwear as Ho Chi Minh, he suddenly made wearing open-toed rubber sandals more socially acceptable. His charisma was central to his ability to lead and draw supporters around himself. Phan Anh's closest allies sat with him at the front of Jack's class; Thang always sat next to Phan Anh and next to him would be Diep. These three were all very good in class and tended to help each other with answering questions. Outside the classroom they also spent a great deal of time together.

During Phan Anh's period of leadership he was protective of other children and never resorted to bullying or to assuming a superior air. He was also unusually kind; on one occasion I saw him take off his sweater and put it on a smaller boy who was new to the school. This was on a particularly cold day when even two sweaters would not have kept out the cold. His behavior set a precedent for other boys to follow, and thus he reinforced his status and set a positive tone of reciprocity within the informal networks that surrounded him. His sympathetic nature created a situation that not only the children but also the guards benefited from, reinforcing the children' willingness to work within and not against the school system. When Phan Anh left the school, his lieutenant, Thang, assumed leader of the group; it was not until his leadership was challenged by another boy that Jack and I began to appreciate the extent to which Phan Anh had created a relaxed and supportive atmosphere in the school.

After Phan Anh left, the group in Jack's class who had previously gathered around Phan Anh now focused on Thang. However, in October 1997 a new boy called Vu turned up at the school. When he arrived in the guards' van, some of the children who did not overtly identify with any of the existing groups showed a great deal of excitement and ran over to the van to greet him. After he was placed in the lockup these boys hung around the cell at every opportunity. Vu was clearly a good friend of these boys and must have been provided with inside information about how the school was run.

It was normal for the more dominant boys in the school to introduce themselves to new boys in the lockup. Yet when Thang went over, Vu seemed to have little interest in getting to know him. A week later, when Vu was released from the cell, he was invited to sleep in the hut with his old friends, and from then on it was quite clear that he and Thang were not on speaking terms—it seemed that Thang had a potential rival. Competition between Thang and Vu for the most coveted position within the informal school structure went on for a couple of months. Vu quickly established himself as a rebel, willing to break rules and ignore the guards' guidelines. This behavior was in marked contrast to that shown first by Phan Anh and later by Thang, both of whom only lightly challenged the system. But soon after Vu's arrival, Thang decided that in order to remove this challenge to his leadership he would have to demonstrate to his peers that he too was not afraid of getting into trouble with the guards.

One month after Vu arrived in the school, Diep, who was in Jack's class, took me over to show me that Thang had been put into the lockup cell. "Look at Thang, he has been fighting. Thang, say hello to Lecar (Rachel), I brought her to see you. Oh, he was very bad, very bad indeed." At some level, witnessing Thang's punishment seemed to give Diep satisfaction. When I asked him why he was pleased that his friend was in the lockup he shrugged and said, "Oh, I am not pleased, but it is funny because he is usually so good." This was the only time that I ever saw Thang in the lockup, but he too seemed to gain satisfaction from being there. When I asked him how he was he said, "Fine, but I fought another boy, this boy here, I was angry."

This was a standard reason for being in the lockup, but by this time we knew each other well and the grin he gave me said that he was pleased to be there and had perhaps engineered it. Judging by the concerned attention of the other boys, his future status as leader had thus been reconfirmed, at least for the time being. It was unlike Thang to fight, and later I discussed the matter with one of the Butterfly Trust's local staff members, who agreed it was unusual behavior for him, and that he had probably done so to appear tough and to legitimize his newly emerging position as leader. As this demonstrates, the system encouraged the boys to learn survival techniques and to toughen themselves up so they would not be seen as weak. It was also important for children occasionally to reaffirm their positions in their informal networks.

After Thang was released from the lockup he clearly continued to feel under threat from Vu, as more boys began to pay attention to Vu and ignored Thang whenever Vu was around. Vu adopted a bullying style in his running of the school's informal network, starting in the usual fashion by picking on one of the outcasts, in this case Sei. Sei, was unusually tall and very self-conscious of his stutter and harelip. He had first come to my attention when some of the older boys from Chinh's class had pulled me by the arm to where he was standing: "Look, Lecar, he is very ugly, talk to him." When I protested, they realized their mistake, stopped teasing Sei, and instead tried to draw the boy into conversation; but after I had walked away, their abuse resumed. Whenever I saw Sei during lesson time he would be doing very menial tasks: cleaning the toilets, sweeping the courtyard, and washing down walls. He did not attend lessons, and Thiep, who always sat at the back of Chinh's class, told me the other boys considered Sei stupid.

Vu took a real dislike to Sei and taunted him, saying that he was too slow to go to school. On such occasions when Vu taunted him, Sei would slouch further into his tall frame and pretend he had not heard the words. Vu laughed at his demeanor, and it was soon established that Sei could be relentlessly teased by almost anyone without anyone coming to his aid. I asked a couple of boys in Jack's class what they thought of this and two boys said that he was "stupid, so he didn't understand." Another boy shrugged indifferently. It was upsetting to watch, and I hoped that the guards would intervene, but I never saw them do so, and because the teasing continued I guessed that they too were resigned to Sei being continually bullied.

During the first class break in the second week of Vu's informal leadership, I saw him openly twist the deformed ear of another boy, Mau. Other boys stood around, laughing cruelly in a way that I had never witnessed before. Both Jack and I were surprised by the change in the school's atmosphere. I thought that the boys seemed altogether rougher and less supportive of each other, and Jack agreed. But this behavior was about to change. Mau attended the same classes as Thang, and although they were not close he was someone whose company Thang always seemed to enjoy. Mau was a peaceful, hardworking person and was also well liked by most of the other children. On seeing Vu bully Mau, Thang, the usurped leader who had been known for his protective nature, jumped in and hit the new leader in the face. Mau then joined Thang in briefly beating Vu.

It was significant that none of the guards came over to intervene as they normally would have, but instead sat nearby in their hut watching television, choosing to ignore the considerable commotion going on outside. By standing back while Thang beat his rival into submission, the guards were clearly showing not only that they were aware of the informal hierarchy and the current tensions among the boys but also that they preferred the atmosphere inside the school when Thang had been in charge. Perhaps because his attack was fuelled by a desire to protect a more vulnerable member of the community, the guards and other boys also viewed Thang's actions on that occasion as particularly appropriate. When the fight was over and Thang had won, he was checked for injuries by most of the boys. Mau was nearby, and younger boys came to his side with the same intention. Vu was totally ignored and as a result made himself scarce, together with his four remaining henchmen. This particular power struggle demonstrated that while informal leadership based on rule by bullying was at first mesmerizing and seductive, it ultimately proved unattractive to the majority of boys. They speedily reverted to supporting Thang, perhaps because it was in all their interests to live within a more peaceful and less aggressive environment.

Later I noticed a change in Mau. Where previously he had walked around with his hand covering his ear, he no longer did so, and now he chose a more prominent seat in the classroom near to Thang. Thang once again sat upright and reverted to his outgoing nature. Other boys crowded around him, and it was once more with his tacit approval that children conversed with outsiders such as Jack and me. Vu meanwhile removed himself to the back of Jack's classroom and avoided the company of other boys.

These moments of shifting loyalties among the boys not only affected them but also had an influence over whether boys felt relaxed in the company of the adults around them. During the two-week leadership battle when

Vu was momentarily in charge, a new hierarchy among the boys had been established based on older and stronger children bullying weaker peers. The atmosphere was tenser, children snapped at each other, and their play fighting ended more violently than it had done before. Afterward, it reverted to the more normal mutually supportive atmosphere.

There was a tendency for boys to pair off with each other and to wrap their arms around each other as a sign of loyalty. The boys gained a great deal from these affectionate relationships. Boys who paired off usually held similar positions of power within the informal hierarchy at the school. Often the older boys played with the younger ones as if they were younger than their years.

As with the children I knew who were still working on the streets, the boys at the school also established family-type networks from which adults were excluded. Their intimate thoughts and reactions to the environment remained solely within a domain that outsiders, including myself, would always have difficulty entering. By being there over a long period I was able to observe the way that children grouped together and how their separate worlds interconnected. Often one couple would be close to another couple, so there existed more intimate links within a larger group of boys.

### Being "Mafia"

During the first year that I was at the school there was a three-month period in which children referred to each other as members of the mafia. The most influential boys in classes run by Jack and Chinh would joke around and point at a child and in a threatening voice say "mafia." Some of the children really took offence if they thought that the term "mafia" was being used with any critical intent, but if the term seemed to be used humorously, the person addressed would duck and laugh and shout "no not me, you, you are mafia." The term was essentially derogatory, however, and seemed to be associated with being labeled a criminal. I was surprised that the children had even heard of the term, but I noticed that the most influential children in the informal network used it to control those they did not want to see gaining too much popularity. Thus members of Jack's class were most likely to use the term to address boys from Chinh's class. The boys consistently called this were very resistant to use of the label, which they took to be negative, because when the term "mafia" was directed at them they knew it meant that their behavior was unacceptable to the most powerful boys in the school.

Khue was one of the boys who was taunted. He was unusually small, with a very cheeky disposition, and looked about nine years old. Actually aged thirteen, he was one of the youngest boys to come through the school. While not posing a threat as a potential leader, he was very independent and, unusually, chose to avoid cultivating alliances within the various groups. This determination to maintain a distinct sense of autonomy was rare. At first because he was so much smaller than anyone else, children would try to play with him, as they might a younger sibling or baby. He was small enough to be carried but would not submit to this role and as a result began to be seen as a nuisance, and hence be teased with the mafia term.

He had been placed in Chinh's class and found it disconcerting when I sat at the back of the classroom where he had also chosen to sit. At the time I think he wrongly concluded that I had decided to pay him special attention, and perhaps to mother him. So he turned to me and said loudly and with great pride in his voice, "I am very bad, and two of my brothers are in a tougher school than this, and my mother and father are in prison." His message was clearly that he was tough and should be respected as such. On one occasion, he left the classroom just after the teacher had gone and returned with a four-foot metal pole. On entering the room he grinned at me, as if to say, "What are you going to do about this?" and proceeded to bang the desks while shouting, "I am mafia, I am mafia." He hit every desk, smirking as he proceeded down the classroom. He was having a great time and clearly wanted a reaction. Coming up to me he looked into my eyes and challenged me to stop him by banging repeatedly on the desk. No one reacted, and I sat there trying not to laugh. This was not what Khue wanted; he wanted to be tough enough to challenge authority and to establish himself as someone to be reckoned with. Partly because he was so small and usually good-natured, no one showed fear and I did not react. After five minutes he gave up, threw the pole down, and slumped into his seat with a look that said, "I've done all I can." But paradoxically, afterward the boys began to show him more respect and instead of being seen as someone to mother he was treated as a nuisance or teased as being in the mafia. As a result of establishing a tough image he felt able to relax a little. He remained unusual in his desire to cultivate the mafia label.

The boys' references to being bad or being mafia were the nearest that most of them came to discussing reasons for having entered the reform school. To some degree these oblique references mirrored those used by the guards when they lectured them on how to become good citizens, or referred to them as social evils. Individual crimes were not referred to; instead boys were told en masse that they were criminals. Members of the NGO and I talked to individual boys, but as Thiep's example illustrates, they found it difficult to discuss any offences, perhaps because it was not in the school culture to do so but also perhaps because of the shame it brought on them and their families.

### Boys' References to Their Crimes

When Chinh, Nang, Jack, or I asked the boys questions about the school and why they were there, they would joke around if they were in a large group and would invariably answer flippantly "because I am bad." The word for "bad" (*kem*) was ingrained on their minds. It was sketched onto walls of the classrooms in a number of places. On the back wall of the classroom in which I ended up spending most of my time, "kem" had been scratched boldly in black. It remained there for the duration of my time, and whenever a child sat on the bench below, the word hung over his head as a reminder of what a child had one day felt the need to inscribe with reference to himself or the children who surrounded him.

None of the boys ever said who had written the word; this did not seem to be important. But on one occasion during the third study period of the day, when I was sitting on the back bench next to Thiep, he took hold of my arm and pointed it to share some of his feelings. He whispered, "That is me, I am bad." I asked him why this was so and he said, "I stole many things before coming here, and now my mother cries." All I felt able to do was squeeze his arm and continue sitting there in silence. At that time the boys were not encouraged by the guards to speak about their experiences, so some of their graffiti served as one of only a few outlets for them to express themselves.

### Changes

As I was coming to the end of my time at the school, a more lenient and less dogmatic approach toward the children's education and general treatment began to emerge, detectable in a number of ways. Because the school was new, most of the procedures chosen to reform the children were still based on a theoretical understanding of reform processes, so initially it came as a surprise to the staff that the behavior of some children reverted to their earlier ways once their time at the school came to an end. This was the case for Sern, Vu, and Phuong, who, as described in chapter 5, quickly went from being model children within the school environment to living in a market in the center of the city, making their living by occasional petty stealing and by helping stall owners by guarding their stalls and running errands. The guards had expected the boys to return home to their parents as model citizens, but none did, and it was only after this particular group left the school that the guards began to appreciate that it was important to be aware of any family-related problems that might have contributed to children originally getting into trouble.

*Phuong's Case.* Vu and Sern did have families that struggled financially, but it turned out that it was Phuong who was in the most difficulty. On his last day at the school he was quite tearful and told both Jack and Chinh that he did not want to leave. This was initially quite a surprise, because most of the children were desperate to leave. Parents or another family member were expected to pick the boys up from the school, but this did not always happen, and by midafternoon Phuong was still in the yard, looking increasingly dejected. Both Jack and I had to leave the school by that time, and we presumed that he would be kept on at school while family members were contacted. But on our next visit we discovered that one of the guards had finally sent Phuong off to make his own way home.

Three weeks later a very scruffy and skinny Phuong turned up at the school to collect his school certificate. All the boys from his class showed real concern and gathered around him protectively. While he tried to put on a brave front with his friends, he privately told Chinh, "I wish I was still living here. I really do not want to leave." He was so unhappy that he had even considered trying to get caught stealing so that he could be brought back. Jack and Chinh alerted Mr. Son, the school director, who was very concerned and was quite angry that Phuong had been sent away from the school without family contacts being followed up. Phuong then told us, "When I got home I discovered that my father was still in prison and my stepmom was running the house. She really did not want me around, and it was only after I begged her that she let me sleep in the pigsty in our backyard. As time went on she became more angry about me being there. She stopped feeding me, and I was forced to eat the pig food."

Phuong was very clear that he did not want to go home and that if no one helped him he would be forced to return to stealing and other crime as a means of survival. He did not want to do this but instead wanted to go to school and continue with his studies. Though he particularly looked to Jack and his Vietnamese colleagues rather than the guards for possible help, it was as a direct result of his situation that the guards started to offer extended social support once children had returned home. Jack was given permission to set up a halfway house to shelter and support children if there were problems that prevented their returning to their families.

Phuong's experience demonstrated to some of the guards that the children they were working with had complex lives and that straightforward approaches to reeducate them in an artificial environment removed from their normal world did little to address their real needs. It marked a turning point in the way children were understood inside the school; although they were still put in the lockup and taught the works of Ho Chi Minh, more time was also spent trying to find out their particular concerns and the motivations that had led to their being placed in the school in the first place.

### The Influence of the NGO

The children were aware that the NGO workers and I occupied a different role from those of the guards, and they responded positively to the interest we took in their lives. For example, the boys in Jack's class were far more relaxed about asking for assistance with their studies than were the boys in other classes. Jack usually responded positively; he did not assume that children knew the answers to questions. By the summer some of the guards were more relaxed with the children and acted in a similar fashion. I believe that this change came about because guards had witnessed the relationships that Jack, Tung, and Chinh were developing with some of the boys. Tung and Chinh got on very well with Bich, another guard, and by August 1997 Bich in turn started to copy their level of interest in the boys. As a result Bich became a particular favorite with the boys. He put himself in charge of cutting the children's hair, and although this also put an end to the individual styles that some of them had developed, they lined up eagerly. There was much joking and laughter, as Bich adapted the manner of Hanoi's street-side barbers. Before cutting hair he would jokingly discuss what style a boy might want, and some of their more radical ideas were taken into account, so that they did not all end up with a shorn head. By adopting this sympathetic approach Bich was helping to break the classical institutional mold.

His colleagues also softened their approach. Toward the end of my time at the school guards no longer paraded the grounds during class time and instead seemed to trust children more. They also took the time to understand individual children's reasons for running away. Tet, the Vietnamese New Year, was always a difficult time for the boys because it is the biggest holiday and family time in the year. The second year that I was there Diep successfully ran away from the school for Tet but left a note with the guards explaining that a member of his family was seriously ill and that he would be back the following day. The next day when Diep returned to the school the guards chose not to punish him, and Mr. Son told Jack that he approved of Diep's behavior and would have done the same under the same circumstances.

### Vocational Training Gains Pace

It was also at the behest of the Butterfly Trust that vocational training was offered to the boys so that they could learn a useful trade in preparation for a return to the outside world. Phan Anh had been the first boy to highlight this need when he confided in Jack that he would have no choice but to return to petty crime on leaving the reform school because he was not qualified to take up a trade and did not have the financial resources either to take one up or to start any training. He lived with his grandmother, who was his only family, and because she was increasingly frail he wanted to work to support her. They were too poor for him to be able to attend school and pay the informally required primary school fees or the required post-primary fees. Apprentices were required to pay their employer while they trained, and training was not an option either. Phan Anh wanted to work as a motorbike mechanic and set up premises outside his and his grandparent's home. He was hardworking and had proved himself to be one of the brightest and quickest students in Jack's English class. When Phan

Anh left the reform school Jack organized funding through his NGO for him to train as an apprentice motorbike mechanic; the NGO also provided him with the funds to support both himself and his grandmother while he was training. Phan Anh's life was transformed by this opportunity: he would no longer be at risk of reoffending, and his status as a legitimate and professional member of society was now guaranteed. His example inspired other boys to come forward and talk to Jack and his team, and it transpired that most of the boys were very keen to learn a trade or to go back to school but did not have the means to do so because of their poverty.

Mr. Son, the school director, eagerly supported the suggestion of Jack and his NGO team that they set up training in motor mechanics and carpentry in the school while at the same time extending such support to boys who had already left the school. Graduates of the school were thus able to take up vocational training as a means to escape reoffending, something that would not have been possible without the support of both the Butterfly Trust team and the reform school staff. It is something that, given the same opportunity, would not have been followed up by child rights activists. When members of UNICEF visited the school and witnessed children taking part in the vocational training program they accused the school and the Butterfly Trust of colluding in child labor.

I could see that these changes at the school heralded a genuine desire to introduce more empathetic reforms for the children and to prepare them for a positive return to the outside world. When Phuong's experiences led Mr. Son to support Jack's plan to set up a halfway house for children, it marked a clear shift in understanding the boys' circumstances, a major breakthrough and one that reflected well on the Vietnamese juvenile reform system. In addition, the boys' experiences in the reform school were not only dependent on the guard-driven formal network but also were shaped by the attitudes they shared within their peer group. This adds weight to my argument that the value of internationally led directives can only be judged by the positive impact they are seen to have at the local level, as judged by the positively altered practices and attitudes of the local administration toward children, and among the children themselves. This impact can only be observed and evaluated within the local community, and by reference to the local cultural norms, not to some international ideal.

## Seven

# Childhood without Discrimination

In this chapter, I look at the UNCRC's applicability to children whose particular circumstances make it more likely that they might be discriminated against, examining in particular some of the ways in which a Vietnamese child's gender or disability can contribute to the shaping of his or her life. I focus on these two areas because along with race, they are probably the most obvious bases of discrimination.

It was just after I arrived in Hanoi that the "girl child" had become the focal point for new projects to be funded by international aid agencies. I had the opportunity at the same time to observe the work of some of the child-focused NGOs that were becoming involved in projects to make mainstream education inclusive, enabling children with disabilities to be educated within a normal school. So it was fortuitous timing that afforded me an excellent opportunity to observe at firsthand the workings in practice of some of the UNCRC's principles in relation to these two project streams.

Two articles of the UNCRC are of relevance. Article 2 states that parties are required to "ensure the rights set forth in the present UNCRC . . . without discrimination of any kind, irrespective of the child's or his or her parents or legal guardian's race, color, sex, language, religion, political or other opinion, national, ethnic or social origin, property, disability, birth or other status." Article 23 recognizes that a mentally or disabled child should enjoy a full and decent life; it also states that the child should have effective access to education while achieving the fullest possible social integration.

One of the problems I found when attending child rights–focused NGO meetings was that there was a tendency for expatriate NGO staff to discuss their immediate environment (in this case Vietnam) in terms of its failure to adhere to all aspects of the UNCRC. But, as I have argued elsewhere in this book, the scale of the UNCRC's ambitions makes its full implementation an impossible task: while some improvements are being made in children's lives there are many obstacles, economic and social, within most societies (including that of Vietnam) that will not be overcome simply because the UNCRC has now been ratified. I observed, however, that incremental successes were being achieved when NGOs focused, intentionally or otherwise, on very particular objectives written into the UNCRC and then worked hard to achieve the goals of one aspect of it, using more tangible, practice-centered techniques. Broadly speaking, this was the case with the inclusive education program I observed in progress, which relates to Article 2 of the UNCRC. The school I visited had been established by the Vietnamese government rather than international aid agencies, while the inclusive education program that had been set up within it was partly funded both by child rights NGOs and by NGOs that did not have any commitment to the UNCRC. So for once there was a broadly based support, both domestic and international, for the programs.

In the first part of this chapter I discuss the circumstances of girl children living in a government-run orphanage; I argue that while it is important to understand the specifics of their lives, this should not be done to the exclusion of the boys who lived alongside them. By overlooking the experiences of "boy children," one might inadvertently attribute particular benefits and hardships to one gender without ever knowing if an experience is actually gender specific or not. To provide an underlying societal context, I have analyzed some of the more general aspects of gender relations within Vietnamese society, since having an insight into some of the ways that Vietnamese society treats men and women differently helps us to understand what kind of aid might be needed, and the most appropriate (that is, culturally specific) form it might take.

In the second part of the chapter, I move on from gender to disability. Here, I examine the workings of the UNCRC by discussing the successes and failures of the introduction of inclusive education programs being supported by NGOs. I do this by focusing attention on the experiences of some visually impaired children who were included within a mainstream school as part of the new inclusive initiative. I discovered that the mainstream school placed more emphasis on visually impaired children developing vocational skills specifically so that they could earn a living on graduating, an approach similar to that of the reform school discussed in chapter 6. Emphasis on vocational training kept these children apart from their sighted peers. This means that the children in the school for the visually impaired were not fully integrated into mainstream society and that their experiences were directly shaped by their very particular circumstances as disabled and often impoverished members of Vietnamese society. But I argue that the project was nevertheless groundbreaking within the context of Vietnam because it successfully laid some foundations from which to challenge age-old Vietnamese prejudices in which any type of physical or mental disability has been understood to exist as a form of punishment from the ancestors for a family's wrongdoings. As one expatriate doctor working for a small NGO in Hanoi told me, children with disabilities are often hidden in their homes and kept away from mainstream society, and in some cases they are allowed to die while still infants.

## The Orphanage

I had heard of the orphanage a long time before I went there, because it was a government institution that did not have any NGOs permanently attached to it: this in itself interested me and I was intrigued to understand the reasons. I found that a number of NGO directors wanted to develop permanent ties to it; for example, one NGO director I met at a workshop on social work told me she was keen to introduce the children and staff to the UNCRC, and another wanted to set up a counseling center for street children in its grounds. Mrs. Ha, the director of the orphanage, was not enthusiastic about any of these proposals. Huong, one of my Vietnamese friends, who had once worked there and now worked for an international child rights NGO, told me that Mrs. Ha was wary of any type of NGO intervention because previous interactions had resulted in her vision for the orphanage being subsumed to the will of outsiders. Huong was one of the few people I confided in about my general critique of the UNCRC and the work of NGOs, and because we were in sympathy with each other's viewpoint it was she who offered to arrange for me to meet Mrs. Ha. She suggested to Mrs. Ha that I could teach occasional English classes to the younger children at the orphanage school if in return she would let me talk to some of the children in her care. I doubted if this idea would convince Mrs. Ha, who was by now very suspicious of any offer of outside assistance initiated by foreigners, but Huong was sure that she could persuade her otherwise. Huong and Mrs. Ha were fond of each other, and as a result of their meeting I was given permission to visit the orphanage on a weekly basis. Mrs. Ha was clearly protective of the orphanage and of the level of access allowed for people like myself. Clearly, some of her sensitivity came from the fact that the institution was far more open than the reform school and therefore more vulnerable to external influences.

### A Relaxed Institutional Style

Rather than upholding a sense of being in an institution, it seemed to me that Mrs. Ha's staff were trying to relax the style of operation. For example, they had opened their school to children in the immediate community to attend classes where they could not afford to otherwise attend public school. Local involvement had made the environment more exclusive and less institutional. However, younger members of Mrs. Ha's staff told me that more could be done to relax the environment of the orphanage; for example, children in their care would benefit from even greater flexibility in their timetable. Because of this Mrs. Ha had been put under pressure to further relax the style in which the center was run (according to Huong she had only opened up the orphanage to the community on the advice of MOLISA, the government department responsible for orphanages, which wanted to create more of a family atmosphere). Learning this helped me to understand the tension that sometimes existed between Mrs. Ha and her staff, who she appeared to treat much as she treated the children. A year after I left Vietnam, Huong e-mailed me to let me know that Mrs. Ha had retired from the orphanage and that the new director was eager to negotiate with her staff members rather than assume she had the final word on everything. While this was good news for the staff I also wondered what this change might mean for the children, who all gravitated toward Mrs. Ha, a strongly maternal figure for them.

### Early Insights into the Status of Orphans

When I drew up to the orphanage on my bicycle to be introduced to Mrs. Ha, I realized that it was the same institution I had passed two months earlier when out on a bicycle ride. On that occasion, I had met some children from the surrounding neighborhood and joined them for an afternoon of learning some of their street games. At the time I had not really paid attention to the orphanage or its inhabitants as they came and went about their daily business. This time, as I entered the orphanage I was immediately struck by the disproportionately high number of girls. Mrs. Ha told me that of the twenty-eight children, ranging in age from two to seventeen, only ten were boys.

When I returned home that day and was typing up my notes it occurred to me that there could be a link between the high proportion of girls at the orphanage and the negative impact of living in a society where more value was traditionally placed on the male child. As a result, I resolved to find out more about why girls were being sent there and why, even if their parents were dead, they were not being brought up by extended family. On both counts what I discovered turned out to be more complex than I had imagined.

Nguyet, a fifteen-year-old girl, was waiting for me at the gate when I arrived on my second visit. She told me that the staff and children were cleaning the orphanage because there was no school, but that I should join them anyway to eat sugar cane and play cards. For over an hour I joined in the playful cleaning process, which included water throwing and tipping of old clothes and garbage from the second floor balconies down to the ground below. Mrs. Ha then announced that the orphanage was now clean and everyone could resume playing. Nguyet invited me to join her and her friends in a game of cards. It was a humid and sticky afternoon as we sat on the stoop playing a fast and furious game. After a few rounds, we paused for a while, each girl resting her hand on the leg or arm of her neighbor, and Lan and Nguyet began telling me about what they had done over the last few days. Lan said she was very happy because she had just been on a trip home to visit her mother. So by Western standards, she was not technically an orphan at all.

*Definition of Orphans in Vietnam.* Until then I had assumed that the children at the orphanage had no living parents, or if they did have parents who were alive they had no contact with them, so I was unable to hide my surprise at Lan's revelation. Before visiting the orphanage I had erroneously assumed that the term "orphan" was universally used when both parents were dead or their whereabouts were unknown. I was not alone in making this assumption. In a conversation I later had with the director of one of the child rights NGOs, the director expressed surprise that children with a living parent would be considered orphans. Mrs. Ha, the orphanage director, referred to all the children in her care as orphans while in the same breath referring to the involvement of a living parent in some children's lives. In Vietnam the term "orphan" refers to a child who has lost only one parent as well as those who have lost both, which is the general contemporary Western use of the term.

This may also explain why there is a discrepancy between statistics presented by UNICEF, which would have used a Western definition for the term, and those of the Vietnamese government. Hopkins (1996, 114) found that in 1993 MOLISA reported a total of 350,000 orphans in Vietnam (about 0.5 percent of the population), while UNICEF estimated that there were 9,600 orphans in Hanoi. (about 0.3 percent of the local population). The disparity of these results, where the Vietnamese definition used by MOLISA implies that there are nearly twice as many orphans as estimated by UNICEF, can in some respect be explained by the fact that that the organizations defined the term "orphan" differently.

It is important that international NGOs working in this field are aware of the local definition of an "orphan," because without this knowledge obvious misunderstandings can arise. For example, the practice of adoption of Vietnamese babies becomes more complicated if it is wrongly assumed that a child has no parents and the facts of familial ties are generally unclear. When I was living in Eugene, Oregon, in 2000 after I had left Vietnam, I happened to meet an American woman who had been in the final stage of adopting a Vietnamese baby girl whom she had already been caring for during a six-week period, when the adoption agency involved discovered that the baby's birth father was in fact alive and unaware that his daughter was being put up for international adoption. The adoptee mother had not known of such a possibility and had falsely understood the baby to be without parents. The biological Vietnamese father subsequently refused to relinquish parental rights and took the baby back to be brought up by his parents. If the agency had been clearer with the adoptive mother about local definitions of the term "orphan" and had first checked its information, the confusion and loss she experienced would perhaps have been less.

*If Children Have Parents, Why Do They Go to Orphanages?* In Vietnam, poverty and societal rules are the two main factors that influence the definition of what is an orphan, and the country is by no means unique in this. For example, it also applied in nineteenth-century America; Hyman Bogen, writing about a New York orphanage of that period, recorded, "The problem of unplaceable orphan children was compounded by yet another situation that the home was just beginning to recognize: more and more single parents were using it as a boarding school . . . this was borne out by its own statistics: only 15 percent of the inmates were full orphans and this total was shrinking" (1992, 47).

Lan, who like Nguyet was fifteen years old, told me that she had gone to the orphanage after her mother remarried, to make way for the birth of younger siblings under Vietnam's two-child policy. Lan seemed unruffled by this apparent shift in her mother's loyalties and told me that her mother loved her very much but that she had had no choice in this turn of events. Lan went home nearly every weekend and still felt close to her mother. On that day she was particularly excited because the week was drawing to a close and on Sunday she was going to be with her mother and half-brother and half-sister.

Although both Lan and Nguyet appeared to have been sidelined by their families, they showed no outward signs of resentment toward the parent who, from my Western perspective, had seemingly rejected them. Instead both girls spoke of their parents with affection. I wondered if they felt that it was acceptable for them to be cast out of the family home in this way because they were girls. Later I realized that their circumstances were also shaped by a number of contemporary and other interlinked societal influences.

## Societal Pressures on Girls' Lives

In looking at some of the girls' experiences, it is useful to step back and remind ourselves again of two important underlying principles that govern the role of women in Vietnamese society: these are the influence of Confucianism and the position of married women within the family. While Lan had been talking about why she had been placed in the orphanage, the other girls sat silently listening while playing with her hair. No one spoke after our conversation came to an end; instead, we resumed our card game for another hard-throwing round in which I lost yet again. Then Nguyet decided to talk about her own situation. She explained that she had moved to the orphanage after her mother died, but that her brother still lived with their grandparents. Like Lan, she still made visits home. Nguyet's mother had died when she was nine years old, and her father had struggled to care for her and her brother but was working full-time and found it difficult to cope. When she was twelve her grandparents took her brother in and Nguyet was sent to the orphanage. She saw her father every weekend and showed great pride in both him and his wish for her to continue receiving an education. She told me that he paid a small contribution toward her education, as did other parents or relatives of children in the orphanage, so he was actively involved in supporting and caring for her. Although I wanted to know more about Nguyet's reaction to her move to the orphanage, I could not bring myself to ask her how she felt about her brother being chosen over her to live with their grandparents. Nguyet would have known that keeping the grandson close within the family was viewed as better insurance for the future, because after his father was dead it would be he, as the male head of the family, who was responsible for everyone, both financially in this life and spiritually in the one that comes after by maintaining the family ancestor worship table and carrying on the patrilineal line. This traditional drive toward the need to have male heirs and therefore to favor them over girl children has intensified with the introduction of the government's two-child policy.

### The Pressure of Being a Single Mother

The more I understood about Vietnamese society the more empathy I felt toward Lan's mother and the life choices she had had to make, which had led to her daughter living separately from her. Particular cultural pressures exist in Vietnam that make being a single mother difficult. It is also clear that any child with only one parent alive is considered an orphan. A survey by the Municipal Center of Social Sciences and Human Studies reported that the number of separated families in Ho Chi Minh City had increased from 14.8 percent of total families in the city in 1995 to 17.3 percent in 1996. The report estimated that at least 6.2 percent of mothers were unwed, and as the following extract from it shows, the authors had clear views about the detrimental consequences for them and their offspring within the context of Vietnamese societal norms:

> At all times they are solitary and have no one to share their plight. Only a few could find some consolation as with common women. But more pitiful are the fatherless children, who are almost orphans. A mother's love cannot substitute for the presence of a father who, by nature, is the pillar of a family. Science has proven that fatherless children usually develop some psycho-psychological abnormalities. They are stubborn and rude, but also shy and worrisome, full of obsessive concerns. They can be easily dispirited and develop misanthropy. "After years of studying fatherless children I have noticed that very few of them had a normal and successful life" remarked Yen, Director of UNESCO Children's Care Center. (Yu 2001, 144)

In this article blame is pointed at the mother, and ominous predictions are made about the plight of fatherless children. If such opinions are widespread, perhaps a mother's decision to remarry—and in some cases give up, or hide, children from her first marriage (girls in particular)—is not so surprising. This practice might also be more commonplace than I had first imagined. My husband was close to a local man and woman who had two young sons, and he understood that the two boys were their only children. But one day when he was having drinks with the family the maternal grandmother walked in with a little girl who was, he was given to understand, the woman's daughter who had come to pay a visit. Nothing else was said, and it was left to him to piece together the story that the wife of the family had been in a previous relationship, and that to be properly free to marry she had had to ask her mother to bring up her daughter.

If prejudices toward single mothers are as great as the preceding report indicates, children like Lan may even have been relieved when their mothers had the opportunity to marry again: to do so would make the family whole again in the eyes of society, even at the cost of preexisting children being excluded from home. Lan spoke fondly of her mother and half-siblings and recognized the advantages her mother's remarriage had given the whole family.

### Avoiding Poverty

The need to survive and not slide into extreme poverty was another significant influence on the choices these families were making. A married woman in Vietnam clearly has higher status than a widow or a separated or single mother, and it is far easier to get by with two wage earners rather than one. Girls in the orphanage were there either because a living parent could not afford to keep them at home and earn a salary to support them or because their living parent had been compelled, for a multitude of complicated reasons, to marry again and start a new family.

### The Influence of Communism

Proclamations from the 1950s promised that traditional cultural practices would make way for more egalitarian attitudes toward women and girls. In 1959 Ho Chi Minh called the Marriage and Family Law "an integral part of the socialist revolution . . . this law aims at the emancipation of women. It is necessary to liberate women, but it is equally necessary to destroy feudal and bourgeois ideologies in men" (Goodkind 1995, 219). In the aftermath of reunification, women in the south, like their counterparts in the north, were invited to join the women's liberation movement. Dung recalls in her memoir-inspired story, "In my precinct, at first, the organization had no trouble rounding up enough united women and turning them into liberated women but later on they ran into difficulties . . . whether you're inducted or not, it will make no difference whatsoever. United or liberated, you'll still go as hungry as before, your husband will remain jobless or keep rotting away in some re-education camp." She goes on to speak of women joining the liberation movement because to show loyalty to the new regime might improve their circumstances as well as those of their families, rather than because they felt it could improve their lot as women (1988, 57–58).

Le observes that throughout the American-Vietnam War, the Communist Party encouraged women to fight alongside men as the "long-haired army" (1989, 16), which meant—for that period at least—previous Confucian definitions of females and males were put to one side (as, similarly, women served vastly different and more empowered roles in the West during World War II). Since the war, the Women's Union, which is the prominent Vietnamese government organization focusing on issues affecting women and young girls, has continued to raise the issue of gender equality on behalf of the general populace. The Women's Union has members who are very actively working at every level of society.

Perhaps because the Women's Union has an apparently strong presence in Vietnam, overoptimistic assumptions have sometimes been made about the level of gender equality that now exists. In the 1980s some social commentators were still very optimistic about the degree to which socialist Vietnam was making inroads into gender inequality and thus departing from the traditional practice of boy preference. Eisen argues that Vietnam in the early 1980s was "a place, where, after exhausting work and furious struggle, women can be confident that they travel the path which will some day arrive at their liberation" (quoted in Goodkind 1995, 343). This seems a remarkably optimistic conclusion to have drawn, particularly in light of some of the experiences of girls like Nguyet and Lan. Dr Nguyen Kim Cuc, vice president of the Vietnam Family Planning Association in Hanoi, has pointed out that "women from both sides in the war are trying to find equality in today's Vietnam, where men still dominate the highest positions of power" (in conversations at Women's Union, Hanoi, 1997).

### Advantages for Girls of Being at the Orphanage

On the face of it, girls such as Nguyet and Lan were in the orphanage because of a combination of traditional and contemporary factors. Certainly traditional beliefs about male preference made it more likely that after a parent died or remarried a girl would be the first to be sent to the orphanage. Vietnam's two-child policy lessened people's chances of having a male child and probably increased the practice of sending girls away. This explanation seemed too simple to me, however, because it did not account for the young girls and women I met who defied any idea that they might be inferior to boys. The girls whose gender did not define the outcome of their lives were more likely to have educated mothers and come from more financially affluent professional backgrounds, adding weight to my argument that gender cannot be treated as the defining factor in shaping a person's life. Other factors also influence the opportunities made available to each child. During the week when the girls were at the orphanage they also attended the local school, for which their families paid fees. Susan Hopkins alludes to the high drop-out rate of Vietnam's children attending school after primary school age. Yet both Lan and Nguyet were planning to graduate from high school, something that because of the high fees involved fewer and fewer children are getting the chance to do. Clearly the two-child policy, these children's ongoing relationships with their families, and the pride some of them showed in the education they received complicated simplistic notions of what it might mean for them to be living in an orphanage. In fact, orphanage life gave them some advantages over children who had to work to pay their rent as well as to attend school.

### Boys in the Orphanage

Most of the academic and NGO literature on gender issues in Vietnam and other parts of East Asia focuses on the experience of being a girl and fails to touch in any detail on the experience of being a boy. In addition, most social commentators who write about gender in this context use the writings of Confucius as a starting point to support their argument that in East Asia women and girls are generally treated as second-class citizens. Across the world, girls continue to experience worrying levels of discrimination. While I strongly recognize that the fact of being female makes many girls' lives more difficult, there are a number of problems with the way in which their experiences are discussed. Examining only girls' lives and omitting boys' experiences from any discussion of gender issues sets up their experiences in opposition to each other. This creates a distorted view of society. There are many reasons for this treatment of boys and girls by both aid practitioners and academics: the first wave of feminism set men and women up in opposing camps, and that type of feminism continues to inform some of the ideas about the "girl child" currently in use among prominent international aid agencies and NGOs. When reference is made to the "girl child," girls' experiences are most often discussed in isolated and generalized terms without reference to wider influences on their lives such as their parents' class and economic capabilities or to their male siblings' experiences. As the sociologist Barrie Thorne points out in her study of American children in the playground setting, "The last two decades of feminist theory have moved the analysis beyond unexamined dualisms and toward much greater complexity. But these insights have not, by and large, been extended to research on children. Relatively static and dichotomous notions of individual and group gender difference sit, like a gigantic magnet at the core [of much child-focused work]" (1997, 157–158). In her observations of boys and girls at play in playgrounds in the Midwest and California during the 1970s and 1980s Thorne found to her surprise that boys and girls did not interact almost exclusively, as the standard literature on the subject had led her to believe, with people of their own gender, and that in fact boys and girls often came together in unexpected ways to play and chat together in the playground. She also observed that much of boys' and girls' activities were quite similar. Thorne concluded from this ethnographic-based fieldwork that too much is made of gender differences and that because of the expectation of differences existing between the sexes researchers have looked for and reinforced differences among children simply by fact of them being either male or female. In the context of Vietnam I argue similarly that while girls are discriminated against for quite particular reasons, some boys also experience difficulties, not necessarily because of their gender but because of other influences, which also contribute to discrimination against girls, such as family poverty, death of a parent, and the two-child policy. Because of these findings, which struck me primarily during my visits to the orphanage, I believe it is a mistake to isolate boys' and girls' experiences from each other; by doing so, we run the risk of focusing exclusively on the experiences of one gender without at a minimum discussing broader and possibly more significant influences at work in children's lives. Thorne's work was based on her observations in playgrounds in the United States, but I discovered something similar in Vietnam, where I found that I could not just use gender as the determining factor if I wanted to confidently analyze why children acted as they did or found themselves in particular situations. I found that other influences such as whether parents were divorced, or dead, or if the family had a low standard of living were as important in shaping the opportunities for children, irrespective of whether they were male or female. And, as I noted in chapter 2, if children's parents were members of the Communist Party and if they had been legally born in the city, they immediately, regardless of gender, had health care and educational opportunities that would otherwise have been denied them.

*Prejudice against Boys without Families*

During an interview, Mary, an aid worker running a religious-based NGO in Hanoi, told me that a year before, in 1997, one of the orphanages she supported in the Northern Highlands admitted two young boys who were about ten years old. Neither boy had any living parents of his own but each had remained in the village where his parents had once lived earning money as runners in the local market. At night some of the village men would forcibly tie them to trees up in the hills as tiger bait. Local people who sought to protect them finally took the children to the orphanage. Both boys explained that because they had no family, the men told them that they were worthless. Most Vietnamese living in the area no longer thought there were any tigers in the region, so perhaps the men's behavior had been nothing more than a cruel joke. Regardless of the men's motives, what they did to the boys was immeasurably cruel and inhumane.

Phuong, of whom I wrote at length in chapter 6, had resorted to living in the family pigsty after his sentence at the reform school came to an end and his stepmother would not consider his living in the house when his father was away. Hiep, who cleaned shoes on the street, told me that his mother was alive but that she could not afford to keep him, so he had left home to ease the burden for her of raising him alone. On my third visit to the orphanage I ran into Tien as I entered the orphanage gates. I had often seen and chatted to Tien as he cleaned shoes in the center of the city but had not known until that moment that he lived in the orphanage. We immediately sat down and started chatting, and as we did so other children gathered around us. Tien told me that he had moved to the orphanage because his extended family could not afford to look after him. Unlike Nguyet and Lan, Tien had no living parents and had reached an agreement with the orphanage staff that he would earn money on the streets to cover the orphanage's basic expenses for him. He felt grateful that he had a roof over his head. Being a boy had not ensured him a future inside his extended family, and his circumstances were on a par with those of the girls who lived at the orphanage because they had no living parents.

After Tien and I had talked, another boy in the orphanage felt relaxed enough with me to tell me a little about his life. Dac Kien was twelve and one of the two boys living there who had a living parent. He was his mother's only son but did not live with her or with his paternal grandparents because, according to Mrs. Ha, neither household could afford to keep him. Dac Kien dreamed of becoming a football player and spent most of his spare time outside the orphanage playing with local boys. As I cycled to the orphanage I would sometimes see him swimming in a nearby lake, always in the thick of a large group of boys. He was very private about what he felt about living at the orphanage and only told me that it would have been difficult for him to go to school if he still lived at home. But being his mother's only son had not prevented him from having to leave after her husband had died. Thus, although the Confucian value system upholds the value attached to a firstborn son, it should not be assumed that because of this a Vietnamese son's life is automatically one of privilege. While this may not be presumed, the more recent focus on the "girl child" by some of the child rights NGOs does create a distorted perspective on childhood, one in which boys, by their very absence from that focus, might be assumed to be doing fine.

Like me, Hirschman and Manh Loi locate Vietnamese culture and social organization within the East Asian cultural orbit, and as I explained in chapter 1 they also acknowledge the tensions that result from Vietnamese indigenous traditions and interactions with Southeast Asian cultures. When looking at the practice of ancestor veneration, they found a strong influence of Confucianism on traditional families in Vietnam, but, significantly, found that the obligations and responsibilities were owed the mother's side of the family as well as the father's. In an ethnography that focuses on the lives of rural Vietnamese women, the anthropologist Tina Gammeltoft observes that "whereas in death rituals, ancestor worship and inheritance matters, paternal bonds are significantly more important than maternal ones, in daily social life maternal family relations seem to be no less important" (1998, 28).

## Is Gender Important?

I started this chapter by asking whether a child's gender plays a discriminatory part in shaping the experiences of boys and girls living in contemporary Vietnam. I have shown that gender does shape children's lives, but that other factors quite obviously also determine opportunities available to all children. An outsider visiting the orphanage for the first time might easily have concluded that girls were suffering discrimination to a greater extent than boys because of their gender, particularly after some of them told me that they had left their families while a brother had been able to stay at home, or a parent had put them in the orphanage so that they could go on to have two more children with a new partner. These experiences were tragic, all the more so because they were shaped by local cultural circumstances, and in some cases would have a long-lasting detrimental affect on the later lives of some of the girls. But boys suffered in similar ways and were discriminated against, for example, because their families were poor, or because they were not the eldest son. In view of this I did not think it was particularly useful for the girl child to be singled out by aid agencies for help to the exclusion of boys; boys too were needy, and they were equally important.

### Disability and Inclusive Education: The School for the Visually Impaired

In 1997 I was invited to work over a two-month period with a child rights–focused international aid agency based in Hanoi to examine the level to which inclusive education was being achieved among visually impaired children. Inclusive education refers to a type of education that includes all children on an equal footing irrespective of their circumstances: whether they work on the streets, live in local orphanages or have a disability. The UNCRC declares a universal right to primary education, but as I explain in chapter 3, after the World Bank entered Vietnam its policies resulted in three-quarters of a million children being pushed out of secondary schools. Access to an education is still dependent on the extent to which parents rely on a child to earn money. Children who illegally emigrate to the city do not have access to formal education because such children do not have permits to be in the city in the first place. Nevertheless, regardless of such problems, which affect a substantial number of Vietnam's children, the government decided (with the backing of aid agencies) to focus on a particular aspect of education: inclusive education for all regardless of the children's disabilities. (I wondered why the problem of residence permits was not also being addressed in the UNCRC inclusive-education-for-all program and why it was that international NGOs persisted in upholding a policy of inclusion that under current Vietnam law was impossible to attain.)

In April 1995 the government of Vietnam issued the Policy of Inclusive Education (decree 26) and gave the Ministry of Education and Training the responsibility for teaching children with special educational needs in the regular educational system and in special schools. Between 1991 and 1995, pilot models of inclusive education were established in twenty-eight districts in seven provinces. In these areas and with the support of an international child rights NGO, the Special Education Center (NIES) focused on training 990 teachers to have a greater awareness of the needs of disabled children within mainstream schools. In 1997 I was asked by this child rights NGO to support and guide three Vietnamese researchers completing follow-up research projects aimed at assessing the extent to which children with disabilities were being integrated into the mainstream education system in Hanoi.

The school I visited was a secondary school in the outskirts of the city; it catered to children from the surrounding area and as well as to children who were visually impaired but came in from surrounding rural areas. Some of the visually impaired children lived so far away that a boarding school had been set up in the school grounds, which meant that some went home for visits at the weekend but the majority stayed at the school throughout term time. This immediately set the visually impaired children apart from their sighted classmates, who went home to their families every day. Experiences in the classroom also set these children apart.

### Classroom Integration

The education system in Vietnam is traditional and formally structured. In all the classrooms I visited the classes were teacher centered; without exception, classrooms were set up with pupils in rows facing their teacher and the blackboard. Children were usually taught through a text and workbook or by following a class activity written on the board to be copied into an exercise book. Most classroom interaction relied on one-to-one communication with the teacher. I observed that children were encouraged to be quite competitive, vying with each other to be chosen by their teacher to answer a question, write results on a board, or be leader of a group activity (which happened rarely). Visually impaired children found it very difficult to follow board activity, particularly because none of the class materials were available in Braille and they therefore could not work through the textbooks alongside the rest of the students. Information was either not read out loud to them or was read out at such a speed that they could not have taken it in properly in order to key it into their Braille typewriters. It was clear that the teacher-centered method of tuition inevitably led to limited involvement on the part of the visually impaired children.

### Reactions to the Researchers

The teachers were obviously aware that we were looking particularly at disability as an area of interest, and they initially responded by making a concerted effort to involve children with disabilities in all activities. This created an artificial environment, particularly within one of the classrooms where two of the children with disabilities were repeatedly asked the same questions, an action that was clearly aimed at impressing the researchers; it did little to help the assessment, however. If one of this pair could not answer, the teacher redirected the question to the other child with a disability, rather than broadening her parameters to include other children in the room. Thus she repeatedly separated those two children and treated them differently from the rest of the class. The classes observed had an average of forty-eight students, and in the integrated setting up to five students were visually impaired. Thus it was difficult for the teachers to offer individual attention to any of their students, and they needed to teach at a speed that was appropriate for all class members. In some cases this meant that slower students were simply left behind, and this often meant that some of the visually impaired children were unable to follow anything that was happening. Some books were not available in Braille, which made it impossible for the visually impaired students to keep up with classroom activities.

### Differentiated Activities

The children with disabilities also took part in separate activities within the overall integrated program. For example, during the afternoon older visually impaired students (between the ages of sixteen and eighteen) took massage classes, which were aimed at providing them with a marketable skill on leaving school. They were also encouraged to take up a musical instrument, which would increase their ability to be active within local community festivals. As a result of learning an instrument these students were part of a school band, and during one of our visits we were invited to watch them play for an NGO group that had visited the school to talk about possible funding.

Considering the school's limited resources it had achieved a great deal in terms of starting the process toward integrating students with different capabilities and physical abilities. Most of the problems I saw were found in the classroom setting and linked to lack of resources needed to obtain high-quality teaching material for children who are visually impaired; another factor was lack of funding sufficient to provide classroom assistants to help the teachers, who were clearly overstretched with such large class sizes to cope with.

It did seem, however, that the visually impaired children really came to life during lessons aimed exclusively at them. I was told by a seventeen-year-old visually impaired girl named Ai that the highlight of the week for the older students was their massage classes. She said that students in the massage classes were really keen to learn the skills because they knew that as qualified masseuses they would be able to return to their homes and lead productive working lives. The moments when they looked uncomfortable and ill at ease with their disabilities were when it was clear that they were being paraded around the school because they were disabled but despite this had skills that their teachers wanted to put on display. During a concert presented for American NGO workers, they looked particularly unenthusiastic. A number of the students had been placed at the front of the band and had nothing to do accept sit facing the audience. The atmosphere was uncomfortable and felt contrived to the extent that, observing this, other members of the research team and I wondered whether a band representing the whole school would have achieved more in terms of respect for the individual and a more upbeat sense of communal activity and inclusion for all. At the end of the concert the visiting aid workers asked the visually impaired children to line up with their hands outstretched for sweets. This was particularly distressing to watch when sometime later the workers ran out of sweets. No one thought to inform the three children still waiting in line, and they were left in a confused queue for five minutes, until they realized of their own accord that gifts were not forthcoming. Once more, my Vietnamese research colleagues and I discussed among ourselves why only the visually impaired children had been offered gifts, because by treating them differently true integration was not being encouraged.

## Children's Interaction and Use of Space Outside the Classroom

Outside the formal classroom setting, visually impaired children were less restricted and moved freely and confidently around the school; in the common play areas, children of all persuasions displayed a relaxed familiarity with each other. When they came across visually impaired children, the children in the school who had sight moved around them and gave them free-flowing access to the corridor or area. This meant that the child with visual impairment did not have to stop or slow down in anyway. At no point was there any complaint, even when the skipping game of a group of girls was interrupted six times in the space of five minutes. However, it was quite clear that children had grouped themselves with those people they most strongly identified with, and within the integrated school the able children and those with disabilities presented themselves as two quite distinct groups. The layout of the school perhaps precipitated such separateness. Because the children with disabilities were more likely to be boarders, they had their own quarters within the school and tended to return to there and to eat in their own dining room during the school day.

During my third visit to the school I was introduced to Ai, who was very eager to practice speaking English with me because she had been sponsored by some Catholic NGO workers to move to the United States and qualify as a teacher for people who shared her impairment. Ai told me that she had been at the school for seven years and that most of her contemporaries were attending the school solely to do the vocational training in massage. Once they finished at the school most would go back to live with their families in their rural villages and earn a living as a masseuse. Ai wanted more for her life than this. After we met at the school we decided to meet regularly over the following two months until she went to America. I would cycle to the school at the weekends to pick her up, and on those occasions as I walked down the silent and empty corridors of the main school and headed into the dormitory area I was struck by how institutional the setting was. With few sighted staff around on weekends and minimal food service available, children could only occupy themselves in a limited fashion. They just lay on their dormitory beds or wrote on their Braille machines. One fifteen-year-old boy sat next to his bed listening to his prize possession, a radio that someone had given to him as a gift. It was the only radio in the dormitory, and Ai told me that the boy carried it everywhere he went because it provided him with a lifeline to the outside world during the days and nights when the school was virtually empty. Usually, Ai and I would either walk from the school to a local tea stand or be picked up by one of her American sponsors in a car. As the car journeyed through the streets of Hanoi she would clutch my hand hard and talk excitedly about going to the United States and about her parents, who were so proud of her. I was struck by the contrast between the opportunities now being offered to her and the limited lifestyle available to some of her contemporaries living at the school. But it was clear to me that her ability to become successfully integrated into wider society and her attempt to gain an education overseas was as a result of two things. First there was an unusual determination on her part in struggling successfully to learn English on her own. She was then able to make the most of the opportunity afforded by the inclusive education program to plead her case in a chance meeting with one of the NGO workers who had visited the school to make a donation, and who eventually became one of her sponsors. So her story was remarkable and awe inspiring. If the Vietnamese government had not established the inclusive education program, none of these options would have become available to her. Yet in some respects, as I have explained earlier, the inclusive education still had much further to go if it were to properly involve all children regardless of their individual needs.

## Conclusions

The children I met in the orphanage and at the school for the visually impaired had a number of things in common. First, neither of the institutions they attended had properly succeeded in fully integrating their members into mainstream society; neither, however, had they given up on trying to further progress in this area. Some of the older children in the orphanage attended local schools, but they still returned to the orphanage at night. Others in the orphanage also worked on the streets, thus raising the question of how they might be categorized should any aid organizations seek to do so. Were such children "street children" or did living at the orphanage discount such a categorization? Visually impaired children stayed at school during the weekends and were really at the school with the sole objective of graduating as vocationally trained masseuses rather than sharing the far more varied ambitions of students throughout the rest of the school. Much of these limitations can be connected to lack of funding to develop a wider range of resources for children with special needs. One of the problems with even beginning to tackle this lack of resources is that Vietnam still cannot afford to provide education for all, even at primary level, so its funding for any type of education is very overstretched.

Another problem Vietnam faces is that because the government signed the UNCRC, as far as the international aid community is concerned legitimate pressure can be put on the Vietnamese government to improve children's circumstances. And because the UNCRC has an overly ambitious breadth of scope, there are too many different areas that cannot be adequately addressed with the limited resources available. So one of my key questions was, if resources are so stretched, should the Vietnamese focus on providing education for all primary-age children (as the UNCRC requires), or would it be more worthwhile to focus instead only on ensuring that disabled children have an education? Or should the government continue to try to do both while in reality failing to do either successfully? This is the dilemma that strikes at the core of the UNCRC's credibility and highlights the type of pressure that its most impoverished signatory countries experience. Of course most signatory countries know that signing the UNCRC also means that they are likely to receive more funding from the UN aid agencies and NGOs that support child rights. But such aid is often not sustainable.

I think on balance that the schools and the orphanage were doing their best and were improving the children's opportunities in some respects, but they were certainly not conforming to all the requirements of the UNCRC. Some girls at the orphanage knew that by being there they could prolong their education before going out to work, and most still had contact with their families. Children at the school catering to the visually impaired were provided with educational and vocational training and, most importantly, the chance to mix with their peers and thus experience more fulfilled friendships than they might have had if they had stayed in their original communities and had no contact with other people in a similar position to themselves. The very fact of moving to the capital and living among friends who were also visually impaired while receiving some of their teaching from adults who were both visually impaired and making a success of their lives as teachers was likely to be self-empowering. Yet when I discussed some of my findings among the visually impaired children with the director of the child rights–focused NGO I had briefly worked for, she told me that "they clearly do not understand integrated education policy" and went on to heavily criticize the program for visually impaired children. In fact, the UNCRC very clearly states that children should be integrated into mainstream society to the extent that is possible. It does not call for absolute integration on an equal footing. In this case the director of the NGO was calling for full integration of all students and misquoting from the UNCRC to add weight to her own and therefore her agency's agenda.

Unlike this NGO director, I retained a level of optimism about children's experiences in both settings because I believe that the real mark of success rested on whether the children I met felt better off than they would have felt had their institutions not existed. As I show earlier in this chapter, girls and boys in the orphanage were quite realistic about the advantages that being at the orphanage gave them in terms of receiving an education and putting off the necessity of working full-time. Students attending the school for the visually impaired likewise were learning a profession that would give them some professional standing in the wider communities from which they had come and would give them more opportunities to be self-fulfilled members of society who could do something to support themselves when necessary.

# Eight

# Institutional Life and Children's Coping Strategies

The first times that I visited both the reform school and the orphanage are permanently etched on my mind because on both occasions, as I arrived, the children, dressed in formal pale blue uniform shirts and navy trousers, huddled together for mutual support and peered at me suspiciously. This was not a reaction I was used to, and I found it puzzling. On both days the weather was wet and cold, and I thought the children looked worn out and miserable. But I quickly learned that what I observed on both days was somewhat distorted by the particularly bad weather and the staff having anticipated and thus planned for my visit.

On my second visit to both institutions few of the children were in the standard uniform but instead wore their own clothing. They told me that they only wore uniforms reluctantly, when outside visitors were expected. I also discovered that the anxiety I had sensed most sharply in the orphanage was because of the younger children's fear that I was visiting with the intention of adopting one of them. So my initial impressions of the children had been based on the atmosphere created by having an unfamiliar adult in their midst rather than the institutional setting itself. From this experience I realized how crucial it is to become familiar with people one wishes to learn something about before prematurely coming to any conclusions about them. It convinced me of the merit of longitudinal fieldwork such as that adopted by traditional anthropologists, where observations are carried on over a number of years before any conclusions are drawn. The tendency of international development programs is to complete short-term fieldwork and research before finalizing the direction a project takes—such as rapid rural appraisal (Chambers 1992). My experiences in the field highlight the inadequacies of this type of approach.

As the days and months unfolded I began to appreciate the level at which children in both places were able to create their own highly effective informal support networks and thus find a way to deal with their experiences within the institutional settings. Most of the children I spent time with during fieldwork were, or had at some time lived, in an institutional setting. The boys who lived at the reform school received sentences of up to two years, while some of the children in the orphanage expected to live there until they were old enough to live independently or return to their families as wage earners. Meanwhile, the children who worked on the streets lived under the continual threat of being placed under arrest and being sent to a detainee or re-education center. I discovered that as groups were thrown together, they had evolved often quite sophisticated strategies for coping with their situation and supporting one another.

It is commonly assumed that institutional life offers people an automatically negative experience. Clearly, institutions are not ideal environments for children to grow up in, but individually they can vary enormously in the quality of support for their inmates. In this chapter I discuss some of the ways in which children provided each other with support and discuss some of the coping strategies children developed for themselves. I show that even in environments such as the reform school, which is immediately and visibly restrictive, children were successful at reclaiming some power over their bodies and creating their own informal support structure by establishing their own hierarchies, in this case based on gang support. As a result children were very capable of maintaining their own identities rather than allowing themselves to become submerged within a collective, adult-dominated, institutional identity. The children's methods were often highly effective but largely unrecognized by adults, who would have gained a stronger footing among the children during moments when they tried to help them if they had had access to, or been aware of, some of the children's self-created methods of coping with their circumstances.

I do not advocate children being left to their own devices; obviously, they need adult protection and guidance, but if we are to properly understand and respect the children we seek to support, it is important to recognize the value children attach to their own support networks, a factor that is often not sufficiently recognized.

### Institutions in Vietnam

In Vietnam it is still standard for people to be placed in institutions, and this is particularly the case for anyone who is viewed as a threat to the current order. This can include Buddhist leaders, people from different ethnic groups, even dissenting ex-Party members, journalists, and anyone who writes critically about the regime. As Templar writes, "The fear in the leadership and its undue obsession with stability had led to a massive exaggeration of the dangers of subversion from outside and from within the country. For this reason there are still unnecessary arrests, deportations and confinements of some people even religious leaders" (1999, 121).

As the capital city of Vietnam, Hanoi is the location of the nation's central research institutes and ministerial offices, some of which have completed studies on children who live on the street. Some of these reports are illuminating because they show a tendency to treat such children as criminals and to point toward institutionalization as one solution for dealing with them. For example, in his report on working children Chung legitimizes the use of reform schools as a means of controlling what he considers to be a social problem; he goes on to justify this argument by explaining, "They relieve themselves on the street and carry out many uncivilized activities . . . there are lazy people who consider going begging as a form of earning a living . . . the community of street people in general and beggars in particular has caused negative effects on the life of the capital city" (1992, 102). Chung, writing for the Ministry of Labor, Industry, and Social Affairs of the Government of Vietnam, places blame with children or their parents for adopting unorthodox lifestyles. And by making sweeping and unsubstantiated claims of unacceptable behavior, his report also presents the children as stereotypically antisocial, an institutional attitude that

I argue does little to help them or encourage the provision of effective remedial programs.

## Institutionalizing Children

Placing children in large institutional settings is generally considered outdated in the West. Over the last three decades, large children's homes have been progressively closed down so that across Western Europe and North America such institutions are mainly phenomena of the past. Even during the latter part of the nineteenth century, Dr. Thomas Barnardo, the founder of Barnardo's, the British-based children's charity, was arguing that boarding orphan children out to families was preferable to raising them in institutional settings. Today family-oriented care is generally considered preferable to bringing children up in an institutional setting. But this does not necessarily mean that the number of children living in institutions is on the decline. According to the U.S. Department of Health and Human Services, the number of American children living in institutional settings rose from 442,000 in 1992 to 550,000 in 2000. When I first started visiting both the orphanage and reform school in Vietnam I felt that I was stepping back in time.

### Common Traits of Institutions

In his work on institutions, Irving Goffman writes that "all aspects of life are conducted in the same place and under the same single authority. Each phase of the member's daily activity is carried out in the immediate company of a large batch of others, all of whom are treated alike and required to do the same thing together" (1961, 17). Some of Goffman's observations are relevant to both the orphanage and the reform school. Both institutions worked to a timetable, which should not be surprising given the numbers of children involved, and because of the numbers of children involved most activities were, by their very nature, communal. Children ate together at long tables and slept in communal bedrooms either on bunk beds or on long raised platforms. Children were surrounded by other children on a daily basis and rarely had the opportunity to be by themselves. But while I was struck by the lack of privacy, in this respect at least their lifestyle was no different from that of people living in the wider community. Vietnamese people generally consider it an oddity to want to live alone and in isolation from other people, and the routines of life that I observed reinforce this belief. Many Vietnamese families sleep on communal beds, so most of the children were doing exactly as they would if they lived with their families. It is also still common practice for another family member to move in with a lone relative, or for the lone person to be invited to live with other family members. When a Vietnamese friend of mine went to study in Germany and her mother was going to be left alone, my friend's cousin was sent to live with her mother for company. So while Goffman's work on institutional settings is of significance, some of what he has to say in relation to the oddity of doing all activities in the company of other people is culturally specific and not relevant outside Western Europe and North America.

### Misinterpreting Children's Behavior

One of my early mistakes was to conclude that in comparison with Western children, Vietnamese children's behavior lacks spontaneity: that they are physically restrained and controlled by their lowly position in what I perceived as an overtly hierarchical society. Because young children who lived on my street were always held in someone's arms, and because they often looked so solemn, I wondered whether they were ever encouraged to be as extroverted as some Western children can be. By the time a year had passed I had seen enough Vietnamese children in different settings to appreciate that the constraints placed on them are simply different from those generally placed on Western children. My initial mistake had been to assume that there is a universal norm for bringing up children, rather than that this aspect of life, like so many others, is shaped by the cultural norms of the particular society. There is a tendency to conclude, as did William Keeson, another scholar doing research in China, that children who are this controlled in school and in the company of adults are therefore "nonaggressive, compliant, unfearful and without obvious symptoms of anxiety or tension" (1975, 11). I think Keeson's observations are based on misinterpretations similar to those that I made when I first observed the behavior of children in my neighborhood and at the orphanage. Perhaps if he had been able to spend longer with the children and observe them alone among their peers, he would have drawn a different set of conclusions, as I later did.

Similarly, in an NGO report based on a master's thesis on psychological, social, and cultural needs of Vietnamese children, Marcus Bjork concludes,

"Children in Vietnam are, in general, conceptualized as passive objects, not as individuals with special rights and needs"(1997, 10) Like the NGO that supported his study, Bjork is a strong advocate for the UNCRC, using his observation of what he presumes to be childhood passivity to support an argument for Vietnam's move toward fully upholding the UNCRC. In the report he states, "In Vietnam, with its profound Confucian tradition, the idea of empowering the children, and treating them as active subjects, as individuals with knowledge and rights must be almost revolutionary. . . . It will take some time to change and modify these concepts" (ibid., 58).

Confucius taught that it is important for a child to learn how to be respectful and obedient to elders. Although some aspects of Confucianism are influential in Vietnam it is wrong to assume, as Bjork seems to have done, that the Confucian value system has an overriding influence over all Vietnamese children's lives. Perhaps because of this very general expectation, outsiders new to Vietnam are likely to misunderstand or overemphasize the implications of what they see. In her work on Chinese childhood, Sing Lau likewise warns the reader that "there can be too much emphasis on Confucius" (1996, 35), and that "beyond the seemingly perfect face . . . children do manifest many problems of growing up. Suffice to say, gangs, juvenile delinquency, and other self destructive antisocial behaviors are becoming daily items of local and international news" (ibid., 39).

Goffman's seminal critique of the asylum shows how institutions can shape and reconfirm a resident's condition. He argues that the institutional setting is one place in which people become so isolated from the outside that a new way of existing is created. Although I use his theory in support of some of my observations in both the reform school and the orphanage, I recognize, as he does, that an orphanage is not a total institution. For example, Goffman defines an institution as a place "symbolized by the barrier to social intercourse with the outside and to departure that is often built right into the physical plant" (1961, 4); this is only sometimes relevant to orphanages. This definition is, however, of relevance to the reform school, in which children had to stay until their sentence had been completed.

### Isolation

During the time I spent with children in the reform school, I was continually reminded of their isolation and the extent to which they had been physically removed from mainstream society. They were always eager to hear news about Hanoi and often reminisced about their previous lifestyles. On hot days some would talk about going swimming in the city's lakes and eating ice cream, or playing with friends and eating particular delicacies. Sometimes during class time when the children were particularly disheartened, their teacher and NGO worker Chinh put the schoolbooks to one side and the boys instead discussed what they would do first on leaving the school. Simple pleasures such as eating noodle soup on the street or drinking some iced coconut were among the most popular desires.

All of these children felt distinctly different from those living in wider society. Children who came in from the immediate community to play on the orphanage playground equipment tended not to mingle with the children living there. The children from the orphanage had a tendency to hold back and to be quite subservient in their dealings with such children. At the time I was upset on their behalf, because by being so reluctant to take charge of their own play area they were showing how little confidence they had in their ability to mingle with the children from the surrounding community. I would watch as children from the neighborhood came into the play area and took the swings away from them, or told them to stop playing on the slide. When this happened the children from the orphanage would group together and silently observe the neighborhood children, or disappear inside the main building. On one of my visits in February 1998, a neighborhood boy asked me why I bothered to visit the orphanage so regularly. When I said that it was to spend time with the children there, he shrugged his shoulders dismissively as if to say "why bother?" and then ran off to join his friends in their domination of the swing area.

### Institutional Uniformity

In the reform school, all the boys were initially stripped of their clothes and personal objects and given a new short haircut, as if their past and, most significantly, their individual identities, were being symbolically removed. In Michel Foucault's discourse on discipline and punishment he puts forward the view that punishments are designed to change the behavior of a person: "Of course, we pass sentence, but the sentence is not in direct relation to the crime. It is quite clear that for us it functions as a way of treating a criminal. We punish, but this is a way of saying that we wish to obtain a cure" (1975, 22).

In December 1997, when I visited the orphanage for the first time, the children were wearing pale blue shirts and navy trousers that were the same design as the ones worn by the boys in the reform school when I first visited that institution. Because all the children were wearing a uniform on my first visits I presumed that this was mandatory and that it was done in part to give the children a sense of communal identity. Goffman refers to this type of institutional ruling as exaggerating the loss of individual identity: "At admission loss of identity equipment can prevent the individual from presenting his usual image of himself to others" (1961, 30). Under some circumstances it also further undermines a person's sense of self and worth, particularly if the rules about wearing a uniform are not consistently applied. Thus, on later visits to the reform school I found that the children who most stood out among their peers were those who were still in uniform when the majority of children were wearing their own clothes sent from home. For whatever reason, these children did not have any additional clothing, and their lack of their own apparel further accentuated their vulnerability and made them more obviously a part of (rather than symbolically separate from) the institution. Thang was one such boy: throughout the two years I was there he always wore the government-distributed pale blue shirt and navy trousers. As well as further depriving him of his own identity this also meant that he, like the few other boys who only owned the school uniform, was often colder in the winter than those who owned coats and sweaters. On one occasion in January 1999 I turned up at the school with bags of clothing donated from members of the expatriate community, but the boys retained few of them, and within a month the boys who had needed them most were again wearing only their thin and unsubstantial uniforms. None of them were comfortable telling me where the clothes had gone, and I guessed that staff members had probably taken them home for their own families, or, more optimistically, that some of the boys had traded separate items of clothing over the walls to local shopkeepers for food and cigarettes.

## Children Taking Control

The anthropologist Mary Douglas argues that society informs how we are placed as individuals and that this is closely linked to how we physically represent our bodies: "Each social environment sets limits to the possibilities of remoteness or nearness of other humans, and limits the costs and rewards of group allegiance and conformity to social categories" (1973, 15). I did not originally set out to look at local attitudes toward self-identity and the physical body, but I realized the importance of doing so once I observed that some of the boys in the reform school were responding to their lack of freedom by addressing their feelings and gaining some control over what was happening to them by gathering into close-knit groups and using a tattoo common to the group to establish a collective identity. Seeing this, and later discussing the meanings that they attached in various ways to their bodies, gave me access to the thoughts and feelings of children who otherwise I do not think would have been so open with me about how they were coping with life inside the reform school. Children in the orphanage did not have tattoos but did form close-knit groups; in addition they created their own buddy system in which an older child permanently attached him- or herself to a younger child in order to "parent" the younger child. Like the children who worked on the street, boys in the reform school also established family-type networks from which adults were excluded. Their intimate thoughts and reactions to that environment remained solely within a domain that outsiders would always have difficulty entering. However, by being there over a long period I was able to note the way that children grouped together and how their separate worlds interconnected.

Because of the restrictive life in the reform school, boys were often prone to depression, but the repressive atmosphere of the school and, more generally, belonging to a society in which the individual sense of self was less pronounced than it would be in a Western context made it difficult for the boys to talk about their feelings. On one occasion in the middle of winter I noticed that Ly, a boy in Jack's class who was sitting in front of me, was shaking from the cold. He had told me earlier that they had had no breakfast that morning. When Jack came up to him to ask a question, he was unable to respond, and as Jack turned away I saw Ly's eyes fill with tears. Children were not encouraged to cry, and if other children had seen this show of emotion they might have laughed at him rather than show support. Without thinking, I took Ly's hand and led him outside. We sat for a long time on the steps, and he told me that he was going crazy with the boredom and sadness of living there. He missed his family and could see no end to the eighteen months that stretched in front of him. He felt alone and abandoned but was unable to share these feelings directly or gain comfort from his peers.

### Songs and Poems as an Outlet

While Jack's class was small and offered lessons to eight of the most able students, Chinh's group was much larger, with more than twenty students. Partly because Jack was already so close to the boys in his class it was easier for me to gain an affinity with the boys in Chinh's class. His class was crowded, and they were more likely to relax during lessons than Jack's students, because the teacher was physically unable to monitor them as closely. Once the boys got to know me they would sometimes beckon me over during class time to admire their drawings and poems. Talking during class could be distracting, however, so boys usually waited until the break to present their work. Once, Thiep, who was sitting up near the front in Chinh's class, pulled on my sleeve to gain my attention. He had written in his book, "Looking for a good life is difficult." Once I had read it and checked that I had picked up the right nuances in Vietnamese, we simply nodded our heads at each other in agreement. He did not want to discuss his reasons for writing the piece. I think that he simply wanted me to know what he was thinking. Our encounter lasted less than five minutes but was memorable because it occurred during my first six months in the school. I was at a stage when I had begun to recognize how important some of the boys' private support systems such as tattoos were to them, but I did not know what they meant, and I had begun to feel that the boys were never going to relax in my company.

For a three-month period a traditional Vietnam poem was written all over the boys' book covers in Chinh's class:

> The moon promised to commit love to the clouds,
> I will always love you
> Now the moon's still there for you,
> But you turn away, gone now.

Boys would show this to me, then sigh and say that they were thinking of their homes, or members of their family. Diep and Thang, two of the boys in Jack's class, got hold of and attached the poem to a picture of a famous

Vietnamese actress, and if it was seen they would quickly hide it out of sight in mock embarrassment. After I had been visiting the reform school for a year I had to go back to England for a two-month visit. When I told the boys in Jack and Chinh's class about my imminent departure they were excited on my behalf, because, as Thiep and Mau, who sat in the seat in front of him, solemnly reminded me, I would be seeing my family. For most of them that was an enviable prospect, but also an important responsibility. By the afternoon the boys in Chinh's class had written a poem, which they slipped into my hand as I said goodbye:

> Do not forget
> Always remember
> For the memory will linger
> So when all is gone
> It is not forgotten.

I was deeply touched by this gift, and from then on kept the piece of paper tucked into my purse, only to lose it when the purse was stolen by a new boy on my return to the reform school.

### Tattoos

By January 1997 I had worked out which boys informally ran the reform school: they were all in Jack's English class and the majority of children in that group wore a "T" tattoo on their middle finger. Of all the boys in Jack's class, Thang was the one with whom I naturally got along best and with whom I shared a similar sense of humor. I also admired his gentle manner with the younger children. I knew the tattoo was important, and when I realized that he too was sporting the "T" tattoo I tentatively asked him if he could tell me about its meaning. He refused immediately, saying that adults were not to know about the tattoos that the boys chose to wear in the school.

But why should the children I asked have opened up to me and told me what their tattoos meant? Choosing to identify privately with a particular group of people is an essential part of human existence. It is what we all do to varying degrees to set us apart from others. If we find ourselves in an unfamiliar situation, every one of us is quick to seek out others and find common connections. The boys in the reform school needed to maintain

the secrets of their gangs because by doing so they created a familial setting for themselves in a difficult environment and, more importantly, regained some control over their thoughts and bodily actions. Living in the
reform school meant that the boys' freedom of expression was severely limited. They could not come and go as they pleased, and parents' visiting hours
were restricted to Sundays. In these respects the school resembled a prison.

Foucault in his discourse on prison life notes that in the nineteenth century people came to examine criminals' dress and faces and that "convicts
themselves responded to this game, displaying their misdeeds: this was one
of the functions of tattooing, a vignette of their deeds of fate" (1975, 260).
The isolating and emotionally repressive regime imposed upon the children
in the reform school similarly inspired tattoos.

After I left Vietnam, reading about Western prison tattooing and the
choices made by Western prisoners has led me to conclude that in that context the tattoos were done for different reasons than those that impelled
the Vietnamese reform school boys. Unlike Western convicts, none of the
boys was tempted to use a tattoo to record the deed that put him inside the
reform school. Rather, it was used as a means of identifying the individual
as part of a family group, group motifs being far more popular than any chosen by an individual. Writing about tattooing practices in Polynesia, Alfred
Gell argues, "As a technical means of modifying the body, tattooing made
possible the realization of a particular type of 'subjection' that in turn allowed
for the elaboration and perpetuation of social and political relationships of
distinct kinds" (1993, 3). Boys relished the success they had in defying the
rules of the reform school by drawing tattoos. Samuel Steward found something similar among the gang members that he observed: "A tattoo for the
gang members or the delinquent was the visible sign of their rebellion, their
manliness, or their affiliation with the stratum that was in revolt" (1990, 113).
The practice affirmed that they could create an area of freedom within their
restrictive environment: As Gell says, "The description of tattooing practices
becomes, inevitably, a description of the wider institutional forms within
which tattooing was embedded" (1993, 1).

More significantly, as I was to discover, the tattoos the boys chose symbolized loss and wrongs that they were experiencing. The meaning attributed to each tattoo was a carefully protected secret. It allowed the boys some
ownership over their bodies and minds. The practice of group tattooing thus

gave the boys a distinctive and yet secret identity, enabling the group to express a strength of purpose and passively resist the attempts of the institution to treat them in a uniform manner:

> "A tattoo is an affirmation: that this body is
>     Yours
> to have and enjoy while you're here
>     Nobody else can
>     control what you do with it. That's why
>     tattooing is
> such a big thing in prison: it's an
>     expression of freedom."
> Don Ed Hardy (Hall 1997, 5)

It was not until the summer, when they began to strip down to their shorts, that I appreciated what large areas of the boys' bodies were tattooed. The guards banned the practice, but somehow the boys continued to practice their art. They used a mixture of ink, dirt, and blood, and I learned that two boys who were particularly good artists served the others. In fact, when one of the artists left, the quality of tattooing in the school fell dramatically. In the West the wearing of a monochromatic tattoo used to be an indicator that a person had been in prison. Because this style of tattoo is now in fashion outside the prison environment, in the future it may not immediately have that association. In the case of the boys, some of the tattoos had quite a rudimentary design, and they were sometimes ashamed of tattoos that they did not like. I frequently caught Thiep, a boy in Chinh's class, trying to scrape a tattoo off the skin on his hand using the point of a compass. Eventually it became badly infected.

The adults who cared for the children were more interested in preventing children from developing individual freedom of expression than in understanding how each child was coping with the prisonlike environment or the change in lifestyle. When children entered the reform school they were at first asked to wear a uniform and their personal belongings were removed. Most prisons adopt this approach. Gresham Sykes writes of a prison in America, "In the prison the obvious symbols of status have been largely stripped away, and we find new hierarchies with new symbols coming into play" (1958, xiv). Writing about prison tattoos in the United States, Margo DeMello notes that "these tattoos usually look more primitive than tattoos created with a machine. . . . Thus not only does the method of execution signify that the wearer is of a low socio-economic status in that he cannot afford, or has no access to professional tattoos, but the tattoos themselves are on extremely public areas of the body where they can be easily read by others" (1993, 10).

The same arguments did not apply when I was in Vietnam. I never came across a tattoo machine while living there, and it would be unlikely that anyone would have this equipment. It would have been expensive to buy, and most local people would not be able to afford the price of a tattoo that would make such an investment economically viable for the tattoo artist. Therefore, anyone who had a tattoo would have had someone draw it directly on his body. Obviously some artists would be more proficient than others, but most tattoos did not achieve the perfect line that a machine might. Nor would having a tattoo in a highly visible location necessarily signify that a person was of low social standing. During Vietnam's wars with France, the United States, and China, many men chose to have a sun pattern etched into the base of their thumb on the outside of the hand, and on this they had inscribed the year they were born so that if they should die, they could be more easily identified. On seeing this I wondered why people did not choose to write their full birth date. It was perhaps likely that these men did not know their exact birthday. In the past only the year of a person's birth was remembered, because until very recently it was common practice for every Vietnamese person to become a year older at the start of the lunar new year.

I was fascinated by the range of tattoos the boys wore and over time began to see a pattern in the choices they made. Jack's students, who were the most influential in the informal network, had chosen one style, while another group had chosen a different design. Distinctive tattoos distinguished groups, and I realized that if I were to learn anything about the private world of the boys I would have to gain their trust to the point that they spoke freely about these tattoos. The main objective of the guards was to teach children how to conform to the role of obedient citizen. When the children took visibly obvious charge of their bodies through the use of tattoos or by writing poems, this covertly challenged the guards' authority.

Paradoxically, it also permanently linked the children to that period in their lives and provided a stronger bond to each other. The tattoo would remain on their bodies as a mark of identity, reminding them and perhaps also indicating to others where they had once been: "Becoming tattooed in prison . . . plays a crucial role in creating the convict's sense of identity in relation to the prison establishment" (DeMello 1993, 10).

Once I discovered the boys' tattoos, my ethnography took a new direction, and I began to recognize the importance of the practice of tattooing. Through observing boys in the reform school I came to believe that children were quite adept at setting up their own support systems and, more importantly, that adults often underestimate the importance to children of establishing informal systems in any cultural context. Furthermore, an unorthodox method such as offering each other an emotional outlet through tattooing was probably very effective and had the added attraction of being a self-generated and therefore empowering response to their situation. It was a method of providing mutual support that goes largely unrecognized in mainstream society.

### The Meaning of Tattoos

After Thang's rebuff, I did not attempt to introduce the subject again, but instead made mental notes of who wore which tattoo. Seven boys in Jack's class wore the "T," and they had the most extensive authority over other children in the reform school. In Chinh's class the boys who had most influence wore a dot on the web of skin between their thumb and first finger. Some of the younger boys had the word "nho" written from the base of their thumb to the edge of their wrist. "Nho" means "to remember," but what was it they did not want to forget? After a while, although I was disappointed that that area of their lives remained closed to me, I lost my initial urge to understand and decided to be patient and bide my time. I focused instead on aspects of their lives they were happy to share, such as their poems and songs.

One day in June, seven months after I had returned from a trip to England, I was at the reform school as usual and was sitting in Chinh's class. New boys had been released from the lockups, and because it was a sunny day everyone was quite relaxed and unusually cheerful. By this stage in my visits I was comfortable with the boys and was particularly close to children in Chinh's class, so it was normal for me to leave my bag in the room when I wandered around during their breaks. But during third period I realized that my purse had been stolen. I was annoyed and upset but decided to address the problem from within the informal network rather than the formal one, by going to the boys in Jack's class rather than to the guards (who would no doubt have punished all the boys in the school). So I sat down with Thang and his group at the end of morning class and told them what had happened. I reassured them that I would not tell their guards anything and also said I did not want to know who had done it but that I would like my family photos returned.

All the boys appeared outraged, and when Jack and I returned from lunch Thang took me to their classroom. He and Diep sat me down and with serious expressions explained that they had found the thief but that my purse and money were gone. Although they said that they had punished the person they would not tell me how they had done this, and I never found out. To compensate me and to encourage me to continue my visits they had conferred with their friends and had decided to tell me the meaning behind their tattoos. This was a memorable turning point in my relationship with boys at the reform school. I remember feeling overwhelmed and emotional: not only were they demonstrating a willingness to trust me but Thang had not forgotten my earlier, quite casual and one-time request to understand the meaning of his tattoo. As I had guessed, their tattoos represented feelings of loss and a desire to symbolize their lack of freedom.

*The "T" Tattoo: Strength and Optimism.* The group that had adopted the "T" tattoo, and of which Thang was presently leader, was most influential among other boys, and this tattoo was exclusively owned and privately understood among themselves. The choice of the letter "T" represented a rhyme: "Tien, tinh, tai, tu, toi," which translates to "money, love, freedom, prison, I." Put together, this meant, "For now I am in prison, I have no freedom, love, or money, but when I have my freedom I will have money and love." They went on to explain that "tai" means "Phai co dau oc kiem duoc ra tien" ("You have to have a head and brain to make money"). This was an optimistic choice; although it recognized the immediate losses consequent to being locked up, it also focused on the future and on how things would improve once boys in this group had regained their freedom. It also served as a reminder that they would need to use their brains to make money. Thus the tattoo encouraged the wearers to find strength in adversity and reflected their ability to situate themselves at the top of the informal hierarchy within the school. In adverse surroundings they had gained a sense of empowerment among the other boys, and it was therefore no coincidence that they were grouped together in the top class in the reform school.

Some children chose to wear individual tattoos, or no tattoo. Two of the boys in Tang's class had chosen not to be tattooed, and although they were not excluded they were always seated at the back of the classroom and were physically on the periphery of the main group. When I later asked Diep, one of the two boys, why he had opted not to be tattooed he said that the group had invited him to be tattooed but that he did not want to be physically marked with a sign that he had been in prison. Thiep, who was in Chinh's class, had an ace of spades design on his middle finger and told me that it meant the same as the dot tattoo, but that he had wanted to wear a different design from the others. His words prompted me to look at the hands of Vietnamese men more carefully, and in doing so I discovered that a man who worked as a motorbike taxi driver at the end of my street, and with whom I always tried to ride because he was a safe driver, had been in a re-education center in the 1970s. He also wore the "T" tattoo on his middle finger and ascribed to it the same meaning that the boys in the reform school did. I therefore concluded that this was a commonly used tattoo. Having chosen it, the boys had knowingly labeled themselves as convicts and, later, ex-convicts, thus identifying themselves in a broader context. Theirs was a shared pride in this symbol, and by choosing it they defied the stigma that society placed on them for having been in a reform center.

*The Dot Tattoo: Alone in the Universe.* Some of the children in Chinh's class had a dot tattoo in the web that stretched between the thumb and first finger. They were in a weaker and inferior position within the informal network, and their symbol was more discreet than the "T" tattoo and had less positive feeling attached to it. The dot was symbolic of the person, and the web of skin represented the universe stretching outwards. The dot showed the person as isolated and removed from the rest of humanity: standing in the middle of the universe he was alone This group was less cohesive than the group who adopted a "T" tattoo. Perhaps part of the reason for this was that there were far more students in Chinh's class than in Jack's, and children were more likely to change loyalties and to feel insecure in their friendships. Nevertheless, those with the dot had a dominant presence in the class. Seven boys had the dot tattoo, which made it the most popular choice for the class as a whole. The group was disparate and far more private than the "T" group about their reasons for having chosen that symbol.

*The "Remember" Tattoo: Reminder of the Mother Figure.* The last most commonly used tattoo in the reform school was found among boys who were younger, aged between twelve and fourteen. The word "nho" ("remember") was used in association with their mothers. It did not identify an individual as part of a group but carried deep feeling among the boys who chose it. It represented loss of family and isolation from people they cared for, but it also served as a reminder of the ideal mother figure. Two of the children who had chosen it told me that their mothers had died; for them it served as a memorial to the person they had loved.

Once I knew what these three most popular tattoos meant and, more importantly, did not divulge the information to the guards, a new way of communicating was opened up to me. I could ask boys how they felt, referring to their chosen tattoos. I became closer to some of them because I respected and took seriously the meaning of their tattoos.

### Tattoos and Group Identity

Tattoos were important in giving some children greater control over their situation. A tattoo identified its wearer as part of a group that provided mutual support and comfort. When a child was invited to wear a particular tattoo, his life took on a different meaning in the reform school. Scheper-Hughes and Lock refer to "the concept of the social skin to express the imprint of social categories on the body self" (1987, 25). Having the tattoo allowed some of the boys, particularly those in the "T" group, to operate in a way analogous to being within a family. The leader was expected to protect the members, and the second in command was chosen by the leader to safeguard the group's interests. When I first started visiting the reform school, the boys in that group all showed kindness to each other and were protective toward other children. Membership was offered to a small group, all of whom were in Jack's class, but the group's responsibilities encompassed every other child in the school.

This practice meant a great deal to them. Children reclaimed some power from having flouted the institution's laws, by showing that they themselves could determine how to treat their bodies. Tattooing was perhaps a popular choice for these children who were already considered to be rebellious social evils by a society that sought to constrain its members both bodily and emotionally under the guise of Communist philosophy. By tattooing themselves, some of them, particularly the "T" group, established a sense of group identity from which they drew great strength. This identity also provided an internal sense of group culture, enabling them to rebut the external pressure to conform to societal norms rather than their own self-devised rule system.

The way that people understand themselves as individuals and take control over their bodies is influenced by the culture in which they live. While Vietnamese children have physical constraints placed upon them in formal settings, they do sometimes take control of their bodies and are quite free and unrestrained when at play. I learned far more about children's experiences through indirect means, through their reference to headaches or through their use of tattoos. What they chose to tell me reinforced my conviction that Vietnamese children do not feel as comfortable dealing with their experiences individually as they do dealing with them as part of a larger collective. This can be seen as a cultural norm for Vietnam and reinforces my general thesis that an understanding of such cultural norms is essential before outsiders can hope to offer effective support services to any part of the local community.

### A Desire for Reform

The general feeling among the aid workers I spoke to in the wider community was that both the reform school and the orphanage would benefit from external support to make them feel less institutional. While I continue to be very critical of the institutionalization of children, most of my initial concerns about children's welfare in the reform school and orphanage turned out to be groundless. Evidence I have drawn upon throughout this chapter indicates that it was not the institutions that were negatively shaping children's lives so much as the social conditions they had left behind, the daily struggle that their families had with poverty, and wider society's perception that these children were either deviant or vulnerable and in dire need, as some of the largest child-focused NGOs considered them to be.

I also found that the desire to make improvements in both institutions was not isolated to a few international NGO workers but was felt by Vietnamese workers at both places. In fact, the improvements that took place in the orphanage were instigated by local staff and in the reform school by local staff with the support of their affiliated NGO, rather than as a result of any pressure from the wider NGO community and particularly those organizations working in the field of child rights.

Children in both the reform school and orphanage undoubtedly missed living in a family setting. Growing up in a supportive family environment would unquestionably have been preferable, but contrary to my original expectations, there were some advantages to be had from living in these institutions. Children at both the orphanage and reform school were receiving a basic education. In the reform school the NGO subsidized the teachers' salaries, and because of this children and their parents did not have to pay any unofficial money to individual teachers. When Ly left the school, for example, he warmly thanked Jack, Chinh, and Tung for having provided him with a free education. He explained that he had really enjoyed the routine of life in the school and that he would miss having the freedom to attend class.

## Nine

# Children on the Global Margins?

When I started doing fieldwork, I expected the lives of the children I met to be uniformly hard and bleak. However, while most of the children experienced hardships and day-to-day difficulties, they did not fit my stereotype of the rundown and deprived child of the South who is so often represented in Western literature and the media. The children I met during fieldwork struck me as being tenacious, highly adaptable, and hardworking. Yet because of their lifestyles and the fact that most of them did not live with their families, they were assumed to live on the margins of mainstream society. The Vietnamese government sought to bring such children back into the fold by returning them to their families in the countryside or locking them up in re-education and reform centers. Meanwhile, the dominant NGOs campaigned for such children to have their rights met under the auspices of the UNCRC and also became involved in the government programs returning working children to rural areas. These concerned adults were preoccupied with focusing on the ways in which these children needed to conform to their adult- (and often Western-) centered view of what makes for an acceptable childhood. They were not interested in working to these children's strengths, so they focused instead on their difficulties and ignored any contribution the children might be making to society.

My firsthand exposure to these children leads me to believe that they were not living on the margins of their society. Any money they earned was spent within the local economy, and the aspirations they held to further their education or to have families of their own placed them firmly in mainstream society. They were actively involved in mainstream activities, such as attending school and visiting family members, and in some cases showing themselves to be highly responsible in their commitment to sharing their earnings with their parents and siblings. Yet I seemed to be one of only a few people who saw the children in such a positive light. In general they were treated either as social outcasts or as innocents in need of immediate rescue from their plight. If they worked they were arrested, if they had family in rural areas they might be forcibly repatriated. If they lived in the orphanage their contemporaries who lived with their families might consider them second-class citizens. The Vietnamese sometimes referred to these children as social evils, the product of a society being corrupted by the West, while the dominant international NGOs generally treated such children as if their childhoods had been stolen by a society that was failing them, in consequence setting up adult-led and family-oriented intervention programs to help different externally imposed categories of children: the "street child," the "girl child," the "working child."

The children's own voices were absent from these two quite polarized perspectives on childhood, and few individuals or organizations ever showed any positive regard for individual children and the coping strategies they had developed. After spending two years among the children who appear in this book, I cannot subscribe to the dominant view that led to them being either infantilized or demonized. It seems to me that such a view can only come from individuals or organizations who are blindly adhering to a dogma that bears little resemblance to the real world and real issues that these children have to cope with on a daily basis.

### Children Take Control

Jo Boyden and Gillian Mann point out that:

> some children are better able to manage stress because of disposition or
> temperament. Thus, some of the protective factors such as resourceful-
> ness, curiosity, a goal for which to live, and a need and ability to help oth-
> ers are largely matters of temperament and coping style. Generally

children who are able to remain hopeful about the future, are flexible and
adaptable, possess problem-solving skills and actively try to assume control over their lives are less likely to be vulnerable than those who passively accept their condition . . . children who have experienced approval,
acceptance and opportunities for mastery are far more likely to be resilient than those who have been subject to humiliation, rejection or failure.
(2000, 8)

Within their immediate world in Hanoi, the work some children did was
valued by their immediate community and gave them a sense of self-worth
because they were able to improve their lot in a way that they would not
have done if they had stayed at home. Under present circumstances it might
be a family's most sensible choice to allow a child to migrate to the city to
earn money and hence possibly have a greater chance of getting an adequate
diet or perhaps an education. Some of the children I knew were keenly
aware of this and felt profoundly confident about the contribution they were
making to their families. These children challenged a commonly held idea
that their families have abandoned those who work on the streets. Thoa used
his earnings to assist younger siblings through school. Hai usually told foreigners that he was an orphan, but like Thoa he had immediate family who
were interested in his welfare. All of these boys had also established strong
links within their immediate community; they gained support from each
other and from adults in an informal network. These children's experiences
lead me to question Western-informed assumptions about street children.
The children I knew did not view their current lifestyle as fixed. The fact
that they were established in a group and received outside support dispels
the image that a child on the street is automatically lonely and vulnerable.

I reiterate one of my central points: blanket policies are incapable of responding adequately to the needs of the individual child and hence fail all
children. While getting to know these young people I was most struck by
their desire to maintain a high level of independence and control over their
lives. I noticed that they responded most successfully to adults who offered
them arm's-length support and did not try to contain them or ask them to
conform to a more accepted notion of childhood. Thus, Khoa was pleased
to be invited to have a permanent position shining shoes at a café. The café
staff looked out for him, and he in turn was promised regular customers

and made enough money to go to school in the afternoons. Hai, however, would probably have found Khoa's lifestyle too restrictive. Although I met Hai where he worked at least twice a week to go to a café or to chat I could never be sure that he would come at an agreed time. He might have over-slept, or be playing pool. And toward the end of my time in Hanoi it was more likely that he was too stoned to meet me. In fact he did not meet me to say good-bye, and later wrote saying he'd been sick and that he wanted to go to a rehab unit for heroin addicts. Clearly, his needs and his responses to his situation were very different from Khoa's.

Tan, who sold postcards alongside Hai, came from a family that lived on the outskirts of Hanoi. At some point in their childhood each of the boys in his family had sold postcards for a living, and this income had contributed to the cost of their schooling. From Tan's perspective he was following an established family tradition. During my last month in the city he told me how excited he was because his older brother was getting married. This brother had once worked on the streets as Tan did but now worked in a motorbike shop near his family home. Tan explained that it would soon be time for him to stop working on the streets and think about doing some kind of vocational training. He was focused and well supported by family and friends like Hai and the women who sold fruit near where he worked. This was not someone who would have benefited from the government re-patriation program, because he already had every intention of going home. Neither was he someone who would want to attend the counseling center set up by a child rights–focused NGO.

Conversely, someone like Hiep experienced more difficulties during the period that I knew him. He lost his coveted spot by the main lake in town and was subsequently sent back to the countryside; he quickly returned to the city because he did not feel that his mother could adequately support him. So much of his life was lacking the permanence and stability that some-one like Tan had, but like Tan his problems were poverty related, and if his mother had not been so poor she might have been able to support him. Hiep knew that he was better off on the streets, although this realization did not rest easily with him. Unlike Tan, Hiep had come into contact with the government repatriation team, which at that time was also supported by PLAN International, a child rights–focused NGO. By repatriating Hiep they were giving him the message first that his present life on the street was unacceptable and second that he should be living with supportive adult family members. But Hiep's family could not support him, so it was inevitable that he would return to the streets; once he did so, the police locked him up, albeit temporarily. He had no one to validate his life choices and praise his success at living independently. Nevertheless, he always tried to retain a level of optimism and was generous toward the people who assisted him. From my perspective, Hiep's level of resilience was inspirational.

Montgomery, Burr, and Woodhead point out that "the risk of adversity will be amplified by social attitudes that stigmatize the adversity and the children affected" (2003, 12). It is ironic that the very organizations that were so interested in offering children rights, and in this case the right to grow up in an adult-led family unit, were doing so in a piecemeal manner without preparing families for their children's homecoming and thus were contributing to the belittlement of some children and to their lack of confidence. Maybe, as Tim Bond suggests, these children should be treated with more respect and not forced to lead lives that were no longer possible or appropriate (1996, 2). Having spent time with these children, I feel their greatest difficulties arose from the negative attitudes of more privileged Vietnamese, the government's opposition to their presence on the streets, and from misplaced philanthropy and sympathy from well-intended but misinformed foreigners. These reactions ignore and belittle the talents and successes of the individual child and dismiss their informal contribution to the local economy, and, most significantly, the contribution that some of them make to their families in rural areas.

### Collective Responsibility

Initially, when I visited the reform school and orphanage I thought both places were considerably institutionalized. It was tempting at first sight to conclude that Vietnamese children have less independence and individual autonomy than their counterparts in the West. But after spending six months visiting the orphanage and two years visiting the reform school, I realized that my first impressions were based on lack of familiarity with the culture and, most importantly, with the children themselves. In reality, rather than having less autonomy I began to see that unexpected freedoms can be gained under the rules of a collective society and by using a different set of standards informed by local social practices. I am not arguing this point as a cultural relativist who considers it acceptable to tolerate local cultural practices out of respect for societal differences. As Paul Farmer and Nicole Gastineau point out, "Violations of human dignity are not to be accepted merely because they are buttressed by local ideology or long-standing tradition. But anthropology—in common with sociological and historical perspectives in general—allows us to place both human rights abuses and the discourses (and other responses) they generate in broader contexts" (2002, 657).

Once I started making regular visits to both the orphanage and reform school I began to understand more about how children in both environments took control of their lives. Contrary to my first impressions and what was written in some international NGO reports, these children were not passive receivers of adult-dictated attention (Bjork 1997). My fieldwork findings show that children set up their own informal networks and gained power over their bodies through group allegiances and in some cases through other bonding devices such as the use of tattoos.

In the orphanage I gained further insight into the impact of government policy on children's lived experience. Nearly all the children in that setting had one living and involved parent, which threw into question the notion that the term "orphan" has one universally applicable meaning. Before visiting the orphanage, the director of a child rights–focused NGO had spoken of the children in that setting as abandoned with partially involved parents or with no parents at all (interview by author, March 1997). As with the boys in the reform school, the children in the orphanage had their own noticeable informal support networks that adults were neither a part of nor particularly concerned with.

I believe that in some respects these Vietnamese children achieved greater autonomy than did their peers in the West. In formal settings with teachers the children were expected to behave with respect and obedience, but, in contrast and unlike in the West, when they were among themselves, older children were entrusted with the care of very young children without adults feeling a need to look out for them. Also, in the case of the reform school, guards sometimes encouraged boys to sort out their differences themselves within their informal hierarchy so that peace might be reestablished. These types of group behavior are a characteristic of the collectivist society, where all take responsibility for those around them.

Children in both the orphanage and on the streets had a level of physical freedom to come and go and roam their immediate community in a way that is becoming increasingly difficult for children in the West to do. Children in the West are increasingly growing up in the company of their adult minders: in the family home, a cocoon, a safe space in which the child is physically protected from the outside world. (Lee 2001, 72).

### Responding to the Needs of the Individual

I have established that the majority of children in this book, like children in other parts of the world, do not have lifestyles that fit an idealized Western model of childhood. On the face of it, the children I knew in Vietnam had much in common. Most did not live with their immediate families and some worked for a living. Regardless of these similarities, however, one of the most striking aspects of the fieldwork process was learning how different each child's life was from that of the next person, and how much each child's attitudes to life informed those differences. One child who worked on the streets was fundamentally different to the next in attitude and aspiration. For example, while Thoa and Binh earned a living shining shoes so that they could attend school on a daily basis and also send money home to their families in the countryside, Hai earned his money in the same way but spent his excess income on betting and smoking grass. He did not want to go to school and rarely visited his grandmother and younger brother, although he was proud of his brother's success in school and spoke highly of his grandmother. Phan Anh, the original informal leader at the reform school, was grateful for being sent to the school and as a result being given a chance to start his own motorbike repair service to support his grandmother. Thiep could see no benefit in being at the reform school and became so demoralized that he started to refer to himself as "bad" all the time. Ly, however, told Jack and me that the school had provided him with the most consistent classroom-based education he had ever had. Lan lived at the orphanage but was still close to her mother even though she had remarried and sent Lan to the orphanage so that she could bypass the two-child policy. Meanwhile Lan's friend Nguyet coped well with life in the orphanage only until her father died, and later felt more isolated in the orphanage and also among her extended family members. In short these children all coped with and adjusted to their circumstances differently, not only because of who they were but because although they might have seemed to live under the same basic conditions the circumstances that had got them there were often quite different. All this adds weight to my argument that attempting to help children by slotting them into very broad categories does not actually help them very much.

The children who appear in this book faced daily challenges and difficulties to which they often responded differently, so when a generalized approach was introduced to assist them it often failed. For example, while the reform school staff tried to re-educate children to the Communist doctrine, this did little to persuade children to change their ways. As I discussed in chapter 6, successful rehabilitation into mainstream society only began to happen when guards in the school eventually recognized this and followed the lead taken by their NGO partners by creating an outreach and follow-up program tailored to the needs of each child.

Like adults, children face many challenges to their lives. They may come from impoverished backgrounds, be caught up in a civil war, or, on a more mundane level, their parents might have had an acrimonious divorce or they might be experiencing bullying at school. Whatever the circumstances, most people experience adversity at some point in their lives. No one should assume that childhood adversities are more pronounced in the South: children in the West also experience difficulties. The crucial point is not so much the particularities of the adversities experienced by each person but his or her reaction to that situation: in other words it depends on each person's level of resilience. "Situations that threaten one child's well-being may not pose the same risk to another child, and in a different context, may be seen as posing no risk at all. Both the adversities that children face and their vulnerability or resilience in the face of those adversities must be understood by looking closely at the specific circumstances of individual children as well as at broader social and cultural factors" (Montgomery, Burr, and Woodhead 2003, 3). So it must be understood that risks to children's well-being do not inevitably follow from an impoverished environment or from disturbed family relationships.

## The Applicability of the UNCRC in Vietnam

The Vietnamese government and its supporters are eager to criticize and punish people (in this case children) who fail to follow acceptable lifestyles, but at the same time, it has committed itself to full adoption of the UNCRC, which imposes an international standard of behavior on children. This means that conflicts of interest may arise in relation to how the government decides "marginalized" people should be treated.

Respecting a child's right to live and work on the street might be viewed as risky. In the West, child-protection professionals choose to intervene on the grounds that they are serving the child's best interests even when, as is sometimes the case, the child protests that decision. This raises one of the central dilemmas of the Western-driven child rights initiative. At what point should we fully support a child's desire to lead the life he or she wants? This dilemma often amounts to children not being given real rights: they are offered rights that suit the adults involved. For that reason alone it is important to spend time among children to discover something about their lived experiences.

Some Vietnamese government policies conflict with a broad interpretation of the UNCRC agenda. Thus children in the reform school were unjustly treated; for example, from what they said, they often did not have any trial in front of a fair court before receiving their sentences. This was not a problem peculiar to these children. In 1998, for example, I met an American lawyer who had come to Vietnam to teach English and ended up working with Vietnamese lawyers who had established a small support group for people who had been sentenced to prison without trial. He said that the work he was doing was highly risky given the government's human rights record. The difficult subject of bribes for police also raises questions about the arbitrary nature of rights. From an international human rights perspective, Vietnam can be criticized on many levels, but simply introducing a children-focused agenda informed by theories about what childhood should be does little to address the experiences of children and the individual child. And if necessary support systems are not in operation, any reference to rights is a futile exercise. Local support and real understanding are essential if support services are to be of benefit to the chosen beneficiaries. Although the Vietnamese Government has ratified the UNCRC, one can wonder the extent to which it will ever be fully implemented.

### The UNCRC's Local Relevance

The UNCRC was introduced to the population with little regard for the Vietnamese position: the country's recent history, or its existing legislation.

For example, there is a Vietnamese National Law for Children but as far as I could tell it received little attention, and it occurred to me that its mandate may never have been considered or even recognized by UNICEF. One of the expectations for Vietnamese children under Article 13:1 of the National Law on Child Protection, Care, and Education is "to show love, respect and piety towards grandparents and parents, politeness towards adults, affection towards younger children and solidarity with friends." This is entirely in accord with the traditional values of filial piety discussed in chapter 3, but the expectations that a child should take responsibility for his or her actions and show respect toward his or her elders is absent from the UNCRC, which refers to the individual child as having rights but no responsibilities. At the outset of the book I referred to UNICEF celebrating the swift ratification of the UNCRC across the globe. But, as the experiences of the children I met show, ratification does not automatically lead to a convention's measures actually being adopted, and in Vietnam, some of the UNCRC articles clash with local practices. The UNCRC is still only sometimes locally and internationally useful, and it should have been introduced with far more caution to countries like Vietnam, where the individualized sense of self is a foreign concept. It is a mistake to view it as an all-encompassing document with global relevance.

The UNCRC was only ratified in Vietnam in 1990, and much of what it stands for is alien to Vietnamese ideas about how to treat children. It is also clear that only when changes are initiated with the full support of local people, rather than being imposed enforced from above, do they have a good chance of succeeding. Substantial change takes time, especially when it challenges fundamental cultural values.

NGO workers are mistaken if they assume that only internationally driven agendas change lives. On the contrary, I believe it is quite patronizing to assume that an internationally led agenda needs to be present for children's lives to improve. Such an assumption is redolent of neocolonialism, presuming as it does that local change does not occur without outside assistance.

### Questioning the Universality of the UNCRC

The universalists who uphold the UNCRC perceive human rights as self-evident universal norms. Sitharamam Kakarala points out the universalist arguments are generally against tradition and strongly favor modernity (Kakarala 1989). Liberalism and industrialization have become the indicators of modernity, which, it is argued, is a prerequisite for the establishment of a proper human rights regime (Donnelly 1989). Universalists have often ignored the diversity of social and cultural formations in the South, and this in turn has provoked the elites of the South to create alternative forms of human rights that often clash with the tenets of the West, thus introducing further ambiguities and opportunities for misunderstanding (Kakarala 1989).

The Vietnamese human rights academic Tai (1988) points out that because scholars think of human rights as constitutional rights they tend to consider those rights as originating with the constitutions of the Western world. But he asks whether we should be considering human rights laws only from within a constitutional framework. Tai raises the question of whether the Vietnamese already have their own substantial protective measures to address human rights issues. I had been living in Vietnam for a year before I learned about the Vietnamese National Law for Children, and as far as I could tell it received little attention; it occurred to me that its mandate may never have been considered or even recognized by UNICEF.

## The UNCRC and the Politics of Aid

The international aid programs operating in Vietnam are funded by international agencies, and these programs are largely implemented by NGOs with the Vietnamese government's approval. Hence NGOs have an important role in ensuring the successful implementation of programs that support such initiatives as the UNCRC. As I explained in chapter 3, it is helpful for the purposes of this book to make a distinction between two main types of NGOs—on the one hand international NGOs that supported the UNCRC and on the other hand those that do not. I believe that members of the latter group were more likely to familiarize themselves with children in the local setting.

In general, the NGOs that focused on the UNCRC agenda were less aware of the real difficulties and conflicts of interest that Vietnamese people face because they did not spend time doing work outside the areas that related to children. It was easy for them to criticize present circumstances, but it would have been wiser to delve a little deeper into the real issues affecting a society before trying to apply the universal policies of the UNCRC to the local situation. One of my key concerns about how the UNCRC was being implemented focused on its articles being interpreted literally, resulting in unrealistic standards being set. I felt priorities had been distorted when, for example, an NGO within the Save the Children Consortium decided under the auspices of the UNCRC to improve Vietnamese nursery education in a country where even access to primary education was not guaranteed.

Similarly, when members of UNICEF made allegations about the reform school and its supporting NGO colluding with child labor, I felt that this form of overly strict adherence to the UNCRC was both culturally insensitive and lacking in informed judgment. It also ignored a young person's right to choose what he did while locked up. It was the boys who had originally requested skilled training because they recognized its value in obtaining work.

The observations I was able to make in the course of my fieldwork have led me to conclude that NGOs that support internationally led legislation such as the UNCRC are more likely to introduce a predetermined agenda to Vietnam, and those objectives rather than locally derived experience inform the direction of their work. From my experience during interviews and participatory observation, it is clear that UNCRC supporters are prone to demonize what happens in countries where children work or are visible on the streets. It is also the case that the countries most likely to be viewed as "failing" the UNCRC are in the South. In that respect there is also a political element to this form of open criticism. Yet it did not have to be this way. NGO work in connection with the UNCRC could have been managed differently, as I had the good fortune to discover during my final month in Hanoi when I interviewed an expatriate at Save the Children Fund USA. He thought much of what child rights supporters were aiming for was unrealistic and overly ambitious, so his organization was working solely in the area of childhood malnutrition and ways to lower Vietnam's high infant mortality rate. His team was focused almost exclusively on teaching rural people to bulk up their basic diet of rice with locally found crabs, which provide a good source of protein when ground up and added to each meal. As he pointed out, the UNCRC and what it should be about can be open to different types of interpretation. His organization worked in Vietnam under the banner of UNCRC, but he was committed to a step-by-step response to child rights, and it was he who had personally decided that the NGO focus should be on malnutrition, which is referred to in Article 24:2:C but is only one very small aspect of the UNCRC. His treatment of the UNCRC was culturally sensitive and a good example of its appropriate use.

### NGOs That Do Not Support the UNCRC

When I was a sophomore in college I took courses on colonial history, and learned that missionary organizations had most heavily undermined local cultural practices. So I was surprised to have my past ideas challenged and to discover during the course of my fieldwork in Vietnam that international NGOs with religious agendas were most likely to work closely within the Vietnamese culture rather than with a Western-informed child rights agenda at the forefront of their minds.

In putting this case I am not arguing that missionary groups are automatically superior in quality to other types of organizations, nor do I wish to ignore the complex pasts of some such groups. To do proper justice to the history and evolution of missionary and religion-based organizations would take up many pages and detract from the central interests of this book. However, I think it is important to acknowledge that missionary organizations during the colonial period did not treat all local people as automatically inferior. Distinctions have been made between Protestant and Catholic organizations, but even so their practices varied from place to place depending on the different personalities of their missionary priests. Religion-based organizations had many quite varied reasons and differing ethical motivations for working in foreign lands.

The people I met working for religion-based organizations showed more willingness to understand local practices than did those working for other international NGO groups, and they were less likely to presume that universally prescribed methods for bettering people's lot would be applicable in the Vietnamese context. It may have been that expatriates working for religion-based organizations had achieved a level of sensitivity that was informed by mistakes and criticisms of their organizations during the colonial period. Perhaps today's international nonreligious NGOs will also experience a similar process, because they are as yet still a relatively young form of organization not properly accountable to a higher body. Perhaps therein lies the general difference in attitude and approach.

Generally, I discovered that in Vietnam, religion-based organizations were run differently from those that uphold the UNCRC agenda. As well as being smaller in size they also tended to distribute manageable projects to separate teams, each of which was most likely to be run by an expatriate and his or her team of Vietnamese contemporaries. This meant that expatriate team leaders were immediately involved at the local level, and as Jack's example shows they were more likely to learn firsthand about Vietnamese reaction to project ideas. They were also more likely to be required by the NGO to learn fluent Vietnamese, an essential attribute for anyone seeking to understand the local traditions and cultural signals.

There was another significant difference for NGOs with religious backgrounds. In Vietnam, these NGOs are banned from overtly practicing their faith and evangelizing during their work. Their work arguably thus takes on a unique dimension because the fundamental reasons individual employees have for joining that type of NGO (for example a desire to promulgate their faith) have to be sidelined. Therefore, while they are in Vietnam, NGO workers in religion-based organizations have to redefine the direction of their work and focus on humanitarian rather than spiritual objectives. I think this has a profound effect on how people within those NGOs adapt to Vietnam. Everyone I interviewed who worked for an NGO with a religious background spoke of showing caution and being mindful that Vietnamese thinking was different from their own. It was common knowledge that the Vietnamese government would ask people found evangelizing to leave the country, and I think this partly explains the more respectful and reflective stance that people working for this type of NGOs seemed to take.

In contrast, the NGOs that focus on children and upheld the UNCRC were most likely to have an expatriate as director who oversaw all work but did not get directly involved in any particular project. This meant that local knowledge was most likely to be confined to what their project organizers chose to share with them, and as Judith Justice (1989) found in Nepal, this type of communication can result in expatriates receiving unreliable information.

### The Implications of Directed Aid Funding

As well as making direct public pleas for money, NGOs that are not religion based have to bid successfully for project funds from aid agencies if they are to stay active. It is therefore inevitable that to some extent self-interested survival instincts come into play when they bid for work. This is not to say that they are unprincipled: far from it. But there has to be an element of compromise or alignment with the policies of the funding agencies if these NGOs are to survive as organizations, and hence the work they do is influenced over quite short time cycles according to the changing priorities set out by their funders. Clearly, this is most likely to be the case if NGOs receive money from the UN or the World Bank. Conversely, NGOs that are locally run or religion based have more varied sources of income and are less likely to respond to internationally set agendas; because of this they tend to work with consistency over much longer time frames. Thus, Jack's religion-based NGO that worked in the reform school relied on funding from a wide range of sources, but money was used to support ongoing and long-term projects. In his organization it was not the funders but the success or failure of each local project that influenced the direction the NGO took. I argue that the reverse is the case for organizations that are preoccupied with the UNCRC, so when organizations focus on internationally led agendas this amounts to local priorities being sidelined.

One of the questions I originally asked was, "But did it matter that the focus often shifted and that aid was redirected?" I believe that it does matter, but only if an NGO is hoping to address real and not assumed local need. This concern becomes irrelevant if the NGO's real priority is to stay in operation regardless of the quality of work being achieved. In this way one can question the type of work NGOs were doing in support of the UNCRC. Some groups were so preoccupied with delivering on that agenda that their own failings went unnoticed or were ascribed to the failings of others. For example, when a project for a counseling center for street children collapsed, the failure was blamed on lack of local support rather than on the inappropriateness of that form of intervention in the Vietnamese context. Similarly, when UNCRC pamphlets were introduced by an NGO into the reform school, resulting in the director vowing that the NGO involved would not be invited back, the NGO in question was none the wiser because it had already moved on.

## Liberal Attitudes among Local Institutions?

I think it is important to note that during my two years in Hanoi I witnessed the gradual introduction of more liberal management regimes in the two institutions I was able to visit. Clearly, it is not possible to say on the basis of just these two schools whether this was representative of a general move toward less-authoritarian attitudes, but I certainly found it encouraging. Among staff in the reform school, ideas about how children should be treated changed for the better: to start with, the reform school was experimental and was clearly an improvement on the alternative of locking children in adult prisons. In view of this it is easy to see how staff members at the reform school saw their work with children in a positive light. By the time I left for England, children were no longer being beaten up by a guard; his influence, as I mentioned in chapter 6, had been drastically curbed because of the general shift in attitude among other staff and in response to the more humanitarian approach of the NGO's members. Boys were also being given opportunities to enter skilled training programs, and their circumstances were followed up after they left the reform school.

Positive changes were also afoot in the orphanage. A year after I left, Mrs. Ha, the director, retired, and as a result some of the younger staff members began to have more say in how the orphanage was run. On the streets, children's lives continued as they always had. But there was some evidence of change because behind the scenes one of the major NGO players in the government's return-to-the-countryside program had at least written a report on the need to prepare families better for their children's homecoming.

### Challenging the Global Model of Childhood

From the outset of this book I have shown that international ideas about children are largely informed by theoretical notions of childhood derived from a Western cultural perspective that does not tell us a great deal about children's actual experiences. Further, the children's rights agenda had minimal impact on children's lives, but where it did have influence it was often ill thought out. Very few children I knew had any real grasp of what a children's rights agenda could do for them, and my findings show that organizations that try to improve children's rights by relying solely on applying the UNCRC at arm's length are failing to make a positive impact. Rather, my fieldwork shows that it is essential to look first at the world of particular children rather than to apply a generalized discourse on childhood in an unfamiliar setting. Much greater involvement and more thoughtfully designed intervention at the local level needs to be encouraged if organizations intend to do appropriate and useful work. This can be achieved in a number of ways.

First, the most prominent donors, principally the international aid agencies, should be challenged to focus on funding that is of long-term value and not driven by short-term faddism.

Second, UNCRC-supporting NGOs in Vietnam expressed very little interest in having anything to do with religion-based NGOs, even though some members of the religion-based groups had tried to make contact. This is unfortunate, because by sharing expertise properly more appropriate forms of intervention might be developed, and as I have shown the religion-based NGOs frequently used a more locally sensitive approach, with more obvious success.

Third, I came to believe that despite rhetoric to the contrary, internationally directed agendas are often neocolonial in nature and lack respect for local opinion and expertise. So local people from a variety of backgrounds should be involved much more centrally in designing funding programs, and their understanding of the nuances of local culture be built in to any work. My findings show that this is certainly the case with the general application of the UNCRC in Vietnam.

Fourth, and most worryingly, Western NGOs with ethnocentric objectives are unlikely to be aware, or are unwilling to acknowledge, that their approaches might create problems for the very people they aim to assist. This has to change. Indeed as Justice (1989) also points out, where foreigners behave less than adequately in their failure to understand local circumstances, their interests are likely to be misdirected, so that their presence actually strengthens the power of locals who behave badly.

### Some Final Thoughts

It was not until I left Vietnam that I began to make orderly sense of all that I had learned while there, and it took a long time for me to feel able to put what I had seen into perspective. During my first year back in England I found it difficult to adjust to the choices available to me in that context. The first time I went to a supermarket after I had returned from Vietnam I had to turn around and leave because I could not cope with the amount of choice. I remember standing by the apple section of the fruit and vegetable aisle and gaping at the number of different varieties. On a daily basis, of course, most of us juggle to sort our bills, and, if we are still in college, to negotiate more student loans. It's hard sometimes to get by and to make the right choices about a career, perhaps get a first mortgage, and later still we may start to feel a little constrained by life and the limited choices available to us.

The reality is that the children I met and whose experiences fill the pages of this book were some of the better-off working children; they were not sex workers, and they did not work in sweatshops or toil on the land from dawn to dusk. But, with the exception of some of the girls who came from middle-class Hanoi homes, they still live the lives they do because they and their families are poor. Their poverty has many complex reasons that can be easily and comfortably explained away without any reference to the state of the world today and to global influences. But my conscience is pricked when I think of the children I knew, and the countless others across the world leading even more difficult lives. As things stand, most of the world's resources are unfairly distributed in favor of countries in the North, and it is that unfair distribution, the tariffs we apply to raw materials, and our willingness to buy goods made in poor countries by people working at subsistence levels that create and sustain so much of the poverty that forces children to work.

It is easy to direct blame at the faceless multinational companies, our governments, and at the World Bank and IMF for creating the debts of weaker nations, or to point the finger at the leaders of corrupt regimes and the wealthy minority that exist in countries of the South. We should continue to hold such bodies to account. But every one of us plays our part, so why do we not make ourselves more accountable? We can only afford the food we eat and the luxuries that fill our homes because cheap labor was employed to produce them and because we in the North hold countries of the South to ransom when we buy their products at bottom-rate prices. Yet for all that this fundamental imbalance is not even addressed under any article in the UNCRC.

If the lives of working children are really going to improve, then short of having a revolution and complete redistribution of wealth across the world, we really need to pay attention to what locals want and to introduce realistic human rights schemes rather than the grandiose ones that in reality only serve to salve our consciences. As Farmer says, "I love white liberals, love 'em to death. They're on our side, but white liberals think all the World's problems can be fixed without any cost to themselves. We don't believe that. There's a lot to be said for sacrifice, remorse, even pity. It's what separates us from roaches" (2003, 40).

Real change among real people will take time because it needs to be based on knowledgeable respect, on long-term and sustainable support at the local level, and on offering sensible types of intervention. Let's start with the basics: food for all, rudimentary health care, and some basic education. I have shown with my reference to the religion-based NGOs that setting such long-term goals is a possible route to take. But it is not sexy or glamorous, or about the latest types of faddism. It is a type of aid that takes real dedication and time, and it is hard, hard work, often grafting alongside the very people one is trying to help. To quote Farmer again, talking about his work in Haiti and the nuns he met who were also working there: "They were just so much more militant, if that's the word, than the white liberals and academics. They were the ones standing up to the growers in their sensible nun shoes. They were the ones schlepping the workers to the clinics or courts, translating for them, getting them groceries or driving licenses" (2003, 62). My experiences mirrored what Farmer observed in Haiti. The children I knew accepted that they and other members of their families had to work, and to suggest otherwise was insulting or just baffling to them. They were surviving at subsistence levels in one of the poorest countries in Southeast Asia, a country that still does not have the resources to provide universal education or health care. Moreover, internationally supported and funded human rights agendas have so far failed to have any noticeable impact at the local level. So these children had no option but to get out there and continue to provide for themselves and do something practical about their daily problems.

# Bibliography

Adams, G. R., T. Gullotta, and M. A. Clancy. 1985. "Homeless adolescents: A descriptive similarity and difference between runaways and throwaways." *Adolescence* 20:715–724.

African Charter on the Rights and Welfare of the Child. 1990. Organisation of African Unity Document CAB/LGG/29.9/49.

Allman, J. 1991. "Fertility and family planning in Vietnam." *Studies in Family Planning* 22 (5): 311–313.

Alston, P. 1994. *The best interests of the child: Reconciling culture and human rights.* Oxford: Clarendon Press.

Amnesty International. 1991. "Vietnam: Renovation (Doi Moi), the law and human rights in 1980." In *Doi Moi Vietnam's Renovation Policy and Performance*, ed. D. K. Forbes, T. Hull, D. G. Marr, and B. Brogan. Canberra: Australia National University.

———. 2003a. *Human rights report on China.* London: Amnesty International.

———. 2003b. *Human rights report on the United States of America.* London: Amnesty International.

———. 2004. *Human rights report on Vietnam.* London: Amnesty International.

Aptekar, L. 1996. *Street children: A growing urban tragedy.* London: Weidenfield and Nicolson (Independent Commission on International Humanitarian Issues).

Ariés, P. 1973 [1960]. *Centuries of childhood.* London: Penguin.

Atkinson, M., and P. Gaskell. 1999. "OECD report shows aid to poor nations at record low." *Guardian* (Manchester). May 26.

Baker, R., and C. Panter-Brick. 2000. "A comparative perspective of children's 'careers' and abandonment in Nepal." In *Abandoned children*, ed. C. Panter-Brick and M. Smith. Cambridge: Cambridge University Press.

Ballinger, J. 1997. "Nike does it to Vietnam." *Multinational Monitor.* March: 21–24.

Barley, N. 1986. *The innocent anthropologist.* London: Penguin.

Bartoller, M. D. 1976. *Juvenile victimization: The institutional paradox.* New York: Halsted Press.

Bjork, M. 1997. "Concepts of children in Vietnam." Master's thesis, University of Stockholm.

Blanchet, T. 1996. *Lost innocence, stolen childhoods.* Dhaka, Bangladesh: University Press Limited.

Block, B. P. 2000. *The Pain and the pride: Life inside the Colorado boot camp.* Winchester, UK: Waterside Press.

Bogen, H. 1992. *The luckiest orphans: A history of the Hebrew Orphan Asylum of New York.* Urbana and Chicago: University of Illinois Press.

Bond, T. 1994. "The street children's programme: Ho Chi Minh City." Annual Report 1994. Ho Chi Minh City: Terres des Hommes, 1–14.

———. 1996. "Street children in Ho Chi Minh City." Ho Chi Minh City: Terres des Hommes.

Bortner, M. A. 1988. *Delinquency and justice: An age of crisis.* New York: McGraw-Hill.

Boyden, J., and J. De Berry. 2000. "Children in adversity." *Forced migration* 9:33–36.

Boyden, J., and P. Holden. 1991. *Children of the cities.* London: Zed Books.

Boyden, J., and G. Mann. 2000. "Children's risk, resilience and coping in extreme situations." Background paper to the Consultation on Children in Adversity, Oxford, September 9–12.

Boyden, J., B. Ling, and B. Myers. 1998. *What works for working children.* Stockholm: Radda Barnen and UNICEF.

Bradford, A. S. 1994. *Some even volunteered: The first wolfhounds pacify Vietnam.* Westport, Conn.: Praeger Publishers.

Bunck, J. M.1994. *Fidel Castro and the quest for a revolutionary culture in Cuba.* University Park: Penn State University Press.

Burman, E. 1994a. "Development phallacies: Psychology, gender and childhood." *Agenda* 22:11–20.

———. 1994b. "Poor children: Charity appeals and ideologies of childhood." *Changes* 12 (1): 29–36.

———. 1995. "The abnormal distribution of development: Policies for southern women and children." *Gender, Place and Culture* 2 (1): 21–36.

Burr, M. 1995. "Privatization and the management of change in Malaysia and Singapore." Ph.D. diss., Sussex University, UK.

Burr, R. 2002. "Global and local approaches to children's rights in Vietnam." *Childhood* 9 (1): 49–61.

Burr, R., and H. Montgomery. 2003a. "Children and rights." In *Understanding childhood: An interdisciplinary approach,* ed. M. Woodhead and H. Montgomery. Chichester, UK: John Wiley and Sons.

———. 2003b. "Children, poverty and social inequality." In *Changing childhoods: Local and global,* ed. H. Montgomery, R. Burr, and M. Woodhead. Chichester, UK: John Wiley and Sons.

Caseley, J., and N. Buom. 1996. "Survey on the situation of street children in Hanoi." Hanoi: Youth Research Institute. 38.

Cassen, R. 1994. *Does aid work? Report to an international task force.* Oxford: Clarendon Press.

Castell, M. 1996. *The rise of the network society.* Cambridge, UK: Blackwell Publications.

———. 1997. *The power of identity.* Cambridge, UK: Blackwell Publications.

Chambers, R. 1992. "Rural, rapid and participatory observation." Discussion paper no. 331. Brighton: University of Sussex, Institute of Development Studies.

Chang, P. M. 1997. *Bound feet and western dress.* New York: Anchor Books.

Chung, V. 1992. "The child and his problems." *Vietnamese Studies,* n.s., 34 (2): 98–109.

Committee on the Rights of the Child. 2003. 32nd session, Geneva, Switzerland, January 13–31 (http.//www.ishr.ch/About%20UN/Reports%20and%20Analysis/CRC/CRC–32nd session.pdf).

Croll, E. 1995. *Changing identities of Chinese women: Rhetoric, experience and self-perception in twentieth century China.* London and Atlantic Highlands, N.J: Hong Kong University Press and Zed Books.

———. 2000. *Endangered daughters: Discrimination and development in Asia.* London: Routledge.

Cuc, N. K., and M. Flamm. 1996. *Children of the dust: Street children in Vietnam and children in extremely difficult circumstances.* Bangkok: Darnsutha Press Company Limited.

Cunningham, H. 1995. *Children and childhood in Western society since 1500.* London and New York: Longman.

Das, V., A. Kleinman, and M. Lock. 1997. *Social suffering.* Berkeley: University of California Press.

Day, T. 1996. "Ties that (un)bind: Families and states in pre-modern Southeast Asia." *Journal of Asian Studies* 55 (2):384–409.

Delahook, A., R. Frankenberg, and I. Robinson. 2000. "Countering essentialism in behavioural social science: The example of the 'vulnerable child' ethnographically examined." *Sociological Review* 40 (4): 586–611.

DeMello, M. 2000. *Bodies of inscription: A cultural history of the modern tattoo community.* Durham, N.C.: Duke University Press.

Dettwyler, L. 1998. "The biocultural approach in nutritional anthropology: Case studies of malnutrition in Mali." In *Understanding and Applying Medical Anthropology,* ed. P. Brown. London and Toronto: Mayfield Publishing.

De Vylder, S. 2000. "The big picture." *Crin Newsletter* (London), 13:11–13..

Donnelly, J. 1989. *Universal human rights in theory and practice.* Ithaca, N.Y.: Cornell University Press.

Douglas, M. 1973. *Natural symbols. Exploration in cosmology.* London: Barrie and Jenkins.

———. 1986. *How institutions think.* Syracuse, N.Y.: Syracuse University Press.

Duiker, W. 1995. *Vietnam: Revolution in transition.* Oxford, UK: Westview Press.

Dung, H. N. 1988. "To serve the cause of women's liberation." In *To be made over: Tales of socialist re-education in Vietnam*, ed. H. S. Thong. New Haven, Conn.: Yale Southeast Asia Studies Publication.

Dutton, M. R. 1992. *Policing and punishment in China: From patriarchy to the "people."* Cambridge: Cambridge University Press.

Edmonds, E., and N. Pavenik. 2002. "Does globalization increase child labor? Evidence from Vietnam." Working paper no. 8760, National Bureau of Economic Research, Cambridge, Mass.

———. 2003. "The effects of trade liberalization on child labor." Department of Economics, Dartmouth College, Hanover, N.H.

Elder, G. H. 1974. *Children of the Great Depression: Social change in life experience.* Chicago: University of Chicago Press.

Ennew, J. 1994. *Street and working children: A guide to planning.* London: Save the Children.

Fardon, R. 1995. *Counterworks: Managing the diversity of knowledge.* London: Routledge.

Farmer, P. 2003. *Pathologies of power: Health, human rights, and the new war on the poor.* Berkeley: University of California Press.

Farmer, P., and N. Gastineau. 2002. "Rethinking health and human rights: Time for a paradigm shift." *Journal of Law, Medicine and Ethics* (Winter): 655–666.

Foucault, M. 1975. *Discipline and punishment: The birth of the prison.* St. Ives, UK: Penguin.

Franklin, H. B. 1998. *Prison writing in 20th century America.* London: Penguin.

Fyfe, A. 1985. *All work and no play: Child labour today.* London: UNICEF and TUC.

Fyfield, J. A. 1982. *Re-education of Chinese anti-Communists.* New York: St. Martin's Press.

Gammeltoft, T. 1998. *Women's bodies, women's worries: Health and family planning in a Vietnamese rural community.* London: Curzon Press.

Gardner, K., and D. Lewis. 1996. *Anthropology development and the post modern challenge.* London: Pluto Press.

Gell, A. 1993. *Tattooing in Polynesia.* Oxford: Clarendon Press.

George, S. 1988. *A fate worse than debt.* London: Penguin.

Giddens, A. 1990. *The consequence of modernity.* London: Polity Press.

Gilbert, A., and J. Gugler. 1992. *Cities, poverty and development: Urbanisation in the Third World.* Oxford: Oxford University Press.

Glauser, B. 1990. "Street children: Deconstructing a construct." In *Constructing and reconstructing childhood: Contemporary issues in the sociological study of childhood*, ed. A. Prout and A. James. London: Falmer Press.

Global Policy Forum. 2000. "Landmark court ruling condemns Argentina's illegitimate debt." Paper produced by the Global Policy Forum, New York.

Goffman, E. 1961. *Asylums.* London: Penguin.

———. 1963. *Behavior in public places: Notes on the social organization of gatherings.* New York: The Free Press.

———. 1972. *Encounters.* London: Penguin.

Goodkind, D. 1995. "Rising gender inequality in Vietnam since reunification." *Pacific Affairs* 68 (3): 342–359.

Goodman, R., and I. Neary, eds. 1996. *Case studies on Human rights in Japan.* London: Routledge.

Gray, M. 1998. "Creating civil society? The emergence of NGOs in Vietnam International Relations." Master's thesis, School of Oriental and African Studies, London University.

Ha, E. D. N. 1996. "Families and reunion possibility of working street children." Hanoi: Radda Barnen and the Youth Research Institute.

Hall, D. K. 1997. *Prison tattoos.* New York: St. Martin's Griffin.

Hastrup, K. 1995. *A passage to anthropology: Between experience and theory.* London: Routledge.

Hecht, T. 1998. *At home in the street: Street children of northeast Brazil.* Cambridge: Cambridge University Press.

Hendrick, H. 1997. *Children, childhood and English society, 1880–1990.* Cambridge: Cambridge University Press.

Herzog, B. 2004. *Small world: A microscopic journey.* New York: Simon and Schuster.

Hiebert, M. 1995. *Vietnam Notebook.* North Clarendon, Vt.: Charles E. Tuttle.

Hirschman, C., and V. M. Loi. 1994. "Family and household structure in Vietnam: Some glimpses from a recent survey." *Pacific Affairs* 69 (2): 229–249.

Hobart, M. 1993. *An anthropological critique of development: The growth of ignorance.* London and New York: Routledge.

Hodgkinson, P. R., and A. Rutherford. 1996. *Capital punishment: Global issues and prospects.* Winchester, UK: Waterside Press.

Holland, P. 1992. *What is a child? Popular images of childhood.* London: Virago Press.

Hong, E. 2000. "Globalization and the impact on health: A third world view" (database on-line). Available from The People's Health Movement, http://www.phmovement.org/pubs/issuepapers/hong24. August (accessed November 12, 2003).

Hopkins, S. 1996. "Situation and needs of children in Vietnam." Hanoi: Save the Children Consortium and PLAN International.

Human Rights Watch. 2003. "Donors must insist on human rights progress." Human Rights Watch Vietnam, New York, February 12.

———. 2005. "Key human rights issues in Vietnam: A Human Rights Watch briefing paper." Human Rights Watch Vietnam, New York.

International Labor Organization. 2005. *The facts about child labor.* Geneva: International Labor Organization.

Jacoby, G. P. 1974. *Children and youth: Social problems and social policy.* New York: Arno Press.

James, A. 1995. "Talking of children and youth: Language, socialization and culture." In *Youth Cultures: A Cross-Cultural Perspective,* ed. V. Amit-Talai and H. Wulff. London: Routledge.

James, A., and A. Prout. 1990. *Constructing and reconstructing childhood: Contemporary issues in the sociological study of childhood.* Hampshire, UK, and Bristol, Pa.: Falmer Press.

James, A., C. Jenks, and A. Prout. 1998. *Theorizing childhood.* Cambridge, UK: Polity Press.

John, M. 2003. *Children's rights and power: Charging up for a new century.* London: Jessica Kingsley Publishers.

Justice, J. 1989. *Policies, plans, and people: Culture and health development in Nepal.* Berkeley: University of California Press.

Kakarala, S. 1996. "Universality versus relativity: A reappraisal of the debate." *Student Human Rights Newsletter* 1 (3).

Karnow, S. 1983. *Vietnam: A history.* New York: Viking Press.

Kazmin, A. 2004. "IMF ends Vietnam aid over central bank dispute." *Financial Times* (London), April 13.

Keeson, W. 1975. *Childhood in China.* New Haven, Conn.: Yale University Press.

Khanh, D. 1996. "Juvenile delinquency a growing menace." *Vietnam News* (Hanoi), April, 4.

Kidder, T. 2003. *Mountains beyond mountains: The quest of Dr. Paul Farmer, a man who would cure the world.* New York: Random House.

Kilbride, P., C. Suda, and E. Njeru, E. 2000. *Street children in Kenya: Voices of children in search of a childhood.* Westport, Conn.: Bergin and Gaury.

Kirby, P., and M. Woodhead. 2003. "Children's participation in society." In *Changing Childhoods: Local and Global,* ed. H. Montgomery, R. Burr, and M. Woodhead. Chichester, UK: John Wiley and Sons.

Kleinman, A., and J. Kleinman. 1997. "The appeal of experience: The dismay of images, cultural appropriateness of suffering in our times." In *Social suffering,* ed. M. Lock and T. Asad. Berkeley: University of California Press.

Kolko, G. 1997. *Anatomy of a peace.* London and New York: Routledge.

Last, M. 1994. "Putting children first." *Disasters* 18 (3).

La Tour, B. 1993. *We have never been modern.* London: Harvester Wheatsheaf.

Lau, S. 1996. *Growing up the Chinese way.* Hong Kong: Chinese University Press of Hong Kong.

Lavalette, M.1999. *A thing of the past? Child labour in Britain in the nineteenth and twentieth centuries.* Liverpool: Liverpool University Press.

Law on Child Protection, Care and Education. National Assembly of Socialist Republic of Vietnam. 1991. 8th Legislation, 9th Session, August 12.

Le, T. N. T. 1989. *Vietnamese women in the eighties.* Hanoi: Hanoi Foreign Languages Publishing House.

Lee, N. 2001. *Childhood and society: Growing up in an age of uncertainty.* Maidenhead, UK: Open University Press.

Lewis, N. 1995. 2ed. *A dragon apparent: Travels in Cambodia, Lao, and Vietnam.* London: Picador.

Lifton, R. 1961. *Thought reform and the psychology of totalitarianism: A study of "brainwashing" in China.* New York: W. W. Norton.

Long, H. 1997. "Hanoi holds first Festival of Filial Children." *Vietnam Courier* (Hanoi), 12.

Luong, H. Y. V. 1992. *Revolution in the village: Tradition and transformation in North Vietnam, 1925–1988.* Honolulu: University of Hawaii Press.

Mackinnon, D. 2003. "Children and school." In *Childhoods in Context*, ed. J. Maybin and M. Woodhead. Chichester, UK: John Wiley and Sons.

Madeley, J. 1991. *When aid is no help: How projects fail and how they could succeed.* London: Intermediate Technology Publications.

Madrigal, W. 1996. "The research experience of a Ph.D. Student in Vietnam." *Vietnam Forum* (Winter).

Malinowski, B. 1932. *The sexual lives of savages in north-western Melanesia: An ethnographic account of courtship, marriage and family life among the natives of the Trobriand Islands.* London: Routledge and Kegan Paul.

Marr, D. G. 1992. *Vietnam.* Oxford: Clio Press.

Mellor, P., and C. Schilling. 1997. *Reforming the body, religion, community and modernity.* London: Sage Publications.

McEver, K. 2000. "For its disillusioned people, Vietnam tinkers with image." Christian Science Monitors Publication House (http://www.audiojournal.com/csm.html).

Min, A. 1995. *Red azalea.* Berkeley, Calif.: Berkeley Publishing Group.

Minh, H. C. 1971. *The prison diaries of Ho Chi Minh.* New York: Bantam.

Montgomery, H. 2001. *Modern Babylon: Prostituting children in Thailand.* Oxford and New York: Berghan Books.

Montgomery, H., R. Burr, and M. Woodhead. 2003. "Adversities and Resilience." In *Changing Childhoods: Local and Global*, ed. H. Montgomery, R. Burr, and M. Woodhead. Chichester, UK: John Wiley and Sons.

Moore, H. 1988. *Feminism and anthropology.* Minneapolis: University of Minnesota Press.

Moorehead, C., ed. 1989. *Betrayal: Child exploitation in today's world.* London: Barrie and Jenkins.

Morrison, B. 1997. *As if.* London: Granta.

Morrissey, O. 2004. "Conditionality and aid effectiveness re-evaluated." *World Economy* 27 (2).

Morrow, V. 1994. "Responsible children? Aspects of children's work and employment outside school in contemporary Britain." In *Children's childhoods observed and experienced*, ed. B. Mayall, 128–143. London: Falmer Press.

Muncie, J. 1999. *Youth and crime: A critical introduction.* London and Thousand Oaks, Calif.: Sage Publications.

Nardinelli, C. 1990. *Child labor and the industrial revolution.* Bloomington: Indiana University Press.

Ncube, W. 1998. *Law, culture, tradition and children's rights in eastern and southern Africa.* Aldershot, UK: Ashgate.

Neher, C. D. 1994. *Southeast Asia in the new international era.* Boulder, Colo.: Westview Press.

Neustatter, A. 2002. *Locked in locked out: The experiences of young offenders out of society and in prison.* London: Calouste Gulbenkian Foundation.

Nguyen, H. 2002. *A family of rural origin shifted to the city.* Hanoi: Hanoi Local Press.

Nguyen, K. 1987. *Vietnam: A long history.* Hanoi: The Goi Publishers.

Nguyen, V. K. 1999. "PACCOM Plenary." *Indochina Interchange* 9 (2): 17.

Nieuwenhuys, O. 1996. "The paradox of child labor and anthropology." *Annual Review of Anthropology* 25:237–251.

Nugent, N. 1996. *Vietnam: The second revolution.* New York: Weatherhill Publications.

Panter-Brick, C. 2001. "Street children, human rights and public health: A critique and future directions." *Annual Review of Anthropology* 31:147–171.

Pile, S., and N. Thrift. 1995. *Mapping the subject: Geographies of cultural transformation.* London: Routledge.

Pilger, J. 2000. "The price of Vietnam being allowed to come out of isolation was the destruction of its health services." *New Statesman* 129 (November 27).

Prout, A., and A. James. 1990. *Constructing and reconstructing childhood: Contemporary issues in the sociological study of childhood.* London: Falmer Press.

Punch, S. 2001. "Negotiating autonomy: Children's use of time and space in rural Bolivia." In *Conceptualizing Child-Adult Relationships,* ed. B. Mayall and L. Alanen. London: Falmer Press.

Qvortrup, J. 2001. "School-work, paid work and the changing obligations of childhood." In *Hidden hands: International perspectives on children's work and labor,* ed. P. Mizen, C. Pole, and A. Bolton. London: Routledge Falmer.

Qvortrup, J., M. Bardy, G. Sgritta, and H. Winterberger. 1994. *Childhood matters, social theory, practice and politics.* Vol. 14 of *Public Policy and Social Welfare.* Aldershot, UK: Avebury.

Raffaelli, M. 1999. "Homeless and working street youth in Latin America: A developmental review." *Inter-American Journal of Psychology* 33 (2): 7–28.

Rapp, R. 1979. "Anthropology." *Signs* 4 (3): 497–513.

Reid, T. R. 1999. *Confucius lives next door: What living in the East tells us about living in the West.* New York: Random House.

Reynolds, P. 1991. *Dance civet cat: Child labor in the Zambezi Valley.* London: Zed Books.

Rizzini, I. G. 1999. *From street children to all children: Improving the opportunities of low-income urban children and youth in Brazil.* Rio de Janeiro: Center for Research on Childhood-CESPI.

Rothman, D. J. 1995. *The Oxford history of the prison: The practice of punishment in western society.* New York: Oxford University Press.

Rydstrom, H. 1998. *Embodying morality: Girls' socialization in a North Vietnamese commune.* Linkoping, Sweden: Linkoping University.

SarDesai, D. R. 1992. *Vietnam: The struggle for national identity.* Boulder, Colo.: Westview Press.

Scheper-Hughes, N. 1992. *Death without weeping: The violence of everyday life in Brazil.* Berkeley and Los Angeles: University of California Press.

Scheper-Hughes, N., and M. Lock. 1997. "The mindful body: A prolegomenon to future work in medical anthropology." *Medical Anthropology Quarterly* 1 (1): 6–41.

Scheper-Hughes, N., and C. Sargent, eds. 1996. *Small wars: The cultural politics of childhood.* Berkeley: University of California Press.

Seabrook, J. 2001. *Children in other worlds: Exploitation in the global market.* London and Stirling, Scotland: Pluto Press.

Sharma, S., and S. Kumar. 2002. "Debt relief: Indentured servitude for the third world." *Race and Class* 43 (4): 45–56.

Shepperson, G. 1958. *Independent African*. Edinburgh: Edinburgh University Press.

Smith, M.K. 2002. "Thomas John Barnardo (the doctor)." *Encyclopedia of Informal Education* (www.infed.org/encyclopedia.htm).

Solberg, A. 1990. "Changing constructions of age for Norwegian children." In *Constructing and Reconstructuring Childhood: Contemporary Issues in the Sociological Study of Childhood*, ed. A. James and J. Prout. London: Falmer Press.

Stephens, S. 1995. *Children and the politics of culture*. Princeton, N.J.: Princeton University Press.

Stephenson, S. 2001. "Street children in Moscow: Using and creating social capital." *Sociological Review* 49 (4): 530–547.

Steward, S. 1990. *Bad boys and tough tattoos: A social history of the tattoo with gangs, sailors and street corner punks: 1950–1965*. Binghamton, N.Y.: Haworth Press.

Sykes, G. M. 1958. *The society of captives: A study of a maximum security prison*. Princeton, N.J.: Princeton University Press.

Tai, T. V. 1988. *The Vietnamese tradition of human rights*. Berkeley, Calif.: Indochina Research Monograph.

Templar, R. 1999. *Shadows and wind: A view of modern Vietnam*. London: Penguin.

Thakur, R. 1984. *Peacekeeping in Vietnam: Canada, India, Poland, and the International Commission*. Edmonton, Alberta: University of Alberta Press.

Thorne, B. 1997 [1983]. *Gender play: Girls and boys in school*. 5th ed. New Brunswick, N.J.: Rutgers University Press.

Topolski, A. 2001. *Without vodka: Adventures in wartime Russia*. South Royalton, Vt.: Steerforth Press.

Tuong Lai. 1993. "Introduction." In *Sociological Studies on the Vietnamese Family*, ed. R. Liljestrom and L. Tuong. Hanoi: Social Sciences Publishing House.

Tuttle, C. 1999. *Hard at work in factories and mines: The economics of child labor during the British Industrial Revolution*. Boulder, Colo.: Westview Press.

UNICEF. 1989. *Guidelines for the application of the methodological guide on situation analysis of children in especially difficult circumstances*. Bogotá: UNICEF.

———. 1994. *Situation analysis of women and children*. Hanoi: UNICEF.

———. 1995. *UK Committee for UNICEF The Convention on the Rights of the Child*. London: UNICEF.

———. 2002. *For every child*. London: Red Fox.

UNICEF/WHO. 1990. *Plan of action for implementing the World Declaration on the survival, protection and development of Children in the 1990s*. New York: UNICEF/WHO.

United Nations. 1989. *United Nations Convention on the Rights of the Child*. New York: United Nations.

———. 2003. "Committee on the Rights of the Child: Country Report to Vietnam" (http://www.hrea.org/lists/child-rights/markup/msg00154.htm). Available from the United Nations, January 11 (accessed January 29).

Van Deer, P. 1998. "The hall of mirrors: Orientalism, anthropology and the other." *American Anthropologist* 100 (2): 293–299.

Vietnam News Service. 1997. "The plight of un-wed mothers and their children." *Vietnam News* (Hanoi), April 8.

Vuong, T. 1997. "Helping street children find their way home." *Vietnam Courier* (Hanoi), May 25–31.

Werner, E. 2000. *Through the eyes of innocents*. Boulder, Colo.: Westview Press.

Whitmore, J. 1984. "Social organization and Confucian thoughts in Vietnam." *Journal of Southeast Asian Studies* 15 (2): 296–306.

Wilson, R. A. 1997. *Human rights, culture and context: Anthropological perspectives*. London: Pluto Press.

Wilson, R. A., and J. P. Mitchell. 2003. *Human rights in global perspective: Anthropological studies of rights, claims and entitlements*. London and New York: Routledge.

Winters, J. 1996. *Power in motion: Capital mobility and the Indonesian state*. Ithaca, N.Y.: Cornell University Press.

Worden, M. 2005. "Vietnam's Road Show." *New York Sun*, June 23.

Wright, P. L. 1990. *Child slaves*. London: Earthscan Publications.

Yu, I. 2001. "The bilateral social pattern and the status of women in traditional Vietnam." *Vietnamese Studies* 4 (142).

Zelizer, V. A. 1985. *Pricing the priceless child: The changing social value of children*. New York: Basic Books.

# Index

## About the Author

Rachel Burr is an anthropologist and social worker. Between 2000 and 2003 she codeveloped and taught childhood studies at the Open University, UK. Between 2003 and 2005 she was a visiting fellow in the anthropology department at the University of Wisconsin. Since returning to live in the UK she has continued to work for the Open University and to practice social work with children.